The Nancies

SUE PEARSON

Dedication

To my father, the late E.O. Pearson Jr., grandson of Addie Bull Tomlinson, who nurtured the spark of girl-grit within me. And to my childhood best friend, Bill Lanterman, who saw the spark too, and helped ignite it with his unwavering support.

Easter Sunday
6:00 pm, 1865
LaGrange, Georgia

Addie sat down on the wood bench in front of the old church piano, brushed a spot of red dirt from the ruffled skirts of her Easter dress, and placed her trembling fingers on the cold ivory keys. Though she had washed her hands, she could still see the dirt under her fingernails.

She wished she had been able to change out of her Sunday clothes. It didn't seem right to be wearing dirty clothes in church, but then, it didn't seem right to a have a rifle propped up against the piano either.

As the militia solemnly filed into the church, she took a deep breath and exhaled slowly. The scents of the old sanctuary—pine, ladies' perfumes, men's sweat—were usually a comforting musty mix, but this was no ordinary day. Joy at the morning Easter service had changed to dread by afternoon.

Addie glanced at the simple wooden cross on the altar. How on earth was she going to instill courage in the others when she was so scared herself? *Please God, help me*, she prayed. *Help all of us.*

Addie was eighteen years old now, fourteen the year the war started. An easy, carefree childhood had become a distant memory. Had she ever been scared back in those days? She remembered being nervous at her first piano recital when she was ten, but it was more a feeling of giddy excitement. And of course, she was deliriously happy when the crowd cheered her performance. Now, waiting for her cue at the church piano, she was terrified, and there wouldn't be any applause no matter how eloquently she played.

No one in the militia looked at her as they made their way to the pews. Addie could see they were struggling with their feelings, too. Some stared at the floor, others at the altar, and a few looked up, whispering, fingertips pressed together. All were members of a commissioned hometown army, formed to respond to enemy invasion. That invasion was now imminent.

The commander signaled for Addie to begin. As her fingers found the right keys, she forced herself to play aggressively. The music filled the hall with a bravado fitting of "A Mighty Fortress Is Our God." Focusing on the music took away her panicky feeling. *Thank you, God*, she thought. *Maybe this music will rally the troops after all.*

The militia was crowded into the first three rows on either side of the center aisle. Some opened hymnals and sang through the two stanzas, some were silent. All remained standing when the music stopped.

"Please be seated," Captain Morgan began. "The Yankees are closer than expected so we must be ready by sun up tomorrow. We'll muster at the Heard house and move out along Broad Street towards the college. Any questions?"

Corporal Pullen raised a hand, the voice strained and high-pitched. "Captain Morgan, is anyone else in this room as terrified as I am?'

Everyone shifted nervously in their seats. A few dabbed at their eyes.

The Captain nodded. "Corporal, I don't think there is anyone here who isn't scared, including myself, but we have trained for this. Not only are we competent, we are committed. Think of your sons, your brothers, all of the men who have defended the South so courageously these long years. The hour is ours to honor their spirit and protect LaGrange. You are soldiers. I expect to see every one of you as the light of day brings us to our greatest test." And with that, the Captain motioned for all to stand. A rustling of skirts filled the sanctuary as the forty-six women of the Nancy Hart Militia came to their feet. The militia leader lifted her hands towards heaven. "Let us pray."

Addie wondered if her sisters, Delia and Sallie, were feeling strong. She stole a quick glance at them sitting in the front row. Both were officers in the militia. They nodded solemnly to their youngest sister as Delia took Sallie's hand, and the two cast their eyes downward.

Capt. Morgan's voice rang out in prayer. "Dear Lord, bless these brave woman who stand before you, single-minded of purpose. We took a pledge to protect our families and defend our homes, and now the enemy is nearly upon us. We ask for your help. Stay close to us in the confrontation just ahead, so that we may feel your presence and be strengthened in your love. Amen"

Addie's quiet "Amen" belied her thundering thoughts. Her world had changed in a blink of time. Killing or being killed—that was the focus now. Had it been only four years since she and her sisters' major preoccupation was of nothing more than fancy dresses, tea parties, and southern gentlemen? Life would never be that uncomplicated again.

Chapter I

1861

*A*t age twelve, I longed to be thirteen. At thirteen I couldn't wait for fourteen. Now I wish I could have lived endlessly in those years of innocence and frivolity. Of course my birthday arrived anyway last week, and with it the realization that my joyous childhood had come to an end. War is the headline of my fourteenth year.

Addie set the journal down on the side table with the pages opened so the ink would dry. She shifted in the soft cushions of the old wing chair and listened—only silence. She had tried to sleep, but gave up and dressed in the dark. Now in the living room, she glanced at the old clock on the mantle above the fireplace. The moon allowed just enough light for her to see the time.

Four o'clock. Sunrise was at least two hours away.

There was no sound of stirring in the direction of her parents' bedroom or in the room shared by her two brothers, Gus and Orville. The house servants were still asleep in their small cabins outside the main house. They wouldn't be about until five o'clock to stoke the fireplaces, taking the

1

chill off the morning and then readying the detached, backyard kitchen for breakfast.

Addie's parents had given her the journal for her birthday. It was bound in leather and featured a delicate floral design on the cover, embellished with mother-of-pearl. They told her they hoped she would fill the pages with memories of a wonderful life, one overflowing with hope and joy. The shots fired at Ft. Sumter, signaling the start of the war, had changed the tenor of her first journal entries. Sadness and fear had all but erased hope and joy.

Now, a week after Ft. Sumter, we are saying goodbye to our dearest Gus, who will join the throngs of young men eager to fight for the South. I wish I could stop thinking that we could lose Gus. He is the pride and joy of the Bull family. Not only that, but the entire community has pinned such high hopes on him. Many think he'll be governor some day. Not if he's dead. Foolish people. Everyone's acting like going to war is some kind of party. They're all smiling and happy, patting each other on the back. "War Between the States, Civil War" – who cares what they call it? Unbelievable that the adults decided to fight and risk losing the people they love! No one asked me. They treat me like a little girl with only childish thoughts. If they had asked me though, I would have said, "You're all crazy".

Addie walked over to the floor-to-ceiling window and pressed her face against the glass, straining to see the gate at the end of the front walkway. Soon enough there would be soldiers on horseback there, waiting for her brother Gus to join them. She wasn't looking forward to the drama this day would bring, but she knew she had no power to hold it back. She slid slowly to the floor, arms hugging her chest to ward off the chill of dawn.

She must have drifted off to sleep because her drooping head suddenly snapped up at the sound of her mother's voice. "Grits, toast and tea in the dining room, children! Eat quickly. We don't want to be late!"

How long had she been asleep? The household was fully awake. The door to the bedroom she shared with her sisters creaked as it opened, and a red-eyed Sallie dragged herself to the dining room. Delia followed, glancing at Addie in the front room as she crossed the center hall.

"Don't know if any of us can keep food down," Delia said to her. "This is going to be a horrible day. Our sensitive Sallie woke up crying. She's thinking about the hardships of every family in town. We can count on her to let her emotions rule."

"If I see Sallie crying, I won't be able to hold back my own tears," Addie said. Gus was Addie's mentor when it came to music. Without his unwavering support she might not have honed her natural talents. She moved to Delia's side, slipping her arm around her older sister's waist. Delia touched Addie's face tenderly.

"Chin up, sweet sister."

"Easy for you to say. You're the strong woman in the family, Delia."

"Well, I do know one thing. While everyone is cheering the departure of our men today, there are three sisters whose hearts will be breaking."

In the dining room, ten-year-old Orville finished off his grits, scraping the last bit from the bottom of the bowl. He laughed at the sad expressions on his sisters' faces. "You all are a bunch of ninnies! Gus is going to be a war hero."

Addie's mother cuffed her young son on the head. "Darling, Gus is doing his duty plain and simple. Now eat up y'all! I think I hear the men at the gate."

Sallie's lips began to quiver.

"Don't, Sallie. You're going to start something," Addie said, picking up a linen napkin from the table and dabbing her eyes.

"Start what?" boomed a handsome and smiling Gus as he strode into the room.

"I can't stand what's happening. Don't go!" Addie could no longer hold back her feelings. The tears came in torrents.

"Baby sister, this war is going to be over so fast," Gus said flashing a smile at Addie. "I'll be back before you've even had time to miss me."

Delia picked up the newspaper from the table. She pointed to an article on the front page. "Gus, I think both sides have misjudged the resolve and tenacity of our leaders. Robert E. Lee turned down the offer to lead Union forces because his heart is with his Virginia home. If he accepts an offer to lead the Confederate Army, I don't think he's going to send our soldiers home in a couple of months with their tails between their legs."

"No, that's what the other side will be doing when Gus starts shootin'," Orville said as he slapped his big brother on the back and the two laughed.

"Right you are! I'm ready to fight and so are those friends of mine waiting for me out front. Give me a hug, girls. Mama, you too."

It was the hug that unraveled Addie. She clutched at her brother's shirt sleeve and wouldn't let go. Sallie began to wail.

Gus opened the door and struggled down the path with Addie and her sisters clinging to him. His attempts to disentangle and hush them only stirred their sobbing to greater levels.

Addie saw the men looking from one to another, chuckling, then saluting Gus whose embarrassment was plain to see. *Why are they laughing?* Suddenly Addie's musical ear heard what they heard. *We sound like a circus calliope, completely ridiculous—all of us grabbing at Gus, me crying so hard my nose is running and Sallie sounding like she's at a Greek funeral. And there's Delia trying so hard to be stoic, but with the hiccups—not to mention Mother flapping at us like a mad hen, and Orville laughing like a baboon. What a chorus of fools!*

Gus finally reached his horse, the one his father had bought specifically for this day. The dark brown Thoroughbred was named Valiant—a fitting mount for the pride of LaGrange, now joining the cavalry and going off to war.

"Ladies, ladies, please! This pitiful display is going to scare the horses. Dry those tears and lift your lovely Southern heads high. These fine men and I are going to fight for the honor and glory of our town, our state, our way of life and, of course, let's not forget, our dear families."

The men at the gate stifled smiles and handed Gus the reins to his horse. He slipped them over Valiant's neck, and with a foot in the stirrup, swung up into the saddle. He nodded to his companions. "Gentlemen, we must go at once to serve the South."

LaGrange Light Guardsman, Brown Morgan, winked, "Not a minute too soon."

Addie watched as these dashing men of LaGrange whirled their horses onto the road and took off at a full gallop in the direction of the waiting train. She felt drained and tired as the soldiers faded from view. The sounds of the sisters' despair quieted as they all ran out of energy and were reduced to sniffling, little moans, and finally, silence. Delia's hiccups were thankfully gone as well. Addie saw her older sister straighten up. "Damn it to hell!" spat Delia.

Addie's mother shook a finger in Delia's face. "Anne Adelia Bull, how could you utter such dreadful language, and in front of your little sister, Addie?! We are proper ladies and do not use such foul words."

"Well, just "hell" then Mother. Do you see what's ahead of us? It isn't just Gus that's gone now. It's every fit, young man in LaGrange. We are without anyone to take care of us." Delia lowered her voice for added drama. "And do you know what vile and despicable things can happen to women who are alone and vulnerable?"

Addie felt a stir of curiosity. "Tell me."

"She will not!" Her mother clapped her hands over Addie's ears just in case Delia had more unladylike things to say.

Addie struggled to pull away from her. "Quit treating me like such a baby, Mama! I'm old enough to know the truth."

"You know, Mother," said Delia, "we're all going to have to grow up now and we'd better make it quick. No more charm and frivolity and play-acting helplessness."

"Well, my headstrong daughter that has always been the way to attract a gentleman's attention."

Addie found some confidence. "Mother, we will not be attracting any gentlemen. There won't be any of them within miles of LaGrange for quite some time."

"Right you are little sister. The only men coming near us will be deserters, scoundrels and Yankee soldiers." Delia pretended to hold a rifle and fire it.

Addie was surprised to hear Sallie's strong voice. "Sounds like we've got to toughen up and say the hell with ladylike behavior."

Her mother's eyes widened. "See what you've done Anne Adelia! Sweet, sensitive Sallie has resorted to those back alley words."

Delia crossed her arms over her chest. "I'd say Sallie, Addie, and I are beginning to see the fix we're in, and might just start thinking of doing something about it."

Addie felt a surge of strength and composure as she looped her arm under Delia's. Sallie did the same on the other side. Then Addie and her sisters, in long dresses with hoop skirts, nipped at the waist with proper corsets, corkscrew curls perfectly tucked behind ribbons and bows, turned together and walked toward the carriage waiting to take them to hear Gus' speech at the depot. There were no more tears.

Chapter II

Delia scanned the crowd hoping to catch her brother's eye. She wanted to flash him a big smile so he would know that the histrionics at the gate would not be repeated.

The Bull family held a certain reputation in their town. They were, above all, refined and dignified. Her father, Judge Orville Augustus Bull, was a wealthy plantation owner with interests in law, politics, and higher education for men and for women. He was proud to have two daughters, Sallie seventeen and Delia nineteen, attending LaGrange Female College. All his girls were expected to earn college degrees, not to encourage independence, but to ensure they would attract the best men in the State. The accomplished men of the times desired brides who were well-educated and refined— women who would be paragons of virtue, instilling their children with values which would imbue the next generation with civility and righteousness.

If Judge Bull had witnessed the scene at his front door an hour ago, he would have been horrified. But he was already at the depot helping with last-minute details for the farewell ceremony.

Delia spotted Gus as the people began taking their seats. She smiled brightly at him. He started to laugh and shake his head as he waved at his three very pretty, and now very dignified, sisters seated with the rest of his family.

"What's Gus laughing about, Delia?" Her father leaned in close to be heard over the twitter of the crowd.

"Well, I think he's just so happy about the solidarity of his family, Father."

"Papa, you should have seen your precious girls this morning," started young Orville. "They were....Ouch!"

Delia saw Addie grab their brother's little finger and begin to twist it, *hard.*

"We were simply excited." said Addie.

"Yes, we wanted to let Gus know we are so very proud of him," added Sallie.

"It was a grand gesture of love, Father," said Delia. "Your pride and joy knows how much he will be missed." She picked up young Orville's other hand and discreetly delivered a solid and painful pinch. Orville grimaced but remained silent.

Looking out over the crowd, Delia noticed many of the departing soldiers waving to a lady-love, sister or mother. *Was that James Tomlinson trying to get her attention?* She had been preoccupied with thoughts of Gus going to war, but now felt sucker punched by the emotional impact of saying goodbye to one of her dearest friends as well.

She and James had known each other since childhood. His leaving would be almost as hard to endure as her brother's. As children the three of them had been like the Three Musketeers, always involved in some raucous adventure. Each man had fostered a strong sense of self-confidence in her. James' competitive spirit fueled her own, and Gus' unwavering support for her abilities gave her dreams wings. At a time when sons were valued over daughters, wives ordered to obey husbands and prevented by law from controlling their own property, Gus Bull empowered Delia. The incidents themselves were sometimes small, but the memories would loom large for a lifetime, shaping her character.

Delia would never forget their bold exploits in the woods as children. Gus was ten years old, Delia eight. As usual, they had gone off to play with James and fight make-believe Indians in the hills by the river. Crouched down on top of a steep cliff overlooking the water, the three of them stared at the 25-foot drop to the gravel stream bed. Just over the edge of the cliff they could see a ledge about six feet below. Gus and James knew that tucked into that hillside was a cave only visible from the ledge—where it revealed itself like some magic treasure. It was Gus and James' secret hide-out, and until that moment, no girl had been allowed to take part in this bold ritual.

First, Gus leaped from the cliff and landed expertly on the small out-cropping. James followed. Delia gasped. A few inches off the mark and both boys could have fallen to the river far below. She was terrified.

Gus and James were laughing. "Don't worry, Sis, we've done this a million times. You can do it too," Gus prodded.

"Y'all are crazy, risking your necks like this!" Delia looked at the river below and shivered.

"Dare ya! Jump. What are ya, just a *girl?*" taunted James.

"She's mighty tough. Aren't you, Sister? There's a cave down here that no girl has ever seen before. We're inviting you because you're no sissy." Gus was applying considerable pressure.

This entreaty was irresistible. James had dared her. Gus had made her feel so special. She knew she'd get all tangled in her skirt and probably wind up dead, smashed on the rocks in the river. Still there was only one thing to do. She reached through her legs and grabbed the back hem of her skirt. Pulling it forward and up, she tucked it into her waistband. Her pantaloons showed a bit now beneath the baggy sultan style pants she had created. Her heart almost leapt out of her chest, she was so afraid.

"Don't look at the river, Delia, just look at us. We'll catch you," Gus promised.

And so, with a little scream trying to leak out of her mouth, she jumped!. Not only did she hold the sound in, but landed squarely. Upright. Breathing hard. Nobody had to catch her. She was on solid ground and Gus and James were cheering. "Turn around, Sister, this is what we came for today."

Delia turned slowly, still scared she might lose her balance. When she saw the gaping dark opening in the hillside in front of her she began to smile, then laugh. The secret of the hillside cave was hers too now. She had proved herself worthy with bravery she hadn't known she possessed. She was part of the gang.

She looked at the boys. "Only one thing, Gus. Don't you tell Momma or Daddy I hiked up my skirt. I'll get a switching for sure and be locked in my room forever."

James stifled a laugh. "You looked a little like one of those exotic Turks on the tapestry hanging in the parlor at my house."

Gus was chuckling now. "Don't worry. Pants are pants. Not like you jumped naked or something."

Now all three laughed so hard they almost rolled off the ledge in front of the cave. They spent the afternoon in the cave telling scary stories about wolves and ghosts of lost travelers. When it was time to go, James showed Delia how to scale the cliff to get back to the top. There were rocks for handholds and a couple of bushes with stout branches to grab. On the way home they played Indian fighters carrying sticks for guns, shooting at scalp-hunting savages hidden behind trees and big boulders. They won, of course, clearing the southern territory of danger.

They started down the carriage road to the house, all of them tired, plenty dirty, but feeling like victors. Delia thought she'd never had so much fun. She knew what it was like to be a boy, and it was wonderful! She felt free and strong. Presented with a challenge she had conquered her fear this day. And in all her days ahead, she would carry a legacy from this afternoon of children's play. A budding flower in her soul had been nourished—one that would keep growing, and blossom into competence. . .

"Anne Adelia Bull, you are one tough kid!" said James.

"You made me proud today, Delia," said Gus cuffing her on the shoulder.

Delia beamed. Gus made her think she could do anything she set her mind to. She loved him for helping her find her strengths. It happened many times—these small incidents revealing new parts of Delia, each building upon the previous growth, like blackberry canes reaching for the sun.

Delia looked at the train that was about to carry away the two most important people in her life. Was it really so long ago when she and James and Gus had created a world where fighting and daring acts of courage led only to laughter and delight? How did it happen that those childish fantasies collided with the reality of this moment in history? The fighting to come would be terrible, and the acts of courage steeped in red blood.

She was already beginning to mourn the losses ahead—not just the men who might never come home, but the genteel life in LaGrange. She knew the men in her hometown were intensely Southern. The elders believed in a way of life that had taken them into a sustainable era of prosperity with the cultivation of one major commodity: cotton. Of course, cotton wouldn't have been prosperous without the invention of the cotton gin, the development of the railroad, and the hard work of plantation slaves. In 1861, Troup County, and the rest of Georgia, had forgotten that just two decades earlier cotton had provided basic survival not the booming economy that began with improved transportation.

LaGrange had a train depot, and that meant cotton could be marketed long distances with relative ease. Money was flowing. Life was comfortable. The imposition of what the South deemed "unreasonable" tariffs by the federal government on imported products threatened this stability—as did the unthinkable notion of an end to unpaid labor. Southern men vowed to fight for a way of life they feared would collapse under the weight of distant decision-making in Washington, D.C. For many of the young men leaving today, going off to war was a romantic gesture as well—a chance to have an adventure and impress the ladies with their bravado. Delia thought this kind of posturing was, at the very least, ill-advised. She knew she would not be thinking about the adventure of war, only the ugliness of it.

Delia saw Gus take his position behind the podium, glancing over his notes. The chattering crowd quieted as Delia, Sallie, and Addie stood up and began to applaud. Gus blew them a kiss and bent at the waist in a slight bow. Then the entire crowd erupted in applause to show their support for all the brave men departing for war. Gus raised his voice and the throng quieted. "You men of LaGrange will come home soon after this necessary work is done. It is a noble mission to protect our way of life. You and thousands of other brave souls will secure the future for our families and the next generation of proud Southerners…"

Delia thought her brother's speech was inspiring even though her family had been against secession. That was just Gus' way. Old and young, tired and down-trodden—everyone just felt better in her brother's presence. He was, simply, charming. But he was also smart, well-educated and outgoing. Delia remembered how he had changed the course of his best friend's life. She thought of all the times James sat on their front porch capturing their portraits in pen and ink. It was just a hobby then. Gus offered so much encouragement that James began to really believe he might have some talent. Soon enough James was the most sought after portrait artist in Troup County.

Even a casual exchange with Gus often resulted in a huge infusion of self-esteem. He helped the powerless to feel powerful. "We're mighty proud of those hands, Joe. They've built a community." Old Joe would be a worker until his dying day. As a youth he had picked cotton and plowed fields for his slave master. Later he acquired some mechanical skills and soon repaired equipment, built houses, and even made some furniture. Now, at a new master's store, he fumbled with hands that were calloused and disfigured from hard work and arthritis. Delia remembered the big smile on old Joe's face at Gus' greeting. "Don' ya jus' know how to lighten a load. Thank you, Sir, Mister Gus."

The closing applause at the depot was bigger than the standing ovation at the start. *Well*, thought Delia, *you've done it again, big brother. This time you have charmed the entire town.*

Delia pushed her way through the crowd as people began to mill about finding loved ones for a hug or a handshake before the soldiers boarded the train. Delia knew she was running out of time. *Where was James?* She had to find him. And then there he was, waving and making his way through the throng of people.

Finally, they were face to face. He took her by the arm and steered her to the other side of the train away from the crowd. He touched her shoulder hesitantly and tried to speak. Nothing came out.

"What is it James?"

He took her face in his hands and tenderly kissed her. She offered no resistance. James took a step backwards. "Well, aren't you going to say anything?"

Gradually, a smile began to turn up the corners of her mouth, and with it, a hint of mischief crinkled in her eyes. "You've just ruined a perfectly good friendship."

James looked at the ground. "I'm so sorry. I just thought…well…you mean so much to me. I just wanted you to know. I feel stupid now."

Delia was enjoying his embarrassment, but she didn't want him to suffer for very long. "What I mean is, you have just turned a friendship into a romance. I hope you meant to bring about this drastic change because there is no turning back now."

"I do mean it, Delia. I'll think about you every day I'm gone. You are the reason I want this war to end quickly."

Delia felt wonderful and terrible at the same time. She was saying goodbye to someone she might never see again—someone she desperately wanted to see again! Someone she loved. Tears came to her eyes and she wiped them away with a white lace handkerchief. She pressed the cloth into his hand. "My heart is in this. Will you keep it close and bring it back to me one day soon?"

"You have my word." James tucked the heirloom lace into his shirt pocket then climbed aboard the train.

Delia could not imagine continuing her life as before. How could she go back to her family's lovely home and sip lemonade on the porch, sing in the choir, shop in town? Who could read a book or go for a carriage ride when something so ominous was unfolding in the country? Just as she came around the end of the train, she spotted Sallie talking with another young man about to lead his cavalry horse into the livestock car.

"...and I will think of you constantly. Is there anything you want to say to me?" Delia overheard him say to Sallie with a kind of pleading look in his eyes.

Sallie paused for just a second then opened the horse's mouth and looked at its teeth. "William, this horse has parrot-mouth. You know, that's when the front teeth bite too far over the bottom teeth. You're going to have to be very careful he gets some grain and not just hay or he won't get enough to eat."

"That's all?" William looked surprised, and, Delia thought, a bit sad.

"Just take good care of this wonderful equine." With that Sallie patted the horse, turned and walked away.

Delia caught up with her.

"I guess you can say goodbye to William forever, sister."

"What are you talking about, Delia?"

"He was clearly flirting with you and you just as clearly rebuffed him."

"Oh, don't be silly! I don't think he's interested in me. And I'm certainly not interested in him or any suitor for that matter. There are so many fine LaGrange horses going off to war and I'm just so worried about them."

"As always, Sallie, your heart is reserved for the most vulnerable." Delia laughed and took her sister's hand, pulling her along to look for the rest of the family.

Delia spotted them gathered around newspaper editor, Charles Willingham, who was addressing her father in a serious tone. "Judge Bull, we need to get the older men in town together for a meeting about security."

"I gather you do not share the opinion of so many that this war will be short," Judge Bull remarked.

"No, I do not. And we're already getting reports of ne'er-do-wells in other areas robbing unprotected estates."

Willingham ran the LaGrange Reporter and taught classes at one of three local female colleges in the town. He was Delia's English teacher at LaGrange Female Academy.

Delia interrupted. "Mr. Willingham, do you think there is a threat to us here in LaGrange?"

"Yes, Delia, I do, and there are not enough of the elders left to form a replacement militia. This is a sad day for me. I've just said farewell to my newspaper staff. They are all aboard the train."

"How are you going to get the newspaper out?" asked Judge Bull.

"That's one of the reasons I wanted to talk with you. Delia is my best student and a most talented writer. If she's interested, would you allow her to take a reporter's position with the paper?"

"I don't know what to say. The women of the Bull family have never held paid positions," said Judge Bull.

Delia's mother interrupted. "But, dear husband, we women are very busy. We volunteer at the Methodist Church, call on our friends, and raise children."

Delia cut in quickly. "Don't you know, Mama, that everything is changing?"

"But dearest Delia, we still have children to raise."

"Of course, Mama, but with each passing moment, it's becoming clearer, at least to me that women will need to step into the vacancies created by the men. It might be difficult, but then again, it might be quite interesting and educational too. I want to be part of that," Delia said.

"My sister—a reporter. What a laugh! She'll get the hiccups first day on the job," young Orville offered with a mischievous smile.

"Addie, take your brother to the refreshment stand."

"Aw, Mother, just when the conversation is getting interesting you banish me from the grownups," Addie complained.

"Not another word. Take his hand this instant and be on your way."

Addie took hold of Orville's hand and dragged him along toward the table with pitchers of lemonade and plates of tea cakes.

Delia continued. "Father, you know what an advocate of education for women you are, sitting on the college's board of directors. And the reporter's position would be very educational experience for me."

"Yes, Delia...."

"And who else is going to do it? The young male staffers at the paper are leaving, this very minute and...."

"Ann Adelia, you are not going to let me get a word in edgewise. But stop right now. I do see the value in experience with the newspaper. We all know what a talented writer you are, and that's why I encouraged you to study English literature and composition. So, the answer is yes. You have my blessing to take the job."

While Delia beamed, her father shook Mr. Willingham's hand.

"Have you an idea for her first assignment?"

"I do. I think Delia should look into how other Georgia towns are handling the loss of their home guards. Her information may help us decide what to do here."

Delia's mind was reeling. *A real job. Taking over for the men. No militia. Danger.*

The whistle of the train turned all eyes back to the tracks. The train was lumbering away from the depot. Delia felt her heart flutter with mixed emotions—sadness that her dear brother was leaving, delight at the surprise of James outpouring of love, and now this growing excitement about the new job.

Delia's mother waved her hand over the landscape. "Isn't it wonderful the gardens are in full glory to see the soldiers off?" Her parents bantered pleasantly as though nothing out of the ordinary were happening.

"You women and your gardens. But it is very pretty this time of year," Judge Bull conceded.

Delia wanted to bring his attention back to more important matters. "Father, can we stop by the newspaper office on the way home? Mr. Willingham said he would give me details on filing my stories."

"I think we can do that, and it will give us more time to admire the scenery on the drive to the square. I just need a moment with the church elders over by the oak tree to set a date for our next meeting."

"Thank you, Father."

While she waited, Delia imagined the men on the train were gazing out the windows at the blazing masterpiece of spring in LaGrange as the cars rumbled down the tracks. She wondered if some of them were worried that it was the last time they would see their home. She thought that surely the memory of the dogwoods, brilliant azaleas, and magnificent magnolias would bring a tear to many a weary soldier at the front.

So much of the fabric of the community sprung from the way people felt about their gardens and the way they felt about their churches. Both were considered spiritual pursuits "for the glory of God." Delia's family and every other in LaGrange were particular about their gardens and even more particular about their churches.

In LaGrange, social divisions lined up with church affiliations. Though everyone knew each other, people tended to keep company with members of their own congregation. This was especially true of the women. They spent a great deal of time in Bible study groups, choir, and other church activities. There was an unspoken, and sometimes unconscious, pull towards people whose customs and beliefs most mirrored their own.

All around them was happy chatter, mostly young ladies talking about their brave men. Though there was an outward show of excitement about today's departure, Delia suspected many were hiding their worry and woe, as her own sisters were doing, to keep up appearances. As she and her sisters waited by the carriage, Delia overheard a group of young ladies from the Presbyterian Church laughing and sounding like chirping birds. "Why not call ourselves the 'Electa Club Golden Girls'! Doesn't that sound fun?" one said. Another, laughing heartily, "A war effort with real drama and flair!"

Delia couldn't help herself. She was beginning to unravel from the stress of keeping so many feelings tightly reined. "You seem to be having such fun today, ladies. Do tell me what amuses you about all of our young men going off to war?"

Elizabeth "Lizzie" Beck looked slightly stricken. "Delia, we're not at all amused by this war. We are talking about what we can do to help."

Helen Trimble who had laughed so heartily added, "We know this war is going to be terrible. We are going to organize a group of us at the Presbyterian Church to entertain the troops when they are on leave. We'll do plays, poetry readings and such. We want to lift their spirits."

"And we were laughing," Lizzie cut in, "at the thought of calling ourselves the 'Electa Golden Girls' since that sounds so unlike sedate Presbyterians."

Everyone laughed at that, even Delia, who was still struggling with her mood. "The Methodist women are going to do something too, and I thank you for inspiring me today. Best wishes to all the 'Golden Girls.' Good day, ladies!" she managed brightly.

Delia turned to climb into the carriage. Sallie stared at her. "You were quite close to embarrassing everyone, Delia. And now you sound like you want us to become a group of silly actresses."

Delia adjusted her bonnet. "Not at all, dear sister. Though the 'Golden Girls' have given me a challenge to think more deeply about a role for us, and I am positively energized!"

At The LaGrange Reporter on Main Street just off the town square, Delia felt goose bumps as Charles Willingham ushered the Bull family inside. *What an important job!* She would be reporting on the war. Willingham took a little of the wind out of her sails, when he told her,"You'll mostly be writing about the events in Georgia and how they relate to the war." *But still – a real job!* She loved to write and now she would get paid for it.

She could use the newspaper library for research, Willingham told her, and then he would transcribe the Morse code wire report, delivering news that was only a few hours old. Oh how exciting to be at the heartbeat of events as they were happening! This is what the telegraph had brought cities and towns across the now-divided nation.

The machinery began clicking and Willingham sat down at the wire desk, effortlessly translating the dots and dashes into letters, then words. "My telegraph man is on the train today. It's a good thing I forced myself to learn every aspect of the newspaper business when I started The Reporter."

"What's the news coming in now?" Delia was fascinated with the wire service.

"Seems there's a new rash of break-ins over in West Point, and an old man who tried to confront the thieves was hurt."

"That's terrible," said Delia

"It's happening more and more all over Georgia as the brave men leave to fight— the scoundrels move in to prey on the vulnerable. I've queried the interim leaders in West Point, Athens and Gainesville to find out how they plan to defend their towns in the absence of their militias."

Delia was riveted. "And what do they say?"

"Well, in West Point, the interim mayor wrote back to me that the townspeople were relying on the senior men to protect them. You can see what good that's doing now."

"And in Athens?"

"The reply was 'We're praying'."

"Gainesville?"

"Stockpiling what few weapons they can round up."

Delia felt like she had been thunderstruck. Inspiration was crystallizing. Her pulse began to race all the while Willingham was explaining her assignment to continue these queries about hometown defense. She willed herself back to his instructions in time to hear him say, "...and here is the basket where you will file your finished stories." She liked the sound of that.

As Delia's family climbed back into the carriage, her mother took in a deep breath and blew it out forcefully. "It's been a big day. I welcome a little peace and quiet at home."

"Mother, you don't understand? It will be a long time before any of us find any peace and quiet."

Her mother frowned. "Are you getting emotional again, young lady?"

"Mother, what I am getting is *utter clarity* about our situation and what to do about it."

Addie began to giggle. "So what are you thinking, Miss Fancy News Reporter?"

Delia sent her sisters a penetrating look. "It won't be funny when cowards escaping the war or Yankees bent on destruction, come through LaGrange robbing our people and burning down our houses. It is clear to me we need a militia, and I mean to organize a new home guard."

Her mother's eyes widened. "That's outrageous, Anne Adelia! There are only older men and young boys left in town, and any guns have been taken with the soldiers who left today."

"You watch me, Mother. There is yet another group of people left who are strong. We women are capable of much more than we were ever given credit for and we must step in for the men while they're gone."

Her mother paled. "Oh no, I can't be hearing this correctly! The Bull sisters are going to become soldiers?"

"Yes we are!" All three proclaimed at once.

Martha turned to her husband, the sound of desperation in her voice. "You are their father, do something! Tell your daughters this will not happen."

"Martha, I don't fancy that it was I who let Delia take the newspaper job. She would have taken it with or without my blessing. If she's determined to organize a women's militia, I imagine she just might do it."

"I am blessed to have a father who knows me so well," Delia said.

"And I am blessed that my spirited daughter's stubbornness has brought me closer to God," her father responded.

"How's that?" Martha furrowed her brow.

Judge Bull brought his hands together. "I pray a lot."

Delia smiled.

Chapter III

"Addie, I want you to send out the invitations to all the women of the Methodist Church because you have the prettiest handwriting," Delia announced.

All the girls in LaGrange schools were taught the art of calligraphy. Fancy handwriting was expected of cultured young women. Addie carefully and artfully created each invitation with the message "Come learn how you can help the war effort." Sallie was put in charge of refreshments for the meeting, and Delia took it upon herself to contact newspapers and town governments across Georgia to find out what measures they were taking for local security.

Forty-three young ladies showed up at the Bull manor house on April 26th. Carriages with servants standing by lined the street in front of the elegant home. Inside, the front parlor and dining room were overflowing with women eager to find a meaningful role to play in this burgeoning War Between the States.

Addie was in awe of Delia for her ability to lead and inspire a crowd. She took after her brother Gus in that regard. Addie thought Delia had a particular gift with words and an inner passion which clearly lifted the listeners' spirits. At times during the meeting, she thought some in the gathering might faint from the excitement Delia created. "You are incredibly competent women—running not just homes, but whole plantations while your husbands are gone to war. And, I might add, doing an exceptional job with all of it!" said Delia.

Addie knew the young women from the First Methodist Church felt committed to managing the home front. Delia's praise stirred them. "Extraordinary," she said of their flair for designing masterpiece gardens, organizing church activities, and getting high marks in college courses, including mathematics, and philosophy. "It is the men," Delia reminded them, "who want to shield us from hardship, but our married sisters know about the labor of childbirth, and the pain of losing babies to the scourge of disease. If some of us have not yet experienced this physical and spiritual toughening, we know we will one day." There was no doubt, Delia argued, that women were as good as men at meeting challenges, maybe better. Now, she told them, they were tough enough to be soldiers too. And besides, there was no one else in LaGrange to see to their protection. Delia told the group of her newspaper assignment. "Not one town I have contacted has made any plans at all to provide safety to their residents. Most say they think the war will be over in a few weeks. But *I* say we cannot afford to assume this will be a short confrontation. We must prepare for the short-term and the long-term possibility."

The women nodded to one another and began talking excitedly—everyone chattering at once.

"Where will we meet?"

"What about uniforms?"

"Where can I find a gun?"

"What will my father say about this?"

Delia interrupted. "Perhaps the first order of business should be to decide what to call ourselves. Anyone have ideas?"

Posey Alford offered the first suggestion. "The LaGrange Very Light Guards."

Everyone laughed.

Delia said, "I, for one, know what we will not call ourselves: The Electa Club Golden Girls."

Nancy Colquitt was a little confused. "I heard that's what the Presbyterian women are calling their war effort."

Addie was so excited, "Yes, the Golden Girls are going to be entertainers, but we need a name that reflects the seriousness of our mission." Never in her wildest imagination did she think she would be a soldier. Life had taken the most surprising turn! She was nervous and thrilled at the same time. *"What to call ourselves? Oh, I just can't wait to be part of this historic, one-of-a-kind, women-only military unit."*

Everyone thought hard for several minutes, wanting very much to come up with a name worthy of this cause—some forty brave women willing to risk their lives to save their homes, their town and their honor.

Finally, Nancy Morgan spoke. "I have always been proud my parents picked the name "Nancy" for me because it brings to mind a courageous woman from Georgia who became a legend some 85 years ago. Her name was Nancy Hart, and she is a distant cousin of mine. While her husband was off fighting in the Revolutionary War, her home was invaded by a group of brutal Tories. They ran rough through her farm, killed her best hog, and ordered her to cook them a big supper. Nancy did what they said, sure enough. The Tories stacked their guns and hovered over a splendid dinner with the prized hog as centerpiece of the menu. Then Nancy picked up a soldier's rifle and shot one of the rude intruders dead. The others ran like the devil as Nancy prepared to fire again."

The assembled women at the Bull house applauded wildly, shaking the floor boards with their approval of this extraordinary heroine from their own state of Georgia.

Pony Alford began to yell. "We are the Nancy Harts!"

More wild applause.

Delia quieted the exuberant group. "Let's vote then. All in favor of calling ourselves the Nancy Hart Militia, raise your hand."

All hands shot up in the air, still clapping over their heads.

"That's it then," said Delia. "The Nancy Hart Militia or The *Nancies* for short if you want to be friendlier—not that the original 'Nancy' cared to be thought of as sweet!"

This meeting had been such fun. Everyone was chattering and giggling in an undercurrent of pure glee. Sallie Bull broke the mood. "There are more serious matters, Delia. You said you would figure out how we were going to learn to shoot guns. None of us has ever touched a weapon more imposing than a sewing needle. Any inspiration yet, sister?"

Delia tilted her head toward the assembled group. "Well, I thought we'd open the dilemma to the floor. Ladies, any thoughts?"

Silence. Then everyone shouted at once:

"We'd need a man to teach us."

"Someone with some experience in Army training."

"A man young enough to know about modern military skills."

More silence.

Delia offered her thoughts cautiously. "I think many of us know there is only one man in LaGrange at the moment who could fill these needs but...."

Caroline Ware Poythress shifted uncomfortably in her seat. The woman next to her said, "Caroline, you know she is referring to your brother, Dr. Ware."

Caroline stammered. "He can't...he won't...he isn't...able to..."

Sallie wouldn't take no for an answer. "Caroline, he is the only one qualified to help us because of his previous military training during his college years. He was a competitive marksman and won medals for his accuracy. The people of LaGrange have always been so proud of his many accomplishments."

Caroline said, "I don't think, think...not at, not at the present time... or, or perhaps ever..."

Delia was persistent. "Could we at least come and talk to him?"

"Well, I don't think there's a good time. He's not himself, and who can blame him really?" said Caroline. "But my sister Susan and I are desperate to help him. I don't think you would make anything worse by talking to him."

"Then I say we adjourn this first meeting of the Nancy Hart Militia, and reschedule for two weeks hence," said Delia. "The Bull sisters will make it a first priority to meet with Dr. Ware and beg his help. In the meantime we ask that each of you make it your job to find a weapon—however you can requisition it, no questions asked. Next meeting, we will look at our potential as a fighting force. Now I believe our servants have prepared some lovely refreshments out on the side porches. It is a wonderful day, not the least because we have put forth a plan that well may keep all the people of LaGrange safe one day." Delia concluded the meeting with a hearty "Well done, ladies!" The women set aside their worries over poor Dr. Ware and his present challenges, and once again clapped their hands in approval of such a bold plan for protecting LaGrange.

Addie spent the next week thinking of nothing but the new militia. She was so excited about what Delia had started. Her older sisters were going to be important leaders in the Nancy Hart Militia, but first they would have to get Dr. Ware to agree to help them. "I'm coming with you to meet Dr. Ware," Addie announced to her sisters. "The three Bull sisters will present a united front on this first mission." She had assumed she would be included. After all, she had printed the invitations.

"Little sister, you are too young to be a soldier in this militia." Delia frowned at Addie.

"I am not!" Addie bristled. "You are so bossy, Delia! Don't you know there are young boys going off to war? How is it I'm too young to be involved in the Nancy Hart Militia right here at home? Besides, I helped put the meeting together, and I joined in the planning with everyone else. I am going with you today, and if you try to make me stay home, I will go tell Mother you are going out without proper escort."

"You really are irritatingly obstinate, otherwise known as bull-headed, Addie. But I guess there might be a use for that quality in our army," Delia conceded. "But you will *not* be a soldier!"

"How about a bugle girl?" offered Sallie. "She's got the musical talent certainly. Every properly outfitted militia has a drum and bugle corps."

"That's not much of a job, but I'll take it, "said Addie. "You, dear sisters, remember this—I will prove my worth as a real soldier. You'll see."

Delia looked serious now. "We are all going to have to prove our worth. I think most people in town are merely amused when they hear the young ladies of the Methodist Church have started a militia."

The driver brought the horse drawn carriage up to the front gate. Addie and Delia climbed into the seat behind the driver. Sallie followed, accepting the hand of the house servant guiding her aboard. "I hope Dr. Ware will hear us out. He is our only hope of becoming a credible militia. Without him we will no doubt be the laughing stock of LaGrange." When she was settled into the seat, Sallie nodded to the driver. The carriage moved off down the road, hooves beating rhythmic and slow on the old dirt road into town.

Chapter IV

He was vaguely aware that he couldn't get up, but he didn't care. His pants were off and he didn't know why. Perhaps it was just easier to leave them off if he had to relieve himself, but he didn't care about that either. His hair was down to his shoulders, stringy, knotted and wet—from what he didn't know. He could smell decay and taste dirt, so he must be outside his cottage—maybe on his way back from the outhouse. In one hand he held an open flagon with the smell of whiskey drifting under his nose, blending with the soil into an aroma of fermenting compost. This was the one man of fighting age left in LaGrange, Georgia: Dr. Augustus C. Ware, country doctor, patriotic Southern son, and now, hopeless drunk.

Augustus drank to forget that he was once a respected physician with a bright future. He drank to oblivion because that future was gone. Before his accident he was excited about the war. His most fervent desire was to be part of the action, and felt his experience and natural leadership ability perfectly suited him to serve. Still young at twenty-nine, he had gone through a military training program in college before specializing in medicine. He had been a model citizen, serving with the local LaGrange Light Guards as needed, while taking care of the medical needs of LaGrange full-time. He was a trained surgeon, one of a number of doctors in Troup County, population 5,799 at its first census in 1830, but now well past 16,000.

Augustus was obsessed with doing his part in the coming conflict. When Georgia seceded from the Union in January 1861, he applied for a position as a field surgeon with the State Army. In early February he received a reply disqualifying him because of health considerations. Augustus suffered from a respiratory condition which the military noted as "poor health" on his returned application. He wasn't just disappointed by the Army's rejection, he was devastated.

He considered himself healthy except for the episodes of wheezing that gripped him once the cotton fields had been plowed—followed by the dust of wind–whipped fields just before planting time. He felt he had important skills to contribute to the war effort, and was being unfairly denied a chance to participate in a great and noble undertaking. A man could show his honor in a duel over a woman. He could amass great wealth and wield power. Or he could prove his worth by heeding the call to war. He didn't think he would ever duel over a woman. He knew he would never achieve great wealth. So he decided to keep applying, over and over again, until someone finally got tired of hearing from him and stamped his application for service "Approved".

As with many plans, life had something else in store for the country doctor. The weather was fierce that Friday, March fifteenth. Rain pelted his cottage. At times in the storm, the wind jolted the small house, and the wooden frame protested with loud creaks and groans. Augustus had been trying to relax despite the discomforting sounds of the storm, safely tucked into a wing chair by the fireplace. He was reading a medical journal when a messenger on horseback slogged up to the front of the cottage. It was John Harrison who owned the plantation supply store and the cotton warehouse near the depot. John was normally a quiet, calm man but not today. Augustus could see from the window that John was agitated, as was his horse. He dismounted in a hurry and pulled the reins over the animal's head. He gripped the reins in one hand, and led the skittish animal up the stone path to the front door. The horse jigged nervously, spooking at the branches and debris being blown about by the storm. Augustus knew this was not an ordinary visit. Something was wrong. John Harrison, that sturdy rock of responsibility, would never have come out in a storm like this without an urgent reason. When he opened the door, John yelled over the wind. "Dr. Ware, we've had an accident. The roof caved in, and a whole row of cotton bales have fallen on two of my workers. We've got bales and beams everywhere, and two boys that are either hurt bad or dead."

Augustus didn't hesitate. "I'll hitch up the buggy and be along right away. Get back in the saddle. You're safer on that horse's back than on the ground about to get stomped by him."

"You're right about that, Doc." Harrison struggled to get his foot into the stirrup as the horse began to spin in a circle. He barely managed to swing back up. "I've got to go back and help rescue my boys." And with that, the horse fled for home with John gripping reins and mane, struggling fiercely to stay in the saddle.

Augustus was used to emergencies, just not responding to them in big storms. But dedication to healing propelled him. He pulled on his boots, grabbed his only heavy coat, and a hat. The carriage house next to the cottage was shaking, but so far holding together. Ben, the stable servant, was inside trying to quiet Dr. Ware's two nervous horses. One was a sturdy, old bay mare, reliable and quiet as a plow horse. The other horse was a five-year-old chestnut gelding. Eventually, he would replace Dolly when the old girl couldn't work anymore, but the chestnut was young, and not what they call "dead broke." He knew Dolly would be the better choice for the buggy today, but he couldn't bring himself to use her. She was due with a foal in another week and he feared the storm would put too much stress on her. So it had to be Reggie . The youngster was anxious about the weather—pacing in his stall, but then even Dolly was acting wary. Ben helped harness the young horse as Augustus spoke to the animal in quiet tones. The horse's ears twitched back and forth which meant he was listening to all the sounds around him. He seemed to relax some with Ben's handling. "Dr. Ware, you want me to come along?"

"No, Ben. My sister needs you to look after her family's safety here at home." Augustus patted Reggie.

Ben was worried, but deferred to the doctor's judgment. "Whatever you say, Doc. You be extra careful out there. It's frightful."

When Augustus led the horse out into the storm, he could tell the animal was tense, but resolved to do what his master asked of him. About a quarter of a mile down the road to town, a tangle of branches wrenched from the trunk of an elm tree lay on the ground. The branches, some thin, some fairly stout, were piled on top of one another, blocking the way.

Augustus slowed Reggie from a trot to a walk, and then gently pulled him to a halt in front of the two-foot high pile of debris. Reggie did not like the looks of this obstacle. He had been surprisingly calm and obedient up to now. He began to worry, jigging in place snorting and swishing his tail. Augustus knew Dolly would have calmly backed up when asked, and they would have driven around the mess, but Reggie didn't have as much training or experience. When Augustus applied pressure on the reins as a signal to back up, Reggie became terribly confused. He wasn't sure what his master wanted, and there was this obstacle in the way. Reggie jumped it. But of course the buggy didn't. The sound of splintering wood rang out and the wheels locked up. "Whoa! Reggie, Whoa, son." Reggie understood "whoa" and frightened as he was now, he tentatively came to a stop. Augustus jumped out of the buggy and went to the horse to quiet him. "That's all right, Reggie, you were trying to help and you just didn't know. Easy now, boy."

The horse stood still, shaking, but halted. Augustus turned his attention to the trapped buggy. A rather large branch had snapped when the wheels went over it, but now half of it was caught in the spokes. He would have to try and pull it out to unlock the wheels. When things start to go badly from a horse reacting naturally to fear, they generally get worse before they get better. This was no exception. Augustus reached his right hand down through the spoke to grab the branch and pull it free. The sound of the branch scraping and pulling against the spoke was too much for Reggie. He bolted. The last thing the doctor remembered was hearing a primordial, ear-splitting scream. It was his own.

Near town, two young black men lay on bedrolls side-by-side on the floor of Dr. Wimbish's parlor. One of the men wore a splint on his leg. The other had bandages around his chest. They had been trapped beneath bales of cotton and broken roof beams for several hours. After John Harrison returned from alerting Augustus, he had pitched in to the rescue effort with a plantation overseer who had been buying supplies at the nearby feed store. The two black workers were from the Reid Plantation. Samuel Reid rented them out two days a week to help John transfer cotton bales from storage to depot after a sale. They were good workers—strong, trustworthy, and capable of following instructions. John feared they were crushed to death, but when he'd managed to shift some of the fallen 500 pound cotton bales that had toppled, there they were: jackknifed over one another, half- protected by a wood beam. They were alive—moaning and trying to move.

When he and the plantation manager had loaded them onto a flatbed wagon, John suddenly thought about Dr. Ware. Why wasn't he here by now? Hours had gone by. He asked the overseer to take the rig with the workers over to Dr. Wimbish's house across town. "I wouldn't ask you to do this but I have a feeling something has happened to Dr. Ware. Maybe Doctor Wimbish can look after the boys while I go see what's happened."

John Harrison galloped off on his horse in the direction of Dr. Ware's house. Rounding a bend on the tree-lined dirt road, he pulled his horse to a halt. The sight just ahead left him feeling suddenly out of breath. The horse and buggy were still attached by the harness, but the horse was trembling badly and sagging half to the ground on one knee. Dr. Ware was on the ground with his right arm extended into the wheel of the buggy. He had been dragged some distance with the rig. His hand was only barely attached to his wrist by a few sinews of gristle, and there was blood splattered everywhere. He was alive, but unconscious.

In the following days Dr. Wimbish expressed confidence that the workers would recover. Ned had three broken ribs, plus lacerations and bruises. His brother, Theo, had a broken leg. They were grateful to John Harrison for digging them out of the collapsed warehouse and seeing they got medical care. The two plantation slaves had heard stories about some inordinately efficient owners, who when faced with permanently disabled and otherwise useless workers, would leave them to die without calling a doctor. On the other hand, a healthy slave was of great value, so if there was a chance to rehabilitate a worker after an accident, the owner would make sure reasonable medical care was delivered. Ned and Theo were among the lucky ones.

Augustus felt decidedly *un*lucky. He was groggy and sick from the morphine Dr. Wimbish had administered, and yet the pain was inching back into his consciousness. Thick bandages covered the end of his arm. When his eyes fluttered open and he saw the mound of white gauze, he flashed on his last memory: bolting, wheels turning, hand caught in the spokes. Now he felt nothing but weakness.

A Negro woman placed a coverlet over his bruised and battered body. He rested on a sofa he didn't recognize in a house he knew wasn't his. Nearby, two Negro workers lay covered with quilts. Suddenly, the servant woman left him—or so it seemed to him. Actually, he abandoned her as he fell back into a deep and drug-laced sleep.

Hours passed. Or was it days? In such a morphine fog, it was hard to tell. . The black boys on the floor were no longer there. In fact, he was in yet another unfamiliar room tucked into bed under layers of quilts to keep him warm.

He could hear the fireplace crackling with oak logs, popping now and then with moisture suddenly released by the flames. Augustus regarded his bandaged extremity. A fragment of the violence he endured flickered into his drug-challenged memory. Horses were a blessing and a curse! Even if you knew how to handle them, their natural instinct to flee kicked in when frightened—which made for a lot of injuries. The doctor had treated quite a few himself. But he was unprepared for his own calamity. Not that he hadn't dealt with adversity—plenty of that with patients. Plus, his wife of four years had died from pneumonia after turning up sick one harsh winter. His two-year-old daughter, Leslie, succumbed at nearly the same time from indigestion.

Alone now, he had kept grief at bay by keeping a very heavy patient schedule. Lately, the only obvious frustration in his life was being repeatedly rejected by the Army he so very much wanted to serve. At least that had been the only thing troubling him. Now the storm of March 15, 1861 had greatly complicated his life.

He could hear his sisters in the hallway outside his room. They came through the door in a flurry of chatter. "Augustus will want me to read to him," said Susan.

"I doubt that, Susan. The only thing you like to read is the social page," jabbed Caroline.

"Then I'll read his mail to him. Surely, he will be comforted to know at least *one* of his sisters cared enough to bring him his correspondence," sniffed Susan.

"Oh, dearest brother!" exclaimed Susan. "We heard you were finally awake. We have visited you every day here at Dr. Wimbish's house but you've only moaned until just now."

"How dreadful this has been for you and for us," Caroline said solemnly.

"We're not going to dwell on this horrendous accident. We came to bring a little light into your life." Susan beamed. "I picked up your mail from the post office. Thought you might want to catch up on the world."

One letter caught the doctor's still drug-blurred attention. It was from the State of Georgia Army Services. He whispered weakly, "Read that one, please, Susan, dear."

"We are pleased to inform you of our decision to reverse our previous judgment of your military status. We deem you able-bodied, patriotic, and committed to service in the Army of the State of Georgia. We, therefore, order you to report for duty in the Surgical Field Corps at Augusta, Georgia on May 1, 1861."

He managed a crooked smile. "Do you suppose I could be recovered by then? It's only the end of March now, I think."

"Oh, Augustus! "Poor dear brother." Susan began to cry.

Caroline braved the truth. "I guess Dr. Wimbish hasn't had the courage to tell you yet. He couldn't piece your hand back together, so had to sever the last useless tissue that was just dangling from your wrist. Augustus, you have no right hand."

Augustus swooned with the gravity of this news, and began a long period of unconsciousness, self-induced by alcohol. In the days ahead, the servants found him passed out in the rooms, fields, and gardens of his sister's estate. They would carefully pick up the crumpled physician, return him to his sister's cottage, and tuck him into bed without ever stirring him from his stupor. On this particular day, a chilly breeze rippled over his half-naked body, but the only warmth he sought was the familiar taste of whiskey from the bottle clutched in his left hand. His right shirt-sleeve flapped around at the cuff because there was no hand to fill it. He took a swipe at his runny nose, but missed. He began to laugh, then cry, then snore. Suddenly there were strong arms under his shoulders, and another pair lifting his feet. He was being moved. He knew that much. But it didn't matter—nothing did.

Sallie remembered Caroline's promise to the Bull sisters: Augustus would be waiting for them in the front parlor. The home was graceful with tall Doric columns along the front porch. Caroline's husband, Frank Poythress, had inherited a large parcel of land from his father, who was one of the original settlers in LaGrange. The Poythress family had accumulated a huge fortune which included fifty slaves. Slaves were counted as valuable property because they could be mortgaged, rented out, and included in a will as collateral to pass on to heirs. But husbands controlled wives' property. Sallie thought all women should be able to control their own property. She knew there were many who would disagree.

Sallie noticed Caroline's eyes darting left, then right, then down at her shoes. "I'm not too optimistic about this meeting, ladies. Augustus is not well at all, but you may see him in the front parlor."

When they passed through the great hall into the parlor, they were surprised to see Dr. Ware sitting straight up on the blue satin settee. There were two large pillows on either side of him. He looked pale and sallow, and drool dripped from a corner of his parted lips. His eyes opened briefly without registering any recognition of people or surroundings. Sallie and Delia looked at one another then sat down in the Regency chairs opposite the settee. Addie stood next to Caroline, who nervously fingered a handkerchief. Sallie opened the conversation. "Dr. Ware, we are here to tell you how sorry we are about your accident, but more importantly, to tell you how very much we need your help."

There appeared to be some movement from Dr. Ware, but what seemed subtle and hopeful at first, suddenly turned useless. Dr. Ware pitched forward and without the pillows to prop him up, had fallen face-down on the floor. The sound of snoring and the smell of whiskey drifted throughout the room.

Sallie gasped. "Oh, my Lord! He's drunk and passed out on the floor, Caroline."

Caroline began to cry. "Now you know why I've been against this! What am I going do?"

As usual Delia took over. "You can't do anything, but Sallie and I can. Let us take Dr. Ware to our house. Give us a few weeks, and we promise we will return him in better shape than he is in now. What do you say, Caroline?"

She hesitated. "I suppose you could try."

They were an odd sight in the carriage going home. Dr. Ware was wedged between them, once again sitting upright, but only because they held him up. The ladies waved to neighbors as their carriage driver urged the horse around the corner towards Bull Street. Delia placed her hand so that it was invisible behind Dr. Ware's hat, and tipped it forward in greeting to ladies crossing the street. "Just the Bull ladies out with a proper escort, right Sallie?"

Sallie wore a pained expression. "I hope you have a plan, Delia because I am at a loss for words over the mess you have gotten us into."

Delia brightened. "Yes I do, dearest sister. Are you not a student, learning all kinds of things about health and human afflictions?" Delia patted Dr. Ware's shoulder. "Sister, here is your next project!"

Chapter V

In her studies on healing, Sallie had learned about alcohol withdrawal. It was expected that Dr. Ware would be confused, dreadfully sick, and have both tremors and hallucinations the first few days. She sat by his bedside every day, wiping the perspiration from his face, neck and arms. She gently massaged his limbs to foster better blood flow. She gave him a bit of laudanum when the tremors were severe and medicinal herbs to quiet his fevers.

Sallie ministered to him daily in the music room, now turned into a convalescence center. She studied his appearance. He was a man of average height with a slight build.and a handsome, but gaunt face. If his cheeks had any suggestion of color he would have looked regal, but he was deathly pale. She wondered if he could ever practice medicine again.

Gus had written to her about talk of developing hometown hospitals along railroad routes, places to which the wounded could be easily transported. LaGrange was such a town but had no hospitals. Sick or hurt townspeople were treated at a doctor's house. Gus thought that might change and urged Sallie to find a role in the development of real hospitals. "You would make a fine nurse," he wrote.

Sallie had smiled at that. Gus always delivering his encouraging words! Over the years, he had helped her cultivate her gifts, and supported her interest in healing. Sallie was the tender of baby birds fallen from nests, abandoned kittens, and injured farm animals. She enjoyed taking walking trips into the countryside with Melva, the house servant, who took care of the medical needs of the Bull's fifty slaves.

Sallie had watched Melva gather all kinds of plants and forest materials for treating a variety of ailments. She had explained to her that willow bark was useful for soothing pain, and jimsonweed for easing rheumatism. Peach tree leaves helped quiet stomach aches, and chestnut leaf tea loosened the chest in cases of breathing troubles. Sallie had memorized all of Melva's remedies, and begged the black woman to teach her more about healing.

To Melva this was a dangerous undertaking because a young girl could too easily mistake medicinal plants for poisonous ones. Safe collection required years of experience. Melva would let Sallie observe her work, but never mix potions. Sallie learned about poultices for lesions, rubs for sore legs, and even about stitching up wounds. Far from being gory or disturbing to her, it was fascinating and personally satisfying to ease pain or fight disease.

Sallie began to see that talented medical people were heeding a call. She believed that call came from God, and that healing arts were a gift. She struggled with the notion that respectable women were ostracized from a place in professional medical practice.

She remembered the day Gus had inspired her to become a healer. The Bull family had been out in the carriage calling on friends across town when an emergency developed at home. Judge Bull, Martha, Gus, and Sallie had paid their respects to the McMurray family upon the death of their oldest child, Madison. Losing young children was not unusual, but when they reached the age of sixteen or so, many parents believed they were beyond the reaches of childhood diseases. Yet diseases like dysentery, measles, or whooping cough still claimed lives of young and old alike. That was the fate of Madison McMurray who turned up with measles and was dead within ten days.

The family was awash in grief, especially because Madison was their only son. Martha Bull had lost one child, a two-year-old girl, from an illness accompanied by a high fever. Sallie had never seen her mother so broken, with fits of crying and depression that lasted for months. Losing a baby was sad, but Sallie thought losing an older child must be even harder—surviving the usual early childhood perils only to die anyway. She knew her compassionate mother was suffering for the McMurray family. "What a sad day and so emotionally draining," said Sallie's mother. "We all need a rest."

But there would be no rest for the Bull family on this particular day. As they pulled up to their house, the stable servant, Thomas, came rushing from the barn. "Judge, it's the mare. She ain't so good. She been trying to fo'l but something is terrible wrong."

Sallie followed her father into the barn. Morning Glory was the Judge's thoroughbred broodmare. She had delivered fine, healthy babies before, so what was the trouble now? The mare lay on her side, moaning. Her nostrils flared and sweat rolled down her neck.

"She been like dis long time," said Thomas

Judge Bull could only think of one thing to do. "I'll go fetch Jacob who runs the breeding program over at the Harrison place. He's had a lot more experience with these things than I have." And with that Judge Bull got back into the carriage and sped down the lane to his neighbor's.

Sallie's mother wrung her hands and fretted. "Oh, I hate to see Glory in such agony! I'll go get Melva. Maybe she can think of something."

That left Thomas, Gus and Sallie to stand watch over the terribly distressed horse.

"Miss Sallie, you oughtn't to be here. This ain't goin be very nice."

But Sallie wanted to stay. She wanted to get close enough to the mare to see what might be holding up the birthing process. Gus urged her to take a look. "You've got a sense for this kind of thing, Sallie. Get as close as you can and tell us what you see."

So Sallie edged closer to the rear of the mare. She picked up her tail and looked at the opening to the vagina. There was clearly a bulge there with a filmy covering, and something under the caul. With her fingernail, she carefully poked a small hole in the covering. Fluid gushed out and suddenly a small muzzle and one tiny hoof were visible right alongside the head. Sallie had witnessed the birth of several of Glory's babies before and she knew there should be two hoofs leading the head out into the world—almost like a diver heading into a lake. It was instantly clear to Sallie that the other foot had gotten hung up somewhere inside, stalling the birth process.

She knew Glory must be exhausted. Could the mare endure much more? She lay there on the stall floor breathing in short, shallow gasps of air. Time was running out for poor Glory.

"I think I know what's wrong, but I don't know if I should try to help."

Gus knew. "Of course you should, Sallie. You have an instinct for these healing things, and Glory might not last until other help arrives."

"Thomas, put a halter on the mare. You and Gus hold her head. I'm going to get this baby out before they both die."

Sallie rolled up the sleeve of her dress and bent over the mare's hindquarters. She slid her hand into the horse's birth canal beside the unborn foal's head. She felt around the flattened ears at the top, then pressed in deeper along the cheek bones. The mare moaned, but didn't move. Finally, she found what she was searching for: a knee. It was folded backward instead of alongside the head the way the other leg was correctly positioned. Sallie followed the knee to the hoof and gently pulled. Suddenly the small leg sprung forward! Now with both feet pointed outward in the same direction, it was like a piece of machinery slipping into gear. Sallie withdrew her hand and the foal slipped out into the world.

The three witnesses held their breath in dreadful suspense. Was the baby alive? Would Glory survive? The foal took one breath, then another. Glory stretched her neck and nickered.

Sallie's mother and Melva burst into the barn to find everyone smiling as a beautiful bay foal struggled to stand. Glory was on her feet too, licking her newest and most difficult arrival.

Mrs. Bull was shocked by such a peaceful scene. "What *happened?*"

Gus beamed. "We just watched the making of a miracle."

Neither Thomas, Gus, nor Sallie ever told her parents what had transpired in the barn that day. But Thomas told Melva and her heart had melted. Thus began the earnest training of Sallie in the ways of the slave healers. There was much to learn, and Sallie was an enthusiastic and gifted student. From that day on, whenever the Bull family held hands around the table to say grace on special occasions or holidays, Gus would squeeze Sallie's hand as Judge Bull let loose a resounding, "Amen!" And to that proclamation, Gus would add his own—a most enthusiastic "Glory, Hallelujah!" Sallie would catch his eye, knowing it was her brother's way of celebrating her first healing miracle: saving dear Morning Glory. How he made her spirit soar with his love!

In his fleeting moments of consciousness, Augustus Ware knew he had a nurse. This young woman was constantly tending to his misery, rousing him from oblivion. He was helpless to stop her. A large Negro man, whom the nurse called "George," watched over him at night. He was an imposing man, clearly strong enough to prevent a patient from escaping should he become sober enough to try it.

After a week had gone by, Augustus was sober and somewhat steady. He did not speak however, because in his mind, if he uttered one word, it would signal a return to the living world. Now he was only being forced to live, but in this environment of mandatory lucidity, Augustus began to grieve his losses since he could no longer anesthetize his feelings. His wife hadn't been perfect, but she had been perfect for him—never complaining about his dedication to the healing arts though he was gone taking care of someone else's family most of the time. Mary thought nothing of being a single parent to their daughter Leslie. And she had the slaves to help make her life a splendid existence. Mary, like most refined people of the South, did not refer to the household help as "slaves." They preferred to call them "servants." How could she be angry about her husband's absences when Augustus was, after all, doing the thing he loved most in the world? She applauded his passion, and felt blessed to be with a man who had a calling to help many people. And truth be told, she was doing what *she* most wanted to do—enjoy a lovely life provided by the good doctor. Mary's home was to her liking, her daughter was pampered by a Negro nanny, and as a doctor's wife, she was held in high regard within LaGrange's social structure. So it was of little consequence that her husband was seldom home. There were actually benefits: she didn't have to consult him about things like dresses, little niceties for her house—particularly the expensive art. And she was solely in charge of the proper raising of present and future children. *Life could go on forever like this,* she often told herself. She'd simply never entertained the possibility of death at such a young age, and was shocked as it overtook her. Nor would she have been able to envision that two months later, little Leslie would die, leaving her husband with no family. Dr. Ware had been profoundly shocked. Though he saw sickness and death every day, he somehow believed his own family would be insulated from such perils.

Though he was devastated by his losses and physically tired most of the time, his spirit was fully awake to each medical case, seeing it as a complex puzzle to solve. He loved surgery the most because of the daring new procedures that could now be undertaken with the advent of anesthetic drugs. Morphine and ether meant he could operate with less risk of shock. Before this miracle, too many patients died from the body's reaction to overwhelming pain. Because of this, sometimes doctors wouldn't even attempt surgery, preferring the patient die somewhat more peacefully. As things changed, he could see that treatment of the infirm needed to be moved out of the home and into a specialized residence. Many more lives could be saved that way, and Dr. Ware was in a hurry to heal as many as possible.

So much had happened since those good days with a loving wife and daughter. He might have recovered from the loss of his family, starting life over at his sister's estate. But when the accident took his dominant right hand, it took away his passion. If he couldn't practice medicine, life was not worth enduring. Now people around him were forcing him to face old issues and surprising new challenges.

In his room at the Bull home, Delia joined Sallie to tell Dr. Ware why they so desperately needed him. "Not one of us has ever fired a gun, and we're not going to chase scoundrels away flapping our aprons," said Delia. Recounting Dr. Ware's expertise and the medals that proved his sharp-shooting ability, Delia pleaded with him, "You are the only one who can make soldiers out of us." He wouldn't even look at her.

"This will be no gaggle of giggling girls," Delia told him. "We need a drill instructor to bring discipline to this militia." Dr. Ware had led such a regimented unit during college as many institutions in the South offered gentlemen military training as part of their higher education.

"Certainly it's unfortunate you lost your right hand, but you don't need it to teach us the skills we need." Delia argued that the women would do the work if Dr. Ware would just provide the instruction, and when she ran out of practical approaches, she dove into an emotional plea. "To turn your back on us in our pledge to protect this precious town will dishonor all the brave men of LaGrange who are even now fighting for our way of life." Still not a sign he was even listening.

On the twelfth day of the doctor's forced recovery, Sallie took a chance. She thought he would benefit from some sunshine after being held prisoner in the music room for so long. "Dr. Ware," she said, as matter-of-factly as she could, "George is going to take you for a walk." It was a big moment.

Augustus had not walked anywhere for two months—at least not sober. The stump at the end of his wrist was healed now, but his spirit still mightily wounded. He was constantly looking for an opportunity to escape George and this tortuous sobriety. Perhaps this outing was his chance.

The first two blocks of their walk, Augustus felt the arms of the big Negro supporting him. His legs wobbled, but with each step he became a little steadier. Without fully realizing it, they had moved toward the house where he had lived with Mary and Leslie. Since the first glimpse of the ugly, raw stump at the end of his right arm, his only feeling had been the yearning to be released from his misery. But as they got closer, he felt a twinge of sadness, followed by a flicker of longing.

Surprisingly, the house was quiet. The current owners were away on an extended vacation in Florida. Augustus was drawn to Mary's garden. He walked to the center and George helped him settle himself on the garden bench. Breathing deeply, he seemed to find, at last, some remnant of peace. He noticed George moving toward the street, and knew he was being granted a private moment.

Unintentionally, in that one deep breath, Augustus began to live again. Allowing his brain to connect with his senses, he first smelled roses—then gardenias and lavender. Was that honeysuckle? He even smelled the grass, and the earth itself. He yielded to a forgotten feeling: true pleasure. These fragrances were bringing him memories he had thought he couldn't bear... of Mary so happy here, building her masterpiece garden one flower, one bush, one tree at a time. But instead of feeling pain, he smiled remembering her delicate fingers, her graceful hands snipping gladiolas that she would fashion into a spectacular arrangement to grace the foyer...always flowers in the house!

Abruptly, the heady scents withdrew, replaced suddenly by a new fragrance. It came over Augustus like a warm, soft blanket. It was sweet and complex: musk, sweat, soap, tea, talc, lilac—a blend he couldn't name, but did remember. He knew instantly what had enveloped him. Unmistakably, it was Mary. The scent uniquely hers was all around him. She didn't need to be visible to be real. Without a doubt, he felt her presence. If he had been standing when Mary beckoned him in this way, he would have fallen to his knees. His faith had been familiar rhetoric before. No longer. Huge tears streamed down his cheeks—not of pain, but joy. He opened himself up to Mary's essence, and though she did not speak a word, he heard her. *There will be a time of great peril for the people of this town, and the women of LaGrange will need your help to face it. Soon many people will come here who need you in a different way. Your work is not done here, Augustus. You are precious and loved. You must embrace life!*

Just as suddenly as it had left, the scent of the garden returned, with its roses and gardenias flooding his senses again. Mary was gone, but he was back among the living. He sat on the bench for a long time—the tears a kind of salve. Augustus was resurrected, back from the brink, but filled with something new. Faith and hope had replaced desolation and emptiness here in this garden. Augustus felt a hand on his shoulder, tender and warm. George...silently acknowledging the doctor's pain.

"I'm ready, George." Speaking for the first time in such a long time, he knew it was time to return—not to the Bull house, but to the life Augustus had almost forsaken. He had many challenges ahead. But the women of La Grange and their courageous mission would come first.

Chapter VI

Addie pulled out her pretty journal and dipped her pen into the ink well.
June 10

Not two months after the LaGrange Light Guards left to join the Confederate Army, and Delia has written a newspaper article about a deserter who got bored with the training and headed home. He came through our neighboring town of West Point and robbed the women running the bank. One of the ladies fainted and got a nasty hump on the head. Another screamed for help. There was nobody able to intervene. That coward got away with a bag of money, hardly breaking a sweat in the misdeed. That will not happen in LaGrange thanks to Delia talking Dr. Ware into training the Nancy Harts. Of course, she couldn't have gotten through to him at all were it not for Sallie and her healing abilities. We do what we can, and I guess that means I have to play the drum and bugle for awhile. I don't know how or when, but I will figure out a way to be a real soldier. Training for the Nancies begins tomorrow.

The next morning at 9 a.m. Addie dutifully trilled on her drum to signal the start of the first Nancy Hart Militia training. Sallie took the roll call. All forty-six women who signed up for the militia that first meeting were present at the Bull plantation just on the edge of town. To keep the dust and dirt of harvested cotton fields out of their houses, the land owners of LaGrange had their homes built near a town square and kept farming operations separate, a short distance away. Addie's family raised cotton, as did most everyone in the South, but they also raised cattle. Today Addie noticed the overseer of their plantation had moved the cows and calves to a pasture full of lush green grass, leaving the already grazed south field vacant for the women. The bull for the herd looked nervous as he paced back and forth in the west pasture—stopping only when his cows seemed settled in their new pasture. Then he lazily ducked his head into the nearest patch of sweet alfalfa.

Addie noticed Dr. Ware's sisters, Caroline and Susan, talking to Delia, all of them smiling and laughing. Then suddenly Delia put up her hand to signal the buzzing group to quiet down.

"Ladies, it's so good to see all of you here today," said Delia. "Thank you for taking the matter of our security seriously. Caroline wants to speak before we begin today."

Caroline stood. "I just want you all to know how excited my sister and I are to be part of this unique group, but more than that, our hearts are full of gratitude that our brother has agreed to train us."

Addie was thinking how lucky Caroline was to have had the intervention of Delia and Sallie, when Susan spoke her very thoughts. "We have to thank Delia and Sallie Bull for their efforts in persuading Augustus to help us. And so without further adieu, may I present a fit and ready-for-duty Dr. Augustus C. Ware!" Susan beamed.

The women shouted and applauded their approval as Dr. Ware maneuvered to dismount from his horse. Addie worried for a moment that the noise would send his mount running off. She noticed that some of the other women seemed to be holding their breath as Dr. Ware dismounted, as everyone knew a large part of his misfortune was caused by a panicky horse. The noise of this enthusiastic crowd might well trigger a new incident!

Good old Dolly barely raised her head as the doctor expertly brought his right leg over the back of the saddle, released his left foot from the stirrup, and easily slid to the ground.

Addie sensed that Dr. Ware wanted to quell their fears. "Dolly's a good old girl. I'm learning there are many things I can still do with only one hand, patting Dolly's neck. "With your patience and dedication, I think I can help you keep LaGrange safe during what we all pray will be a short conflict."

Dr. Ware informed the women that military training was not always exciting, but rather, full of marching drills, equipment repair, and keeping uniforms clean. "Have you decided on a uniform?"

"No," said Delia, "There seems to be some disagreement in our group. I think it would be very professional to wear uniforms. They could look like dresses with full skirts but actually have seams up the center to separate the folds into large pant legs. We'd have a lot more freedom to..."

"I just think our men would prefer we look like women, wearing our pretty dresses." Sallie flashed a smile that was met with approving glances from the other women. "Bonnets too," offered Lucy Latham.

Addie thought it was a silly argument. She tended to agree with Delia that uniforms would bring respect, not ridicule, but nobody was asking her opinion. It was just more confirmation that the group thought of her merely as a child mascot for the militia. She would surprise them—oh yes, she would! And to do that, she was determined to pay close attention to everything their expert had to teach.

Dr. Ware held up his arms to signal an end to this argument. "I didn't realize this was such a controversy, so let's concentrate on soldiering skills first. Show me what we have in the way of marching material, ladies. Please form a straight line, and Addie, would you begin a lively beat so The Nancies can keep step?"

The line wasn't exactly straight, and the women weren't exactly at attention, but they did march off when Addie led the way, setting the drum beat. Behind her, she heard a shriek. "Disgusting!" said Lucy Latham, as she stopped abruptly to avoid stepping in a pile of cow dung. Delia couldn't stop in time and plowed into Lucy just as Sallie stepped on her sister's hem. The three landed in a heap on the ground.

Addie started to laugh, but stifled it quickly when she saw the stern look on Dr. Ware's face.

Dr. Ware surveyed the wreckage of his marching formation and sighed. "All right troops. Obviously we have a lot of work to do for our drills. We won't accomplish perfection in a day. Let me have a look at the weapons you rounded up since your last meeting."

The group gathered under the shade of an oak tree, laying out the few guns they'd scavenged from their homes and barns. There were only seven of them, all old—flintlocks, and most of them rusty. Addie saw Dr. Ware's expression change from curious to grim. "Ladies, I'm not sure if a bullet would exit from the front or the back of these weapons." He let out a sigh. "This is going to be a challenge. You must have better weapons, but I suppose we'll worry about that another day."

Addie asked, "How are the better weapons different?"

"Well, they're not rusted for one, but they are also more efficient." Dr. Ware explained that with the pressure of war, manufacturers would work to develop weapons with superior range and killing power. "Flintlock guns are being replaced by a percussion-type firing mechanism. Rifles and long guns with repeating actions and better ammunition now improve the range of fire. Lighter and more effective cannons are being hauled by ox cart onto battlefields." Dr. Ware had been part of the South's special attention to military training, and an officer of any rank was held in high esteem. In fact, military standing assured one's social acceptance. Now at war, the strategists were sure this readiness would help the South win quickly. The men of the North held the same view.

"So, ladies, we have a lot of work to do. I think we will spend the remainder of our time today learning the basics of these flintlocks and have a firing demonstration."

Addie struggled to rein in her excitement. She couldn't wait to fire a real gun but she would have to. *Better to appear calm and stay quietly focused on the lesson.* Lucy wasn't able to contain herself. "This is so exciting!" she gushed while everyone around her broke into giggles. *Everyone is excited,* Addie thought, *but they are acting like silly little girls.*

Dr. Ware raised his voice. "Ladies, there will be no giggling in this militia. You are to take your jobs seriously, and learn how to be disciplined soldiers. Our first order of business today is gun safety." Dr. Ware proceeded to instruct the women on the parts of the gun, the striking mechanisms, the handling of gunpowder, and the importance of keeping the weapons clean. Addie paid careful attention—a flintlock gun had three main parts: a lock, a stock, and a barrel. She leaned in close as Dr. Ware showed how the gun worked. A hammer on the top part of the weapon was fitted with a piece of flint. Pulling the trigger released the powerful spring that held the hammer, and the hammer dropped with force enough to produce a spark.

In turn that spark ignited the gunpowder in a metal spoon-like fitting called a pan. The lit gunpowder then traveled into the gun barrel through a small hole where it exploded, expelling a lead ball with deadly force. "Ladies, these are the mechanics of firing, but things can go wrong."

Addie's attention was rapt. Dr. Ware told the group that too much gunpowder might produce too big an explosion, but too little, not enough of an explosion. And if the small hole into the barrel was obstructed with dirt or debris, the gunpowder would simply fizzle out in the pan. "It's called 'a flash in the pan,' and it means the gun will fail to fire."

Dr. Ware knew the modern percussion-cap guns were far superior, but he understood that those weapons were needed at the battlefront. These flintlocks dated back to the Revolutionary War, but they were still powerful, and would have to do for now. Looking over the seven guns, he picked out the three he thought could be fired safely. He asked for volunteers. This first lesson would not be actual target practice for all, but rather a chance for the women to observe the action of the guns.

Addie wanted so badly to volunteer, but knew Delia wouldn't allow it. Careful study would have to suffice for now. Betsy Haralson came forward along with Leila Pullen and Posey Alford. Dr. Ware taught them how to tamp the lead ball into the barrel, and how to place the hammer in the half-cocked position for loading the gunpowder. He emphasized that when the gun was fully cocked, it was ready to fire and advised them never to point at something they didn't intend to shoot. "I need to warn you, these guns are quite loud and have a substantial kick," he said, before showing them how to brace the gun so that it wouldn't knock them down or badly bruise a shoulder.

As Addie and the rest of the group watched, Dr. Ware walked the three volunteers in a line side-by-side further down the field. Separating them by ten feet for safety, he began with Posey, showing her how to shoulder the gun, brace herself, and pull the trigger. He helped by placing his left hand on her right to steady the weapon. Facing the unoccupied pasture ahead, she closed her eyes and pulled the trigger. *Boom!* Posey stumbled backwards, but Dr. Ware kept her on her feet. Utterly astonished that she had actually fired a gun, the observers began to clap and cheer. Posey turned and curtsied to the crowd of eager soldiers-in-training.

Next it was Leila's turn. Addie thought her face looked flushed, and wondered if Leila was nervous. This time Dr. Ware offered the same instruction, but let Leila steady herself by bracing the weapon with both hands. Those hands were quivering slightly. Leila took a deep breath, squeezed her eyes shut and fired. She sat down hard, her big hoop skirt flying up in front. Dr. Ware helped her to her feet. "Ladies, you have to keep your eyes open when you fire. It not only helps you with your balance, it enables you to see your target. Now Betsy, you are last today." Dr. Ware repeated his instructions and asked Betsy if she was ready.

"I surely am."

Dr. Ware began the prompts. "Ready!"

She steadied herself.

"Aim!"

She picked a point on the horizon off in the distance. Addie thought, *keep your eyes open, you ninny.* Betsy closed her eyes.

"Fire!"

The explosion was loud and the recoil sent Betsy spinning wildly like she was an unwinding ball of twine. There was a brief guttural moan, then a thud. Now it was curiously quiet. No one spoke as the group surveyed the fields for the source of the strange noise. No one in the group appeared injured. The cows, briefly startled with each firing, seemed fine now. The women looked out over the fields. Addie spotted a large mound of black in the grass, and was fairly sure she knew what it was. "Oh my!" she said. It was the bull, strangely still. Betsy did not make the connection. "Is he sleeping?" she asked.

Dr. Ware shook his head. "I don't think so."

"Well, what on earth happened to him?" Betsy looked at the doctor then scanned the group, sure someone would know what happened.

Delia had an inkling. "I think you plugged him, Betsy."

"Impossible!" said Betsy. "If he's dead, he must have had a heart attack."

Addie could contain herself no longer. "If he was watching you fire your first shot then I suppose that's possible," she laughed.

"Please Addie, a little respect!" said Sallie.

"Enough arguing and speculation. Let's go have a look," said Dr. Ware. He led the group to the west pasture where the impressive purebred bull once grazed in peace. He now rested in eternal peace, felled by a gunshot straight between the eyes. He was dead on impact with Betsy's wild shot.

Betsy began to wring her hands. "Oh, I feel so bad for the poor thing."

Addie said, "At least it was quick."

Dr. Ware turned his eyes heaven-ward. "Mary, I hope you have some help for us. The Nancy Harts are going to need it."

The Nancies, of course, thought Dr. Ware was appealing to the Blessed Mother Mary, and so launched into prayers of their own. Heads were bowed, voices murmuring..."Dear Lord, please forgive us..." "guide us..." "Dear Jesus, we're so sorry..."

Delia muttered, "Papa's going to be angry."

"I'm so sorry, Delia. Can you forgive me?" Betsy sounded genuinely stricken.

"Accidents happen, Betsy," said Delia. "At least we'll eat well this week."

Just as death was permanent for the bull, so too, was the nickname Elizabeth Haralson had earned today. It would follow her all of her life: "Bull's-Eye Betsy".

Chapter VII

Addie counted silently after the lightening flash...*one...two...three... four-* but still jumped at the thunder crack. *Was it one mile per second?* The storm was close. In other times, she'd found summer storms comforting, knowing that in the aftermath the temperature would drop and the air would smell wondrously fresh. But now, with the war underway, all she could think of was the sound of cannon fire and Gus in danger.

"Addie, help me close the front windows!" her mother called. "Looks like we're in for a drenching." The two of them struggled to close the tall windows as the wind picked up and the skies darkened.

Suddenly the back door flew open, but when Addie ran to close it, she saw Melva and George coming inside with daughter Frances. They were soaking wet. "Woo-ee! We's a sorry sight ain't we?" Melva held up a letter.

"Jus in town to get some supplies and such when we seen this big ole storm a comin." George said, "Missus, this is for you."

Addie's mother laughed and reached for the letter. "Oh, praise the Lord! It's from Gus."

A letter from Gus always brought such happiness; but now, watching her mother read the letter, Addie watched her expression darken like the skies outside. Tears began to streak down her mother's face.

"Mama, has something terrible happened?"

"No, darling. I'm just a bit overcome. Gus has promised me he won't die in the war."

"Why is he talking about such depressing things?" asked Addie.

"Well, I had written to him about my stubborn daughters preparing for a fight, and my great worry over him heading into battle. I told him I could not stand losing another child—not sons, not daughters. Baby Martha's death was almost more than I could bear. And now this dreadful war...." Mrs. Bull dabbed a handkerchief to her eyes.

Addie sat down on the sofa next to her mother. Holding her close she whispered, "Don't worry, Mama, Gus always keeps his promises." With the thought of her brother's integrity, she was stricken with a wave of guilt—triggered by the mention of her baby sister. Addie had a secret, and now the memories of that fateful day had returned to haunt her. She was only six years old then. How could she remember everything so vividly? But she did.

Young house servant Luella had been in charge of the children, though she was still a child herself—just eleven years old. Addie couldn't remember Luella doing anything bad to them except scare them with spiders and bugs. After all, Gus did the very same things. .

But on this particular day, Addie had done something very bad. Baby Martha was sick, but no one suspected how the illness would progress. She remembered being in the nursery with little Martha while the baby cried on and on. Luella had checked on her and gone to get the baby some water. Addie thought Martha was just being a cranky two- year-old. Her mother would have known what to do, but had gone into town to consult a pharmacist about medicine. To young Addie, the baby's crying was just irritating. She'd tried to soothe her little sister, but nothing had worked. Finally, anger rose up in her and she slapped little Martha's face—hard. The poor baby cried louder than ever. Addie was horrified! The baby wore herself out crying, and after awhile she stopped. Her little cheek was bright red where Addie had landed the blow. *How could I hit the baby? What a horrible thing to do!* She remembered her mother's horror when she came home minutes later and saw the baby's red cheek.

"What happened here, Addie?"

Though the choice she faced made her squirm, she answered, "Luella did it!"

Luella was dismissed immediately, sold to another plantation owner. The very next day little Martha's fever spiked and she fell into a stupor. The family's vigil was short. She died that night, and Addie's guilt was nearly unbearable. In her six-year-old mind, God had taken baby Martha because she had lost her temper and hit her sister. Then there was the shame of the awful lie she'd told to cover up her contemptible act.

Now hugging her mother so many years later, Addie couldn't get away from her dark thoughts.

Why did I ever think it was all right to blame Luella? Did I think she wouldn't mind being blamed for slapping the baby? How despicable of me to think that way! A servant—a slave—had seemed, in that moment, to exist for my convenience. And for that, and the loss of baby Martha, I can never forgive myself.

Rationally, Addie understood she wasn't to blame for Martha's death. Time and maturity had brought more reasonable judgment. But there was still a six-year-old child within her that could not shake the torment of that day. There was only one way to redeem herself, and that was to accomplish something important in her life.

Addie's mother continued reading Gus' letter. With a puzzled look she asked, "Addie, what does Gus mean? He says 'Addie's cooking prowess is music to my ears.'"

Addie laughed now. "Oh, Mother, I wrote to him about how all the cooking lessons had improved my skill." She was happy with his playful, disguised message.

All through her childhood, she had felt especially close to Gus because it seemed he was the only one who took her seriously. Once, around the dinner table, she'd asked why public kissing wasn't allowed. "It seems like such a joyful, friendly custom among the slaves" she added. Her mother had almost fainted. From this and other instances, Addie learned not to ask her parents about certain things. But she could ask Gus *anything,* and he would tell her the truth. Gus was the one who told her about sex, and why adults worried that kissing would lead to it, which in turn, might lead to babies born out of wedlock. She was twelve at the time, and just beginning to understand what it meant to be attracted to boys. Gus didn't think kissing was bad. "I've stolen quite a few," he told her, "and that was that."

Addie was fascinated. "And nothing more happened than that?"

"Just some giggling," said Gus.

That sounded harmless enough to her, and she resolved to keep any future kissing a secret from her parents.

Another question, more perplexing to Addie than kissing and sex, was why she could only play the piano and harpsichord. Addie loved music, and unlike some other children her age, actually looked forward to practicing. In fact, she could play any tune the instant she heard it. She was exceptionally talented, called upon by her parents to entertain at their many parties. She didn't mind, as she loved playing and loved the applause too, but wanted so much more. Classical music and the hymns were lovely, but she longed to play the uplifting, rhythmic tunes the slave families shared at their gatherings. She wanted to play a harmonica, a banjo, or a drum, or belt out something powerful on a trumpet. The boys were allowed to play the brass instruments, but not the girls. Harpsichord, piano or violin were the ladylike instruments that girls were expected to master on the path to refinement. Gus had played the trumpet as a teenager. "Why is it I'm not supposed to play any of the wind instruments?" she asked him.

"Because some people don't think girls have the breath control. They think you'll faint or damage your lungs." said Gus.

"I think that's silly."

"So do I. Just one minute Addie." Gus took off with a grin, and returned with his old trumpet. "I haven't played it for years, and I think it longs to be kissed by your lips!"

They laughed until it hurt.

"Just one thing, little Sis."

"Oh, I know. I'll only play it in the barn or sneak into Effie's cottage. Mother and Father will only hear the piano," Addie promised.

Effie was the household cook. She and her family lived in a small cabin behind the Bull home, near the kitchen. She and her husband spent evenings on their front steps with their eight children and other relatives, playing music with a lively beat. Of course, there was the occasional sad Negro spiritual, but Effie's family favored happy, playful music—just the kind Addie longed to make.

Addie offered a deal to Effie and the others. "I'll help you with your chores if y'all will teach me to play these great instruments. What do you say?"

"Girl, don' you go gittin' me in trouble with your Mamma." Effie smiled at Addie.

"Banjo, harmonica, trumpet and no trouble, I promise." Addie crossed her heart to seal her sincerity. Effie thought the deal was a little bit scandalous, but deliciously so. She knew in the worst case, if Mrs. Bull should find out, the consequences would not be that harsh. Martha Bull was a gentle mistress of the plantation, unlike some who actually beat their servants for the slightest perceived misbehavior. Some were beaten for no reason other than to keep the slaves afraid of the masters.

Addie devised a clever plan. Everyone in town knew Mrs. Annabella Dawson Hill was working on an important project for the ladies of LaGrange. Mrs. Hill was well-known for her incredible cooking. Most of the wealthy white women of the day had servants to cook all the family meals, and Mrs. Hill's reputation for fine cuisine had all the ladies clamoring for her recipes. She ran an efficient household and relied upon a talented cook to carry out her instructions. Whether it was dressing a turkey, or shucking oysters, or mixing home remedies for indigestion, Annabella was deemed an expert. Her methods were unquestioned—so much so, it became de rigueur to use her recipes and follow her rules because everything Mrs. Hill did was considered to be in the finest of taste. Her project, a new cookbook, was eagerly awaited. It would not only be a tool to teach servants, but for young ladies of the mannered estates to one day please their husbands. When Mrs. Hill invited other ladies to contribute their favorite recipes, they were thrilled! Who wouldn't want to be part of such a prestigious publication?

Addie's plan to become a one-girl band was inextricably linked to her mother's excitement over Mrs. Hill's cookbook-in-progress. "Mother, I'm going to watch Effie make some corn bread dressing." "Mother, Effie is expecting me to learn how to prepare chicken and dumplings today. It may take a while." "Oh my, "Effie's teaching me peach cobbler this morning. See you later."

Her mother thought it was wonderful that Addie was so interested in the domestic arts. "You're going to best your sisters in the culinary arts and make some man very happy one day," she told her. " It would just be splendid if her youngest daughter joined her in contributing to Mrs. Dawson's book. Thus Addie had her mother's blessing to go to the cook's cottage or the kitchen to whip up something creative. She just didn't realize it wasn't food.

How Effie laughed teaching Addie to play the banjo! "You are good, girl!" In no time Addie had joined the family of musicians on the front step, playing tunes like "Old Grey Mare" and "Looka Dar Now." She had never felt so free or so happy. It seemed ironic that music bestowed a feeling of freedom when these friends of hers would never be truly free. They were amazing people who had every reason to be unhappy, yet took joy where they could find it in life—and they often found it in music. Addie adored them all. "How will I ever be able to repay you for all you've given me?" she asked Effie one night as she hugged her.

"Juz be happy and love whilst ya got love to give," Effie said, hugging her back. Addie had found her calling in music, and all because of Gus and his old trumpet. She would never forget his unflagging encouragement and support.

Occasionally, Addie's mother questioned her about her frequent trips to the cook's cabin, and the sounds that wafted on the early evening breeze and through the Bull manor windows. "Addie, dear, Effie's plucking on the banjo again. I don't know how she can sit and recall recipes for you when she's busy playing those silly tunes."

"Effie says cooking and music both have a rhythm, and it helps her remember ingredients to strum that banjo," said Addie, giving her mother a sweet, earnest look.

"Is that so? Curious way to cook," said her mother.

"Oh, we surely are cooking, Mama!"

By the time Annabella's book, <u>Southern Cooking with Mrs. Hill</u>, was published, Addie was an accomplished musician on six instruments: banjo, harmonica, fiddle, fife, trumpet and drum. She had learned dozens of songs, and delighted in playing them by ear. Every so often, as she sat at the piano playing some hymn, with her sisters gathered around working needlepoint or reading a book, "Ever of Thee" would suddenly spin into "Camp Town Races." Delia and Sallie would convulse with giggles until they heard footsteps in the hall. "Amazing Grace" was all Martha or the Judge would hear as they checked on their refined and respectful daughters.

Addie laughed aloud at these treasured memories just as another crack of thunder pierced the air. "What's so funny, Addie? Are you trying to coax me into a better mood?" asked her mother.

"Oh, I was just thinking if Gus could have seen his sisters at our first militia training, he would have been rolling on the ground laughing." Addie kept her secrets—the ones that made her happy. And the ones that made her ashamed.

Chapter VIII

If I can just distinguish myself as the drill leader with my drum and bugle skills, Addie told herself, *then maybe I can impress the Nancies with my dedication to the unit.* She had another idea too. When *the Nancies* gathered at the town square to practice formations for the first time, Addie brought along her family's pony, Molly. She had groomed the little black mare to a high shine and braided her mane with bright yellow ribbons. Sitting astride the pony carrying the state flag, with her drum and her bugle strapped across her chest, Addie made her entrance. The women smiled and laughed as she trotted Molly across the square, then turned and faced the unit, bowing her head grandly to her fellow soldiers. Then dropping her reins, she put her bugle to her lips, sounding the call to drill. The women applauded appreciatively, pleased with Addie's extra attention to detail today.

"Couldn't we have a quadrille team?" Lucy Latham was bursting with excitement over the idea of a mounted color guard team.

"Where are we going to get the other three horses?" asked Ella Pitman. "All the fit mounts in the area are gone to the war front."

"Wait!" shouted Betsy. "We've got Belle. She's blind, but she'll go anywhere I ask her to. I know she's old, but she's steady and calm. She wouldn't care about the flags or all the commotion."

"Yes, because she's blind," said Posey Alford dryly. "My family still has the big Belgium to plow the fields. He's pretty unflappable. I'd love to ride with Addie."

Delia thought it was time to point out the obvious. "Ladies, don't you see? Our color guard would look so much more polished if they wore pants instead of riding with their skirts all bunched up around them."

Sallie jumped in. "There you go Delia, trying to insinuate uniforms when the rest of us don't want them!"

Addie noticed Dr. Ware had arrived to begin the training. He looked mighty vexed.

"Are you ladies arguing about uniforms again?" he said with a hint of exasperation in his voice.

"I was just talking about the practicality of it if indeed we have a color guard," retorted Delia.

Sallie countered. "I know you, Sister. You wanted to open that door again...."

"Whoa, whoa, whoa. Let's be men...er, I mean let's be disciplined about this and hear one argument for and one against uniforms," offered Dr. Ware. "Delia, you first."

"Well, I recently attended a meeting of the newly-formed Ladies' Home Society so I could write a newspaper story about towns preparing to tend the wounded from the warfront. Our group from the Baptist church will be organizing hospital supplies and helping the men recover, though God willing, few will be in need of it. Anyway, the women have designed uniforms. Not pants, but dresses in gray homespun with dark blue sashes at the waist. So you see, I'm not pushing for pants necessarily, just a professional look."

"Oh, I've seen those uniforms," said Leila Pullen, "and they are just plain ugly."

Lucy blurted out the truth as she saw it. "With the war on and no one to dress up for, I still want to wear my lovely dresses and feel pretty. Can't we be pretty and competent?"

Addie noticed many women nodding in agreement, and knew Delia would not win this argument over uniforms.

"We need to move on, ladies," Dr. Ware said, clearly ready to settle it now and forever. "Let's put it to a vote. All in favor of uniforms raise your hand."

Addie's hand shot up, but there was only one other. Delia, of course.

"All right then. If you are going to be pretty, you'd better be pretty darn good. That's the only way you will be taken seriously. Next order of business is to elect officers. Any one have nominations for your commanding officer?" asked Dr. Ware.

"Well, it was Delia's idea to start this militia..." said Sallie.

"I'm much better at the organizational phase, not the leadership part," said Delia. "I think we ought to elect Nancy Brown Morgan since she is a direct descendent of the original Nancy Hart. Wasn't she a cousin, Nancy?"

"Yes, I was actually named for her. I'd be proud to be your commander but perhaps we should take more names," Nancy offered.

A chorus of protest followed.

"Another vote, soldiers," Dr. Ware said.

Every hand flew up instantly.

"Congratulations! Captain Nancy Morgan of the Nancy Hart Militia." Dr. Ware shook her hand, and the women broke into wild applause.

Addie was happy that Delia was voted Third Lieutenant. Even with the bickering over uniforms, Delia was still a respected member of the group and they had showed her that. Sallie was also elected as an officer, which only strengthened Addie's determination to have all three Bull sisters march in this one-of-a-kind army.

"Discipline is the most important part of any army," said Dr. Ware. And to achieve that aim, the word is 'drill, drill and more drill,' so that is exactly what we will do today."

Once again, Addie was directed to set the pace of the marching with her drum. She dismounted from her pony, tying Molly to a hitching rail on the periphery of the square. Dr. Ware organized the women in five groups of nine, shoulder-to-shoulder, and then placed a line of soldiers along each of the four quadrants. With five groups and four quadrants, one group would have to sit out a maneuver, joining the formation on the next round.

"Hup, two, three, four..." Posey called the rhythm aloud while Addie kept the beat with her drum. The two lines facing one another marched forward, then stepped through and past the advancing line as the other two lines completed the same maneuver. When all the women faced the outside of the square, Posey yelled, "About face!" The women obeyed, and began the march through the center once again. In the beginning some flustered moments ensued as the four lines took off at nearly the same time, almost colliding. Eventually, they worked out a smooth rhythm, including the transitions between entering and exiting lines.

A crowd gathered as people tending to business stopped to watch the Nancies. Young Orville Bull stood near a group of other youngsters who had laughed and jeered when the women came close to running into each other. Now, after just an hour, the unit was looking smooth and crisp.

"You're not laughing now, are you, dimwits?" Orville taunted. "My sisters helped put this militia together, and when they all become sharpshooters, you had better run home crying for your mamas." Orville could be flippant at home, and call his sisters unflattering names—all in fun—but nobody better disrespect them in public.

In the following weeks, it was "drill and more drill" just as Dr. Ware had promised, but there was target practice too. Now each woman got a chance to shoot. The kick of the rifle still surprised them, but gradually they were getting better. Addie noticed a big improvement in their skill level. They might not always hit the target, but at least they kept their eyes open. And she kept hers highly focused as well, learning how to handle a firearm by keenly watching the others.

At the end of the first few months of target practice, Dr. Ware told the Nancies he would be turning more of the leadership over to Captain Morgan and the officers. "The Battle of Bull Run last month has made it clear we cannot tend the wounded in private homes as we have done in the past. We have to set up well-run hospitals in towns across the South, and I have been asked to direct that effort in LaGrange. I'll check in on you now and then, but at this point, you are proficient enough to keep practicing as a group on your own."

And so The Nancy Harts continued drill formations and target practice with unwavering enthusiasm. Addie was pleased she had mastered the precision of the matching formations, but still she yearned to handle a rifle. Though they were not training as an attack force, Addie joined them in learning how to advance and hold a line. One day, they unexpectedly learned how to make a hasty retreat in a surprise encounter with the enemy. Ella Pitman, along with many of the other women, still struggled with the noise and kick of her musket. One particularly hot and humid afternoon near the Bull family plantation garden, Ella stepped up for her turn at shooting a target, which was a tin tray hung from the center of a grape arbor. Ella squeezed the trigger, and the kick of the charge jolted her to the right. She hit a target all right, but not the tin tray. Instead, she shot right through the middle of a large hornets' nest that was hidden amongst the grape leaves. The hornets attacked ferociously, and the women ran faster than they ever thought possible, petticoats and hoopskirts flying. A few who tripped and fell were "shot" by the enemy. Ella swooped down on her fallen friend, Delia, who was shouting and flailing at the wasps.

"Come on Delia, get up and run!" Ella commanded, pulling Delia to her feet.

Delia was red in the face and angry. "I've gotten stung at least six times and it's all your fault, Ella! I hope some wasps fly under your skirt and sting you 'til you can't sit down anymore. I'm so mad at you!"

"Hey, it was an accident and....Damn!...*nation*!" Several hornets had indeed flown under Ella's skirt as she'd bent down to help her friend. The excruciating pain was exactly what Delia had just wished upon her. Ella took off running, pulling at her skirts. All the way down the path layers came off: petticoats, skirt, and finally, the pantaloons. As she stopped momentarily to tear it off each layer and kick it out of her way, the stinging continued.

Delia's mood brightened at the sight of Ella streaking off with a bare behind gleaming in the sun, running only in her fashionable French shoes and blue ruffled blouse. What had seemed seconds ago like a major debacle now verged on the ridiculous. She stumbled to her feet and began running with the other *Nancies*. A giggle began to bubble up into her throat.

Everyone shrieked and swatted at the swarm as they ran to a nearby pond. It was an effective maneuver as the hornets veered off from the water. When the women realized they had outsmarted the hornets, they suddenly connected with the new relief of cooling water.

Delia was laughing uncontrollably. "Ella, you really must stand up and take a bow for that performance!"

Ella was red-faced with embarrassment and in considerable pain. She sat waist deep in the shallow water at the edge of the pond feeling very foolish. Then it dawned on her that accidentally shooting the hornets' nest was funny, and running half-naked down the path to the pond was hysterical! She imagined what she must have looked like to the others, and suddenly, was laughing at herself. "Thank you, Delia. Your wish is my command." And with that, she stood and bowed to the group. Addie's hand flew to her mouth, covering a little gasp. The ladies, who would ordinarily have been shocked by a display of nakedness, understood completely why Ella had removed her clothes, and they roared with laughter. Addie dissolved into giggles and said, "Good thing Dr. Ware is busy elsewhere." The women sobered momentarily—imagining the good doctor witnessing this scene, then the laughter bellowed even louder.

"Bravo, ladies. That was our first skirmish!" laughed Captain Morgan, "and we are all still alive."

"And most of us dripping....with Southern charm, don't you know," added Leila Pullen.

"And at least one of us showed us a new twist on the phrase 'a flash in the pan' which, with Ella's able demonstration, will henceforth be known as 'a flash in the pond,' don't you know." Young Addie was having the time of her life.

The giggles gripped all of them, including Ella, who then started pulling off Leila's clothes. A free-for-all followed, amid gales of laughter. They pulled at each other's clothing—bonnets and shoes came off, and even a few skirts and blouses were shed as the brave soldiers of the Nancy Hart Militia reveled in this silliest of predicaments.

Chapter IX

Delia came away from the "flash in the pond" with a new insight, one without a bit of humor in it. She fully understood that *the Nancies* needed better weapons. She was certain that if Ella had been handling an Enfield rifle, instead of that rusting relic from the Revolutionary war, the hornets would have been undisturbed. If she could be the spark for such an outlandish idea as an all-women militia, why couldn't she think creatively about acquiring the right weapons?

She remembered the day at the depot, which had brought such clarity to the situation they faced. Reacting to the silly girls of the "Electa Club" helped bring her idea into sharp focus—the idea of the Nancy Hart Militia. How could she say goodbye to the men of LaGrange, and just go on home as though nothing important had happened? How could she sip lemonade on the porch, sing in the choir, shop in town, read a book or go for a carriage ride when something so ominous was happening in the world? The Electas seemed to be taking this monumental change so lightly. She couldn't and wouldn't.

She knew she shouldn't criticize the women of the Presbyterian Church. In reality their group was providing a worthwhile service to the soldiers. It had been just three months since the men of LaGrange left to fight. The first terrible battle had been fought at Manassas Junction, Virginia, and wounded men were returning to LaGrange.

Central places for treatment and recovery were being set up in area churches. Doctors and nurses were needed, as well as volunteers to cheer up the wounded soldiers. Delia told her sister, Sallie, to heed Gus' sentiments. "Good nurses are in demand and you would be perfect. Why don't you ask Dr. Ware about a position in one of the new hospitals?"

A week later, Delia was pleased to hear that Dr. Ware had hired Sallie to be his surgery assistant. "Dr. Ware expects me to develop such skill that I would become, in effect, his missing right hand Sallie told her. "It's almost like learning to be a doctor, rather than just a nurse. What a wonderful opportunity."

Both the Methodist and the Presbyterian Church buildings were turned into hospitals. The Presbyterian women, who had formed the "Electa Club," had plenty of work cheering up the wounded soldiers. They traveled to each hospital, putting on plays, singing, dancing, and in so doing, tending to the morale of the Confederate soldiers. The men responded heartily with applause and cheers.

The ladies of the Baptist Church were useful volunteers as well. Their Ladies' Home Society helped acquire and tend to medical supplies. Many of the soldiers' wounds were wrapped in bandages made of lint, a labor intensive operation which involved the scraping of cotton or flax cloth. The Ladies' Home Society didn't mind the tedious work as long as they were useful in stocking medical supplies.

Delia was busier than she had ever been in her life, tending to her militia duties as well as her job with the newspaper. At the LaGrange Reporter she had first look at casualty reports, and always held her breath when she scanned the names of the dead and wounded. She had almost fainted from relief when neither Gus nor James turned up on the casualty list after the Battle of Bull Run. Other battles had ensued, of course, but with winter coming, perhaps there would be a lull in the fighting. Yet in Delia's mind, this posed a new worry: the first winter in those awful camps. Already she'd heard reports of rampant disease among the troops in close quarters. She wrote to Gus, hoping he would heed the advice Sallie was offering these days.

Dear Gus,

Sallie is following your encouragement. She is working as a nurse with Dr. Ware and learning so much. You mentioned how unsanitary the camps are, which compels me to share Sallie's instruction to wash our hands more frequently—something about the transmission of sickness through simple touch. Dr. Ware has been reading some interesting findings by a German doctor named Lister, and is now insisting on cleaner conditions in all local hospitals. In fact, the government inspector closed a hospital operating in the basement of our church. The plank flooring was laid on top of the dirt, and therefore wasn't sanitary enough. Sallie is assisting in surgery now, and only re-uses ether masks on patients if they've been washed in a disinfecting solution. Evidently it's possible that a patient can breathe the germs of his sickness onto a mask, and the next patient can breathe it in. Sallie and Dr. Ware think this disinfecting process can interrupt this transmission. They also say that washing their hands, not just with water, but with soap, has an effect. So, wash your hands and continue to stay healthy. And duck your head when the bullets are flying!

Your Loving Sister Delia

Delia was working on a story about the hospitals in LaGrange as they were developing a reputation for good medical services. With increasing frequency, sick and wounded men were loaded onto trains and shipped south to the hospitals of LaGrange, as well as to neighboring Newman and West Point. The men who required amputations, Delia knew without a doubt, were comforted by Sallie's compassionate and skillful care. Most were worried about pain, but Sallie reassured them that the new medicines would keep them comfortable.

For her story on the hospitals, Delia was allowed to observe Dr. Ware and Sallie in surgery. At first it was wrenching to watch. The cutting and bleeding were so grisly. But Delia gradually relaxed when she saw that the patients felt no pain. The team used ether during the surgery, and morphine later to manage pain. Delia saw that Dr. Ware's patients were more worried about coping with life after losing a limb. "Let me show you what I thought I'd never be able to do after I lost my hand," he would tell them. Then he proceeded to hold a needle with the claw of his prosthesis and thread it with his left hand. If that weren't enough to impress the patient, he would pick up a scalpel with the claw and neatly carve his initials, A.C.W, on a potato. And if the patient still didn't respond positively, he would try some humor. "Never thought I could do this!" he'd say, proudly picking up a bedpan with his metal hand. "Never really wanted to though" he added. At this point, most patients couldn't help laughing or a least managing a smile.

Dr. Ware's experience of overcoming great depression also provided inspiration for his patients. It was obvious to Delia that his example supplied a large measure of hope to these physically and emotionally damaged men. Clearly, Dr. Ware felt life was still worth living, and he was respected by all who worked with him. In this endless toil of patching up war-torn bodies, he was making the best of a bad situation.

These days, Dr. Ware was so busy in the hospital wards, he didn't have much contact with the Nancy Hart Militia, but his heart was with them. He still offered to help in any way he could. When Delia was packing up after her day at the hospital, Dr. Ware asked her to step into his office. "Delia, you know how committed I am to *The Nancies* and how proud I am of their growing skills. So I hesitate to say this, but you need to get Enfield rifles. I know it sounds impossible, but those old guns are dangerous—not so much to an enemy, but to the soldier firing them."

"I know, Dr. Ware. I've been thinking the only way to get Enfields is to import them from England, the way the Confederate Army is doing."

"But the blockade..." Dr. Ware began.

"Well, from news accounts, the Yankee blockade of our ports is not very effective at the moment. Weapons are getting through to our soldiers in the field—so why not to *our* soldiers here in LaGrange?"

"Those are dangerous thoughts, Delia," warned the doctor.

Delia liked dangerous thoughts, and was inspired by the actions of a few brave women. She had read accounts of the Southern war correspondents, Felix Gregory de Fontaine and Peter Alexander. Each described the courage of a few women who were moving in and out of the military camps as spies. Some posed as wives visiting loved ones. Others plied a trade popular with lonely men. Still others masqueraded as men to infiltrate army units. They actually dressed like a man in a soldier's uniform! These impostors were clever and got away with it—or knew when to disappear. As for the women who used their feminine charms, well...the men didn't suspect that such women—pretty, refined, soft-spoken females—would undertake such great risks.

But some did, and as a result, Generals got word about enemy troop movements from these visitors. Information on strategy and supplies was smuggled into kitchens and bedrooms. If men were running the blockade, thereby making successful trips to England and France, why not a brave and ingenious woman?

Delia considered herself as clever as any woman—or man for that matter. And she was well aware that both England and France considered cotton an essential part of their economies. After all, her family had grown wealthy because of it. Textile mills were doing a booming business, turning Southern cotton into cloth which could be sold all over the world. Now, with the blockade of Southern ports along with the South's stockpiling, cotton was hard to get, but not impossible.

"Delia, the blockade is surely going to tighten as the war continues," Dr. Ware warned. "Getting through is going to become increasingly difficult."

"I agree with you," she said, looking him in the eye. "So I think we must act now while we still can!"

She knew her family, with its money and political connections, could put her in touch with the right people—people who, for the right price, might trade cotton for Enfield rifles, ammunition, and medical supplies. At any other time, this scheme would be appalling, but with talk of a major Northern offensive in the year ahead. Delia and Dr. Ware both knew the war was only accelerating.

"As the war drags on, we should be more concerned than ever about armed readiness at home. I don't know if I can convince my father to help *the Nancies,* but my family has the right connections," Delia confided.

"Perhaps I should get involved then. Shall I speak with your father?"

"Father will want details, so let me think this through first. Then I'll set up a meeting. Thanks for backing me up on such a dangerous idea, Dr Ware."

"Well, these are dangerous times." he said solemnly.

In the weeks that followed, Delia fleshed out a plan to procure Enfield rifles for the militia. When she felt prepared, she invited Dr. Ware and her father to meet her at the newspaper office. She could be more forceful there, on her own turf rather than in the home where father ruled. Perhaps Mr. Willingham might even back up her facts, strengthening the argument for her plan.

"Papa, promise you will hear me out," Delia pleaded before the discussion began.

"Knowing you, darling, I think I will have a hard time getting a word in edgewise, but I do promise to listen,"

"The Nancy Hart Militia needs modern rifles. Don't you agree, Dr. Ware?"

"Yes, I do. In fact, Judge, I think the women would be safer if they were handling better guns. I worry about those old muskets exploding on them."

"Mr. Willingham knows my research is very careful," Delia continued, "and I have determined that we—that is you and I, Papa—can go to England to trade cotton for Enfield rifles."

"But the blockade..." began Judge Bull.

Delia held up her hand. "Remember, Papa, you said you would listen."

Mr. Willingham intervened. "Our information tells us, Judge, that the Yankee blockade of Southern ports has not been effective. It may be at some point, but supplies and munitions from European ports are getting through to our troops."

"Not only do *the Nancies* need better and safer weapons," added Dr. Ware, "but our hospitals need more medical supplies. You could accomplish both in one mission.

Delia forged ahead, laying out the rest of the plan. "I'll pose as a wealthy Southern woman of leisure, traveling to England with her father. My only mission in life is to dress well, and everyone knows that the latest fashions only come from Europe. That would be the ruse. But in reality, we would be negotiating a deal to trade Bull family cotton for militia and medical supplies.

"Don't you see, Papa? Nothing is 'business as usual' anymore. We have to look after our own interests, and since we've got a negotiating chip, we must use it!"

"I wish I could say this is a preposterous idea, Delia, but our world has changed. You are smarter, or perhaps just more outspoken, than a Southern lady ought to be, but you are also right about this. If a farmer is supposed to make hay while the sun shines, then it would be wise for us to leverage cotton while we can." Delia and her father had frequently discussed the economics of war. The "famine of cotton" the South had been trying to orchestrate had finally hit textile mills in Britain very hard. Delia was counting on her father's frustration that his role in the war was little more than reading about it in the newspapers and pouring over Gus' correspondence. She was betting big that he wanted a chance to get involved.

Fortunately, her scenario made sense to him. European travel was not an unlikely event. The Bulls, like many LaGrange people, were not strangers to traveling abroad. Their network of social contacts and business connections extended across the Atlantic. In fact, they made an annual trip to France and England each year so that Mrs. Bull could keep up with the latest fashions. In this one trip, she took care of the wardrobe needs for the entire family, buying up everything from fancy French hats to fine silk fabric for dressmaking. Judge Bull regularly checked on his European cotton customers, along with his other financial interests, and over the years, many friendships had been forged— friendships which could be more valuable than ever now.

"What do you say, Papa? asked Delia, her voice hopeful.

Mr. Willingham and Dr. Ware turned to the Judge expectantly.

"I must be insane, but yes, let's do it!" His face, Delia noticed, was lit with new excitement. It was his adventure now too.

Chapter X

Delia was about to step into a world filled with stealth and dangerous dealings.

She couldn't afford to be ill-prepared when they set sail for England. All through the winter, she read everything she could about the effect of the war on Europe. She asked Mr. Willingham to get her several editions of *The Times* of London, and also keep up-to-date with the dispatches from the Confederate Press Association.

The European governments, she learned, weren't ignoring this war, but were trying to stay out of it—like parents with quarreling children. Both the United States and the Confederacy desperately wanted European support. Yankee spies and informants were everywhere in Britain and France. And while the foreign governments were trying to remain neutral in the War Between the States, they were also making money from supplying warships and munitions to both sides. It was a risky position. There were rumors that at least two war ships were being built in Liverpool for the Confederacy.

"Papa, do you know anything about this?" Delia asked, knowing her father had many key contacts in the Confederate government.

"I will share this with you since we are partners in crime, so to speak, but don't tell anyone else. What I've heard is that our Confederate agent, James Bulloch, is involved in a complex scheme to sneak the ships out of Liverpool. But there is a problem, as you might imagine. He has to persuade key officials in Britain that our Southern cause is just and worthy of their support, however clandestine. It turns out my friend, Henry Hotze, may act as go-between."

"I met Mr. Hotze in Montgomery, Alabama, during high-level government meetings. He was a Swiss-born gentleman with important relationships among the wealthy and was influential in Europe. Evidently Confederate leaders felt he would be more useful in Great Britain than working as a propagandist for the South."

By late winter of 1861, Delia feared they would miss their window of opportunity. The blockade was tightening. So far, not one departing steamer from any southern port had been stopped, but getting back in was riskier. Southern supplies were still getting through to the troops, but the European ships were frequently being fired upon. "Papa, we have to go now. If we wait until summer, when there is sure to be more traffic on the seas, we may have lost our chance." Her father agreed that it was now or never.

Delia wanted to limit information about their trip to a very few people. Her father, along with Dr. Ware and Mr. Willingham, cautioned her that discretion was essential as northern spies had turned up in the smallest of communities in recent weeks. Railroad towns like LaGrange were strategically important and that made them vulnerable. Of course, the Bull family knew about the trip, but the Pitman family was also drawn in to the mission as extra wagons and hands would be needed upon return. The Pitmans spent summers in Florida near St. Andrews Bay attended by more than a dozen servants. They drove to their private estate in six wagons full of people and home goods. Since they knew the route so well to the Gulf coast and back, they agreed to make their wagons and servants available to rendezvous at Mobile, Alabama and carry war supplies back to LaGrange. Delia and her father felt comfortable accompanying their cotton bales on the train from LaGrange to Mobile. But it was a different matter to bring the rifles and other valuable supplies back through the same route. Along that rail line were several places where the track gauge changed, which meant that goods had to be off-loaded and then reloaded onto different trains. They simply didn't want to risk rail-hands stealing their hard won supplies. So the Pitmans offered a measure of security for the trip home.

The only other person Delia let in on the plan was the commander of the Nancy Hart Militia. Nancy Brown Morgan worked Tuesdays and Wednesdays clerking at the general store since the owners were at the war front. Because it was Tuesday, Delia knew exactly where to find Mrs. Morgan. George drove the Bull sisters into town and pulled the rig up to the hitching rail, just outside LaGrange General Goods. Inside Nancy Morgan was just finishing up an order. "Be with you in just a minute, girls," she said.

"We'll just look around," replied Delia. She turned to her sisters and spoke quietly. "Don't say anything about our trip to anyone. Let me do the talking. Understand?"

"Delia, do you think I'm stupid? Of course I won't say anything." Sallie turned to Addie pressing a finger to her lips. "Shhh."

"Speak for yourself, Sallie. I'm tired of you two always telling me what to do," whined Addie.

"Good day, Rose." Nancy Morgan saw her customer to the door. "Now, what can I do for the lovely Bull sisters today?"

Delia glanced around the store, making sure they were alone. "Captain Morgan, since you know all too well about the appalling state of weapons in the Nancy Hart Militia, I'm letting you in on our plan to get a load of Enfield rifles."

"What!? You have Enfields?" Nancy's face lit up with excitement.

"No, not yet, but we will soon have them. My father has agreed to trade cotton for rifles in England. We leave for Liverpool shortly to arrange the deal."

The door flew open and Lizzie Beck almost tripped over the threshold. "Ladies, do I hear something about 'a deal' being made in Liverpool?"

"Oh no," Sallie whispered to Delia. "She is the worst gossip in the Electa Club Golden Girls."

Addie spoke up loudly. "Yes, Lizzie, Delia's got a *deal* brewing in Liverpool."

Delia frowned at her youngest sister, but Addie continued confidently.

77

"Mother and Father agreed to let Delia go to England this year to buy fashions since the war makes it awfully hard to find good fabric. So, we were just asking Mrs. Morgan if she would like a few bolts of silk or taffeta."

"Yes, that's right, Lizzie," said Nancy. "I was just about to show them the pitiful supply of yard goods I am left with here."

Delia held her breath. *Would Lizzie believe this lie?*

"Oh," said Lizzie, pursing her lips. "I thought I heard something about Enfields"

Delia tensed as Sallie fidgeted with the bow of her bonnet, but Addie just giggled and said, "Oh my, no. Delia said she was certainly going *far a field* to stay in fashion."

"How silly of me to misunderstand," Lizzie said with a wry smile. "But isn't it dangerous to travel these days?"

Delia marveled at her sister's cleverness. Now it was her turn to pick up the conversation, relieved it had taken a different turn.

"It's not the leaving that's dangerous, it's the coming home," Delia said. "But the blockade is not well-organized, so ships with goods are still getting through. A lot of people are putting off leisure travel, but I think we will be fine."

"Well, it certainly sounds like you've done your research and are happy to assume the risk—all in the name of fashion!" Lizzie giggled.

"Well, don't you agree, Lizzie, that no matter what happens in life the most important thing is to *look* good?" Now Addie matched Lizzie's giggle. Delia tried hard not to roll her eyes.

On the way home, Delia couldn't get over how aggressive and quick-witted Addie had been. What wonderful qualities! She hadn't expected such nerve from sweet Addie. An apology was in order.

"Addie, I guess I shouldn't have told you to keep your mouth shut. I didn't know how fast you could think on your feet! While I stood there gaping, you pitched a perfect story. Now Lizzie will be buzzing about the Bull sisters' new dresses and be in a snit that she can't compete."

"I just knew Lizzie would buy my tale because she really *does* believe the most important thing in life is to look good."

"Well done, little sister. I must do something nice for you in return," said Delia.

"Let me be a soldier," Addie said, her face suddenly serious.

"Delia, you have to admit she is quick..." Sallie began.

"She's still too young," Delia interrupted.

"You are bossy and mean, Delia," Addie retorted, "and perfectly fit the title 'Superior Officer'."

"And don't you forget it," said Delia patting Addie's hand.

This skirmish among sisters was forgiven and forgotten by the time Delia and her father boarded the train headed for the port of Mobile.

"Delia, please be careful!" Addie pleaded, hugging her sister.

"Let Father's restraint be your guide please," said Sallie, "you can be impulsive."

"You are such worriers," said Delia. "I plan to enjoy every little minute of this trip!"

"She's going to be a handful," Mrs. Bull whispered to her husband with a troubled look.

"Yes, Darling, that is one thing we can count on." Judge Bull smiled and winked at Delia.

In Mobile, the Bull family cotton was off-loaded from the train and set aboard a steamer bound for Liverpool. The early March voyage across the Atlantic in a side-wheel steamer promised to be boring, but gratefully uneventful. Delia stayed in her cabin the first five days, adjusting to the rolling and pitching rhythm of the ship—staving off seasickness as best she could. Just short of a week, however, she felt well enough to get some air on the deck, and take in the scenery.

Day twelve they arrived in Liverpool and soon made the connection they hoped would lead to a successful mission. In the lobby of The Charles Hotel, Judge Bull extended a hand to Henry Hotze's firm and friendly one. Hotze very much reminded Delia and her father of Gus—not only with his ability to instantly put people at ease, but because he was a handsome figure, tall with a muscular build and an engaging smile. Delia guessed he was about thirty. If she were not so intent on seeing her mission through, she might have viewed Henry as a possible suitor. Though she had no romantic interest in him at the moment, she didn't mind a little harmless flirting.

"How wonderful to see friends from home!" said Hotze. He turned to Delia and lifted her hand to his lips.

She smiled coquettishly. "And I thought I would come here and charm *you*. Clearly, you have beat me to it, Mr. Hotze."

Henry feigned surprise. "Please don't let that stop you, Miss Bull. I welcome your attentions whatever your intentions."

The Judge coughed loudly and stepped between his daughter and Henry. "Young man, we are here to talk about serious..."

Henry spotted someone he had just seen on the street earlier—someone he didn't know, but who seemed to be listening intently to this conversation between friends. "Judge Bull, do me the honor of attending a gathering this evening. It will be a grand, loud party with the Fleet Street business people, and we can talk about everything there—from the most serious to the most frivolous. Will you come?"

Delia quickly jumped in. "But of course Daddy and I will come. I didn't travel all this way to sit in a hotel room with a locked trunk of dresses! We have come for some serious fun, shall we say, and you are *just* the man to see that we get plenty of it. Isn't that so, Daddy?"

Judge Bull patted his daughter's hand. "Delia, my sweet love, once again, and as always, you are right."

The party was indeed loud—and just as lavish. Hosted by a group of government officials and bankers, its purpose was to welcome a diplomatic party from the Azores. Elaborate horse-drawn coaches delivered a steady stream of elegant guests to the entrance of The Charles on State Street. "The refined upper class of Great Britain, do *so* love a big celebration," Henry had told her, "that few will question the obvious: why such attention showered on a delegation from a small group of islands? Islands that have little commercial benefit to England?"

Heads turned to stare as Delia made her entrance...and eyes followed. She wore a spectacular gown of lavender silk and lace with a modest hoop skirt, and a delicately- pleated train. Elbow-length sleeves, with a poof of fabric at the shoulder, added a bit of artful whimsy. The deep-V neckline showed off a generous décolletage. She was a dark-haired American beauty, a genuine Southern lady. Delia had "good bones"—the kind most women envied and men admired. Her cheeks were chiseled, her eyes wide and deep-set. Her eyebrows were naturally arched, and her lips naturally pink, though she had scraped them with her teeth to deepen the color. Her height added to her scene-stealing presence. At five-foot and seven inches, she was a tall, slender willow compared to the shorter, and more Rubenesque European woman. Delia didn't have to work very hard to look gorgeous, and the other women could instantly see that. They were as envious as the men were enrapt.

Delia didn't care much about the attention nor the hubbub she had created. She was, however, obsessed with the food! This was no homegrown affair with pork and turnips. Silver trays decked with cheese pastry puffs, lobster canapés, truffles, caviar, and more glided by her wide eyes—and at every turn, another handsomely appointed waiter. She knew she should be ladylike, but it was impossible. So long deprived of fine food in these war years, she couldn't resist these scrumptious morsels.

Suddenly, the charming Henry Hotze was by her side—just as a waiter tried to pull his tray away to circulate the food. Delia kept diving for one more item, and then, giddily, another.

Henry laughed. "I'm so glad you are enjoying this party!"

Judge Bull raised an eyebrow. "I'm afraid I'll have to speak for my daughter tonight since she is busy savoring delicacies she's not likely find anytime soon in LaGrange."

Hotze bowed. "Then that alone was worth the trip, Judge Bull."

James Bulloch turned from the bar and walked quickly over to Henry's small gathering. "I thought I heard a Georgia accent in this crowded room. Henry, please introduce me."

"Delighted! Judge Bull, may I present James Bulloch, our agent in Liverpool?"

"It's getting to be a small world, isn't it Mr. Bulloch?" said Judge Bull. "I was pleased to learn another Georgian was appointed to such an important post here in Liverpool. Allow me to introduce my oldest daughter, Anne Adelia Bull."

"Please, Mr. Bulloch, you can call me Delia. I'm reporting now for our newspaper, and have followed the mentions of your work here in England."

"Thank you, Delia. I hope you and your father don't know *too* much about my activities. A lot of what I do is supposed to be secret, at least from the Federals. Henry and I are collaborating on a very important deal."

"Can you tell us anything about it? I promise it won't wind up in the newspaper!"

"Hmm, a writer. As it turns out, Henry and I have a need for someone creative and persuasive with words."

"James, I think we should share a little about our current dilemma with these good people. I'm certain they can be trusted, and I suspect they may want to be involved."

"Well first, let me tell you there are deals being made all over this room tonight," said Bulloch. "It is as secure an environment as we can find these days, but still we must be vigilant."

Delia was eager to hear whatever Mr. Bulloch had to share. "Deals are being made to set up ports in the Azores, places for blockade runners to land and load up British supplies bound for the Confederacy," he explained. "These docking ports have been quite successful in Bermuda and Nassau, but now I need a secret place to send my second warship, the *Alabama*. "I'm not sure if I can sail it out of Liverpool at all.

"The U.S. Consul in Liverpool, Thomas Dudley, is closing the net around me in an effort to impound the warship," said Bulloch. "My plan to get the ship under sail depends on a favorable deal in the Azores—an agreement to shelter her until a British supply freighter can rendezvous and transfer the guns and ammunition aboard."

Henry jumped in. "We came here tonight to put the right people together so we can finalize the arrangements. Always safer to talk in a noisy crowd than arranging something private, and thus more suspicious. We're being monitored carefully by U.S. agents in Europe."

"So how are you going to get the ship out of Liverpool?" Judge Bull asked.

"A wink and a nod are not enough to get us past British inspectors. Not with a cargo-hold full of war materials," said Henry.

Bulloch smiled ruefully. "Yes, the English play a complicated game, so Union spies think the British government is still neutral. Somehow, I have to get the inspector to allow us out of the harbor with an empty ship under the ruse of testing the engines. Then the ship just continues on its practice run all the way to the Azores."

"And then, I suppose," said Delia, "a British ship with munitions cleared for delivery to, ah…perhaps Guatemala or the new British Honduras, mysteriously shows up right next to your vessel?"

"You are quite well-read, Delia. That's how it's done. A little sneaky, but people like the inspector get paid along the way, and we get the ship loaded with arms for the Confederacy," said Bulloch.

"Still, we have to be extremely careful, warned Henry. "We have to drum up sympathy among the population here, so nobody gets carried away and blows the whistle on our deals. Which is exactly how you might be able to help us, Delia."

"How so?!" Delia could barely contain her excitement over joining this risky, but vitally important mission.

"We want to make sure the inspector is sympathetic to the South," said Henry.

"Not only the ship inspector, but if we can sway as many Brits as possible, our job here is much easier. Henry will author a series of editorials for major newspapers here in England, but we need a ghost writer whose words are powerful enough to get the job done. So, Delia if you can write persuasively and influence public opinion, there will be a payoff for you," offered Bulloch.

Delia was quiet for a moment. She wasn't hesitant to help, but wanted to be sure she established the terms of any "payoff." While she lifted a tea sandwich from a passing tray, Judge Bull jumped in to fill the silence. "My daughter would like to return to LaGrange with more than just memories." Looking around to see if people might be listening, he continued. "Delia would like some shoes, a few draughts of medicine for community health needs, some food items we can't get at home and …."

"And guns," Delia said abruptly through a mouthful of food.

The men were surprised. They knew Delia's payoff would be more than silk slippers and hair ribbons, but a woman talking about guns was shocking.

"We can certainly help with the fashions and the health supplies, but Enfields are another matter," said Bulloch.

"Of course, and that is why my father brought a load of cotton from LaGrange along on this trip," said Delia

"Can you help us find a buyer?" asked Judge Bull.

"I'm certain we can work everything out, but I'm curious about the weapons," said Bulloch. "Why would a refined Southern lady need a load of Enfield rifles?"

"I'm arming a home guard," said Delia

Hotze chuckled. "Most able-bodied men in the south have left their homes to join the Confederate army. Are you putting together a militia of little boys?"

"No, grown women," Delia shot back.

Hotze and Bulloch looked at each other in amazement. With a slight bow to Delia, they said in unison, "Brava!"

The deal was sealed. Delia would write a series of pieces calling upon British sympathies for the Southern cause, though the byline would be Henry's. Then he would arrange for a blockade runner connected with the Azores negotiation Bulloch was conducting. Cotton from the Bull plantation would be exchanged for the best rifles of the day, along with kegs of black powder and cartridge material. The medical supplies, by comparison, were not difficult to acquire, nor were the food and shoes. It all depended on the right price. Hotze knew that Britain's textile mills were in danger of shutting down because there wasn't enough cotton. And if that happened, the country faced dire rates of unemployment. In mid-1862 Europe, no raw material was more in demand than cotton. The Bulls had an irresistible commodity.

Everything depended on the success of Bulloch's scheme to get the cruiser *Alabama* out of port in Liverpool. It sat empty so as not to alert the U.S. Consul Thomas Dudley and his cadre of spies and informants. Its false papers tied ownership to the obscure principality of Monte Largo. Bulloch needed someone on the inside at customs—a sympathetic inspector who would look the other way. His luck was tied to Delia's literary skill. In three days, she managed to craft ten inspiring editorials that appeared everywhere in Great Britain under the byline of the esteemed Henry Hotze.

"The South is not fighting for anything but self determination. If we win our voice, we win our future and yours. An independent Confederacy will bolster the economy of all Europeans. Free trade with the South will ensure Great Britain is no longer ensnared by the greedy tariff mongers in the North. The South will keep England in cotton with textile mills humming and families able to feed their children."

Customs officer and inspector Oliver Wright thought self determination was a fine idea. After reading quite a few editorials, he concluded that the North was a bully—and a greedy bully at that. He wanted cotton in his port and a strong economy. Wright heard rumors that a certain newly-built ship in his jurisdiction wouldn't be allowed to leave port upon completion. Wright knew very well where the ship was bound, and for what purpose. So before an order to impound could be delivered, he authorized a "trial cruise" to test the seaworthiness of two ships. Bulloch had his inside man. The cruiser *Alabama,* and another lighter, swifter vessel, left Liverpool for a short trip around the harbor and never returned.

The *Alabama* and the smaller *Midnight Mist* were both empty for the trial cruise, which ended at the Azores. There to greet them was a tender from Britain with a huge supply of guns, ammunition and other wartime necessities. Henry Hotze had made the necessary arrangements through Bulloch to set aside forty-six Enfield rifles, twenty barrels of black gunpowder, crates of cartridge material, as well as jars of ether, chloroform, and shoes, cloth, and food items. After unloading it all from the tender, the ships sailed for Bermuda to begin separate missions.

In Liverpool, Delia worried and continued to plot. Now that the deal for supplies was completed, she wanted some measure of control over her precious cargo, and that meant keeping watch over it. If this were Gus' mission, he would accompany the cargo all the way back home. Courage and determination—hadn't Gus taught her that she possessed those qualities herself?

Gazing out the window of her hotel room, Delia remembered that when she was ten years old, Gus had challenged James and her to a horse race over the fields and down a forest path, one that included several streams and fallen trees. All the Bull girls were taught how to ride, but side-saddle was the only acceptable style for proper ladies. Though it was awkward at first to sit on a horse with one leg draped over the front of the saddle, many ladies became accomplished horsewomen. With enough practice, some even joined the men on fox hunts, jumping obstacles as they raced to follow the hounds through forests and fields. Staying balanced in the saddle was the trick to riding side-saddle, and it took time to master this odd perch. Riding astride took a bit of mastery too, but wasn't quite as difficult. With a leg on either side of the horse, the rider's weight was distributed more evenly.

Delia, Gus and James had ridden their horses out beyond the cotton fields of the Bull plantation to a wide, open pasture. It was a bright, crisp fall day with trees just beginning to turn color. The wooded hills around LaGrange were still lush with the faded glory of summer, but there was a slight chill in the air that added to the excitement. Delia counted on her pony to be calm and forgiving when she struggled with her balance. She had only recently started riding lessons, and knew mastering side-saddle required practice on a quiet mount. When Gus called for the race, Delia knew her pony was quiet enough for her to gallop side-saddle, but "quiet enough" also meant "slow enough" to assure last place in this competition.

Delia wanted to race, but there were problems to solve. "I'll race you, but only if you change horses with me," she told Gus. "You know Daddy's Thoroughbred is a better match against James' black horse."

"All right, we'll have heats then," he said. "You take Max here in the first race against James' War Hero. Then I'll take on the winner. But you won't have a chance, Delia, riding side-saddle over those logs in the forest. War Hero will leave you in the dirt when you fall off, so just ride with my saddle. You know what to do."

So, Delia picked up her skirt. She contemplated the makeshift sultan pants, but thought they might restrict her legs. She made a quick decision. "Tarnation! Nobody here cares," she announced, stuffing the hem of her skirt into the waistband of her pantaloons. She was only a little nervous, as she knew she could ride better with her legs on either side of the horse. She just hoped nobody would see her unladylike riding attire.

Gus looked on with great amusement. "James, you had better watch out. It looks like Delia is serious about winning this race."

James feigned concern. "I'm really scared of a half-dressed girl who is more likely to land in a ditch than jump over it on a horse."

Delia knew it was good-natured fun, but she certainly wasn't going to give anyone the satisfaction of seeing her fall off her horse! "James, I'm going to ditch *you*...in the dust!"

She handed Gus her pony and putting her left foot into the stirrup, swung her right leg over the seat and fixed the ball of her foot onto the other stirrup. She felt much more secure in this position balanced evenly over the big horse's withers. When the two of them lined up side-by-side, the horses knew what was expected. Maneuvering like this meant time to run!

Gus held his arm up in the air. "Ready...Set!"

He dropped his arm. "Go!"

Max and War Hero launched into a gallop from a standstill. At first, the fields were flat so the running was easy, and Delia felt pure exhilaration. She squeezed Max's sides with both legs, urging him forward and he responded, pulling away from James' horse. Heading into the woods, she was in the lead by an easy ten lengths. Delia had never jumped before, but Max had, with Gus aboard. She was scared, but thought he would jump the log just ahead, so she just hung on tight. Perhaps too tight. Her nervousness made Max lose confidence. He came to a sudden halt, tossing forest debris into the air. Fortunately, Delia was not part of the debris he launched. Because her seat was more secure, and her legs firmly around Max's barrel, she stayed on through the sudden stop. She quickly surveyed the scene, pleased that she hadn't landed on the ground, as she would have riding side-saddle. Suddenly, something big and powerful flew by her. It was War Hero, soaring over the log. "See you later," James called, laughing.

"Later has arrived, you silly boy!" shouted Delia. She wheeled Max around and dug her heels into his sides. No clutching now. She rode fearlessly. With her urging, he took a mighty leap over the log, adding a spurt of speed that made it clear this race wasn't over yet. War Hero slowed as he approached a ditch, trotted down into it, then galloped up the other side. Max saw it, but didn't slow. Delia kicked, and the horse jumped across the ditch. The distance between the horses was closing now—Max just four lengths away. Two more logs, then a bank, and out into the open again, heading for the finish line. Delia couldn't afford to show any fear or hesitation, as Max would sense it and shut down. The rest of the race, she reveled in being part of the power and force of this amazing animal.

She nearly caught him too. Max was within a half a length of War Hero when they crossed the finish line. James was hooting and hollering, patting his horse, alive with the joy of winning. But Delia was excited, too. For her, winning wasn't what mattered. She had walked through the fire of her own fear and felt her own power. Her self-confidence had bloomed that afternoon—a flower that would not fade with the seasons, but only gather more color and richness with the passage of time.

"Well that was quite a horse race!" said Gus.

In their excitement, Delia and James hadn't noticed Gus. There he was, sitting on Delia's pony, Molly, riding side-saddle. Delia thought it was the funniest sight—a boy in a lady's side-saddle! She laughed so hard she fell off of her horse.

Delia watched Liverpool Street below, bustling with carriages. How she missed Gus. She could surely use an infusion of his support. He had shown her she was every bit as capable as a boy. Now that she was a full-grown woman, was she as competent as any *man*? The situation facing her was nothing short of dead serious. She and her father had planned to return home together on a passenger ship, but now she knew she had to make sure their war supplies reached LaGrange. Without supervision, such drastically needed commodities could easily fall into eager hands. She wanted to keep watch over it herself, but there would be obstacles to overcome. Delia thought of Gus. He wouldn't hesitate traveling on a blockade runner. Well, then, neither would she! There was only one safe way to do it, and she could imagine Gus laughing with gusto over her bold decision. Delia smiled slyly. Then that was it. She had her plan.

At tea time, she met her father in the hotel lobby. "Papa, you've believed in me and we've come so far. Will you trust me one more time?"

"I've had a hard time overcoming your stubbornness, Delia. What is it you want now?"

"Buy me some clothes."

"Sweetheart, I always buy you clothes."

"Men's clothes."

"You can't be serious."

"That's exactly what I am. We have to make sure our supplies get home, and the only way to do it is to travel with them. It will be much safer for me if the people onboard the runner are all men. So, I'll dress like one and act like one."

Delia hoped her father would envision the possible fate of a woman in the company of rabble rousing seamen—or, God forbid, her being taken prisoner by the enemy during a blockade run. She thought he might see the wisdom in traveling with a son instead of a daughter.

"Papa, we've come so far, but don't you see, someone has to watch over our new rifles."

"Yes, I do see that, but why couldn't I escort the cargo and send you home on another safer ship?" said Judge Bull.

"Papa, *every* ship bound for any port in the south is carrying supplies the Yankees don't want us to have. I'd be in even more danger alone on another ship."

Judge Bull paused and rubbed his forehead, as though he felt a headache coming on.

"Don't tell your mother I encouraged this, Delia," he said sternly.

"Then that means you'll find me some suitable clothes."

The tailor at the men's shop tried to talk Judge Bull out of such drastic alterations, but the distinguished Southern Gentlemen insisted he had been losing weight since the war started. "But, Sir, taking these pants in six inches at the waist, then tapering and shortening the trousers, is just too much."

"Don't worry. If they never fit, I'm sure my son can use them. Don't you think so, Delia?"

"Papa, I think they will be perfect for Andrew."

Delia and her father boarded a cruise ship bound for the Azores the following day. It was an uneventful Atlantic voyage, at least until they docked. As the pair departed the large ship, they took note of two smaller ships being readied for sail. One was the *Alabama,* about to be commissioned for service in the Confederate Navy. The other was the *Midnight Mist,* beginning its career as a gun-runner.

Chapter XI

Between sunset on a day in late March and sunrise the following day, Delia vanished. In her place, "Andrew" Bull accompanied Judge Bull as they boarded the *Mist*. Delia decided that clothes really do make the man. The altered pants were not a perfect fit, but they worked just fine. The shirt and jacket from her father were large, but certainly hid her female curves. She couldn't bring herself to cut her hair, so had twisted it into a tight topknot and jammed a seaman's cap down over it. Glasses, and eyebrows thickened with make up added to the disguise while men's gloves concealed her slender fingers Heavy boots finished the look of a slightly gawky, but otherwise distinctly male passenger.

Now on board, Andrew and Judge Bull surveyed the vessel they hoped would carry them and their precious cargo home. The ship was smaller and sleeker than the *Alabama*—one of the new blockade runners specifically built for speed and maneuverability. Many were getting through the Northern patrol boats with these faster ships. Still, there was risk. When ships were intercepted, crews were taken prisoners of war, cargo confiscated and sent into enemy hands.

The blockade runner, *Midnight Mist,* pulled out of the Azores in the early morning fog. In stow was a careful plan for the week-long trip to the Gulf coast—and beyond that, to the off-loading destination. Avoiding detection in the final miles involved traveling at night, in fog, without a moon, or optimally, all three. The *Mist* was operated by a crew of fifteen seamen, and carried wartime supplies for a number of southern agents—six of whom were aboard for this particular trip. Judge Orville Augustus Bull and his noticeably quiet son, "Andrew Adolphus Bull" rounded out the group.

"Does he speak?" asked Captain Tyler Forest as he welcomed them. The boy wouldn't meet his eyes.

"Not much. He's very shy. But he takes very good care of his old, broken down Papa. We will need private quarters since my disabilities demand I get as much rest as possible." The Judge thrust a thick envelope into the captain's hand. Forest's jaw dropped when he glanced at the rolls of cash inside.

"Sir, you and your son may stay in my stateroom for the voyage since it's the only private quarter on the ship. Everyone else has bunks below, and now I will join them since your offer is too generous to refuse."

"Thank you, Captain. Andrew thanks you, too." Judge Bull nudged his son, who quickly nodded to Captain Forest.

Judge Bull should have anticipated the first drama of the voyage, but didn't. Several hours of the trip passed before the bustling crew settled into a quiet routine, and the few passengers found their way around the below deck bunk room and galley. The islands of the Azores were no longer in sight, just an endless horizon of azure blue. Andrew and Judge Bull stood at the rail looking eastward over the calm seas. Just enough breeze to power the sails, conserving the anthracite coal that fueled the steam engine. Anthracite burned so cleanly it sent up very little smoke, thus making the ship harder for blockaders to detect.

"Well, son, so far so good," Judge Bull said heartily. "If the weather continues to cooperate, there will be no worries about running low on fuel. The wind can power us from time-to-time until we get within sprinting distance of the coast."

Delia grunted, "Uh huh," practicing the low ranges of her pitch and keeping conversation to a minimum. When she turned toward the Judge, she caught sight of something that wouldn't have startled most men, but certainly jolted her. Several crew members were leaning against the rail, fumbling with their pants. Delia was panic stricken. Her mouth flew open, but she stifled the shriek with a hand to her throat. Her enormous eyes were full of shock, and all color had drained from her face. When her father looked to see what catastrophe might be underway, he, too, was startled, but not altogether surprised. The crewmen were having a pissing contest.

"Aye, mates, on the count of three, all hands below." And so, on the count of three, the men put their hands in their pants, pulled out private parts, and began to pee over the side. Distance would determine the winner. "Andrew's" face reflected the feeling of panic he felt. His hand flew over his mouth as he averted his eyes. Seeing his reaction, one of the sailors laughed so hard he peed on his own foot. He was disqualified, and Delia fled to her stateroom to recover.

"What's wrong with him?" asked one of the men in midstream.

"Sick," said Judge Bull. "I think he's seasick."

"Well, if the boy is sick in this calm ocean, there's a sea of trouble ahead," said another sailor. "Better see he drinks enough water so he can join us here at the railing! Better to pee than puke."

Delia stayed below. Mortified by the sight of the men's private parts, she realized that she hadn't thought through certain details of this venture. She might be bold, but she was still a lady. Actually, she *wasn't* a lady on this trip, but suddenly wished she could have it both ways—be a man and be *treated* like a lady. Of course she couldn't, so she would have to work harder at being a man.

Judge Bull thought it best that Delia stay below and feign seasickness, but after another twenty-four hours without appearing on deck, some of the crew began to worry. They asked the captain to inquire.

"We've noticed Andrew is not even coming up on deck to urinate. If he's that sick, it could mean trouble for everyone." Illness was an unwelcome visitor on any ship, and this particular ship had no real doctor, just some crew members with first aid training.

Judge Bull was horrified by this new attention—not that his son might be sick, but that his son might soon be discovered to be a daughter. He raised his voice so Delia in the stateroom below might hear him. "Captain, the boy is just shy. He can't pass water in front of other people. I've tried to make him manlier, but if it hasn't happened in all these years, it's not going to happen on this ship."

Delia's mind was working very fast. If she didn't find a way to urinate more like a man, instead of in a bucket behind closed doors, she'd be found out.

The captain continued. "Shy or not, it could be seasickness or worse if he isn't drinking enough fluids. I don't mean to embarrass anyone, but this can be a serious—or even deadly matter."

Suddenly, Captain Forest and Judge Bull heard the familiar sound of fluid streaming overboard. They looked over the side of the deck to see a thin ribbon of dark liquid spurting forth from the porthole.

Judge Bull was equally surprised and amused. "That *you*, Andrew?"

"Yep," came the mumbled voice from below.

The captain accepted this somewhat quirky behavior, but with new reservations. "You know, Judge Bull, that stream is awfully dark. Please get Andrew to drink more water. He's probably dehydrated. My mind is at ease though, to see that he is relieving himself. I'll tell the crew not to worry."

Later, in their stateroom, Judge Bull congratulated his daughter. "Nice job. I shouldn't ask how you performed that miracle."

Delia sported a devilish grin. "I'll show you." She picked up a cup full of tea and filled her mouth with the dark liquid. Then pushing on the porthole, she stood close to the opening, pursed her lips tightly, and forced the tea from her mouth. It formed a perfect stream out the porthole and into the sea, but she had to repeat it quickly to get the proper amount.

Judge Bull stifled a laugh. "No one will ever believe the adventures my son 'Andrew' has gotten me into! And that's one we will *not* talk about with the ladies at home. And by the way, you had better water down that tea or else the drama will continue.

The crew thought "Andrew" odd for his modesty, but tried to get along. Some attempted to strike up conversation with him, but since they got merely grunts in return, gave up the effort. Mostly, Delia was pleased to know what it was like to be treated like a man—except when the crew told off-color stories or sang ribald songs about loose women. It didn't embarrass her so much as anger her that men could be so crude and disrespectful. Once the shock had worn off the pissing contests, they didn't seem so bad by comparison.

Delia and her father knew there were three southern ports that had been successful for the blockade runners: Wilmington, North Carolina; Charleston, South Carolina; and Mobile, Alabama. Charleston was most active in terms of getting goods to port and beyond, but she had selected the Mobile voyage because of Captain Forest's experience. Because he had run the blockade near Mobile before, he had accurate charts for approaching the bay. Mobile Bay was protected with barrier islands, and therefore, several choices for entering the main channel existed—though some were easier because of water depth.

As *The Mist* successfully passed Key West at the tip of Florida, Captain Forest let out a sigh of relief. "Mates, that was our biggest problem—getting past the Union blockade headquarters at Key West. Everybody must be sleeping there. I didn't see a wisp of smoke anywhere on the horizon. A couple of days now, and we'll be whistling Dixie in Alabama."

Three days later, they were in position to dash for the entrance to Mobile Bay. Captain Forest explained his strategy to the crew—how *The Mist's* final run would take place on a moonless night.

"We'll head straight between Dauphin Island to the west and Fort Morgan to the east. If we get in there, we'll have a good twenty feet of water under us and some measure of protection from the guards at the fort."

"What if something goes wrong and we can't get in there?" Judge Bull asked.

"We can go down the long side of Dauphin and slip in-between the tip of that island and one called *Petit Bois*. Trouble is, the water gets shallow there, only 'bout six feet. We need seven to get through because of this load we're carrying. But if we have to, we might still make it." Captain Forest scratched his chin and smiled.

Delia hoped that was a sign of confidence since her own spirit sagged with the barest suggestion of running aground.

They were very close now. All eyes strained in the darkness to see the silhouette of another ship or hear the hum of other engines. Nothing. Then suddenly, a rocket signal flare went up into the darkness from somewhere off to the left of *Midnight Mist*, followed by shouts and the roar of engines.

"Let's get 'em boys! Those rebels be damned!" rang out from shadowy forms in the night.

They had been spotted by a blockader. Delia and the Judge stood on the deck, peering through the darkness to see the Yankee patrol boat. Then like a hulking menace, its fearsome outline arose, blacker than the night itself. Like some awful apparition, it was not there one minute, and the next, a looming monster right at their stern. Two-thousand yards separated the boats, but only a thousand between *Midnight Mist* and the best entrance to the channel.

"Hang on, mates! This is where the fun begins." Captain Forest almost seemed to be enjoying himself.

The Yankee boat began to fire on the blockade runner, not because they were within range, but to raise holy hell and put fear in the rebels. Captain Forest yelled, "Full speed ahead," but the small ship was struggling to put any distance between the two vessels. In another ten minutes, the patrol boat would be upon them.

"Looks like our only chance is the shallower channel between *Petit Bois* and Dauphin," Captain Forest shouted.

"But I thought you said it wasn't deep enough!" Judge Bull's voice was suddenly hoarse from anxiety.

"Well, we'll have to lose some weight so we can run faster and sit lighter on the water. You all have some tough choices to make and you need to make them fast. We'll be captured if we can't lighten this load. Do you want to wind up in a Yankee prison or lose some of your cargo?" Captain Forest swept his steely gaze over the passengers. "Make up your minds now, friends."

A jumble of words spewed from the group. "Dumping? But *what*? How much?" The captain delivered directions. "Dump half of everything you've bought or all of the heaviest cargo, which would be your weapons."

Delia knew this predicament was a possibility from the start so was ready to be part of the decision-making. Making her voice as low and gruff as she could, she said, "I vote half the guns, half the ammo, half the food, half the medical supplies—over the side."

A chorus of voices agreed, and the captain ordered the dumping to begin. As precious cargo splashed into the sea, Delia's heart sank. She wouldn't be bringing back a new rifle for each of *the Nancies,* but twenty-three Enfields were better than none. Dr. Ware would be upset about choosing guns over medical supplies, but he would understand. Her father agreed. Now amid the tension and splashing, something palpable was happening. *The Mist* was pulling away from the gunboat. She was flying! Delia felt exhilarated by the speed—or was it the relief? They'd come so close to being captured!

Captain Forest ducked *The Mist* into the intricate turn past Dauphin Island. He ordered the engines cut so he could listen and watch for the blockader. Delia wondered...*Had it gone into the main entrance now to lay in wait for The Mist? Surely the Yankees wouldn't risk the guards at Ft. Morgan. But maybe they would.*

"We wait here 'til we know where the Yanks are prowling," said Captain Forest. He ordered all of them to sit or lie down, and be quiet—not a cough, not a twitch. The only sound was a gentle lapping of water against the boat, which could easily be mistaken for water against the marshy beaches of the channel. They waited, barely breathing.

Engine noise and occasional shouts pierced the quiet. "We know you're out there Johnny and we're coming to get ya!" someone yelled.

"Aye, they're following us in past Dauphin," whispered Captain Forest. "'Tis a beautiful decision."

Two minutes passed. Then three. Suddenly, the shouting was distinctly more intense, and there was a great scraping and crashing sound. Then silent engines as voices screamed out. "We're on the sand!" "Do something!" "Damn those runners!"

Captain Forest shouted an order. "Fire up those engines! Full speed ahead!"

The ship darted out of the shallows for the last sprint to Mobile Bay. The Yankee boat had run aground making a turn into the shallow channel pursuing *The Mist*.

"Guess their captain didn't want to risk the guard at Fort Morgan after all. Thought if we could make it around Dauphin, they could too. Too bad their ship is bigger and heavier than *The Mist*. We won! They lose!" Now out of danger, Captain Forest bellowed a victorious shout into the crisp dawn air.

Delia gasped. In the faint morning light, she could see sailors dashing toward canon stations on the beached vessel. In seconds, she heard a deafening boom and instinctively covered her head. Looking out from aft of *The Mist*, the ball fell short by ten feet. Passengers and crew began to cheer—joined by "Andrew's" distinctly female octave. "Papa, can you believe this! We're going to make it!" Lost in the ecstasy of the moment, she didn't care if her secret was out.

The Mobile Bay dock was full of great whooping and joyful shouting—the exultant workers ready to secure *The Mist* in her berthing.

"Way to go! Those Yanks will have a good long wait for high tide to float them out!" Though it was a close call, another successful runner had gotten through. The North must be getting more aggressive. Up to now, two out of three ships were getting through—most slipping by unnoticed. It appeared the blockade was tightening yet again.

At the dock in Mobile Bay, the Pitman family met Delia and her father with a line of wagons, ready to transport their hard-won supplies home. Who was accompanying Judge Bull in this daring escapade? It was supposed to be Delia, but this was a young man holding the Judge's hand and smiling jubilantly. There was something odd about his voice though. "Well, hello, Ella! It certainly is a great pleasure to see you here this morning." And with that "Andrew" bowed and took off his cap, spilling Delia's long dark hair around her shoulders.

Ella could hardly believe her eyes. "My gracious! It *is* Delia. Wouldn't you know you'd wind up joining the merchant marine?"

Looks of surprise rippled all around the dock and even up on deck of *The Mist*—quickly dissolving into smiles and guffaws. So good to laugh together in such dreadful times—times that gripped their lives like a heavy vice. And still, none could imagine the horror that lay ahead.

Chapter XII

Delia and Ella delighted in each other's company: Delia relieved to be a girl again, and Ella bursting with excitement over her friend's daring escapade. Dresses, teas, music lessons, and ladylike deportment seemed so frivolous amidst the increasing gravity of war. The discipline of the Nancy Hart Militia had given these women a new kind of self confidence.

"I can't wait to see what you can do with an Enfield," Delia told her. "You have mastered those ancient muskets with some pretty fancy shooting, hornets not withstanding."

Most all the women in *the Nancies* were developing harder bodies, with muscle definition that reflected their months of regular drills and long marches. Like the rest of them, Delia and Ella both felt physically strong for the first time in their lives. Leading *the Nancies* made Delia feel mentally strong as well. She was discovering just how capable and competent she was, accomplishing things she had never dreamed she could.

"Don't tell anyone, Delia," whispered Ella from their perch on the wagon seat, "but I think you formed a fine male figure on that ship. I wish I could have come along."

They were both well aware that men could be freely adventurous, while women were prohibited from risk-taking. However, war and necessity had altered this custom—so for now, the women of The Nancy Hart Militia could experiment with adventure. Delia, and now Ella, along for the ride home, were savoring the thrills while they lasted.

The trek from Mobile back home to LaGrange took many days. In their horse-drawn wagons the Pitman/Bull entourage moved twenty miles a day. Soldiers headed into battle could travel twenty miles in a day, but not in the relative comfort provided by horse power. Elisha Pitman had plotted their course carefully, so that each day's end delivered them to a comfortable inn or wayside stop. "The town up ahead is a dusty bump in the road," he told the group, "but they have hot water and bathtubs the girls will appreciate."

"How about good food, Mr. Pitman?" Delia asked." I'm still dreaming about caviar canapés in Liverpool."

"I expect it won't be that fancy, but we'll get our fill," he assured her.

When they pulled into the hamlet, the servants took the loaded wagons to the livery, staying with them all night to keep watch over the imported goods. Delia and Ella shared a room, and after luxuriating in hot baths and clean clothes, joined their fathers in the dining room for ham, biscuits, sweet peas, and yams.

"Every bit as good as the paté and rosemary biscuits in Liverpool!" Delia proclaimed. "Shipboard food with a bunch of seamen leaves a lot to be desired. Unless you love beef jerky day after day!"

Everything on the inn's menu was outrageously expensive. Meat was cured with salt in the South, and before the war, a bag of salt that cost two dollars was sixty now. The dinner they were having was a dollar a plate the previous year. Now this simple fare was twelve dollars a person. The Bulls and Pitmans, however, didn't feel an inordinate amount of pain over this inflation. They still had wealth, though the difficulty of selling cotton was taking a toll on each family's fortune.

"So, Elisha," said Judge Bull, "do you think you'll chance the blockade to sell some of your cotton now that we've done it?"

"I'll wait and see. I'd sure hate to have my load aboard one of the few runners that gets caught. And I still think this war will be over before the end of the year. Then cotton will be king again!"

Though their bank accounts weren't growing, their confidence was, bolstered by the conviction that the South would prevail. So they didn't complain about exorbitant costs. That was merely the price they had to pay for the right to govern themselves state-by-state.

The next morning, Delia awakened from a dream with a gasp. She had been back on a familiar street near LaGrange Female College. Suddenly, gunboats emerged on the horizon and cannon balls began hurtling relentlessly towards her—from the right and left, over her head, and through her feet. She tried to catch them with her hands and throw them back, but each time she reached for one, it disappeared in a puff of smoke. Her efforts were futile, leaving her feeling ineffective...a failure. Now, fully awake, she was relieved. She was *not* ineffective. She had just carried out a dangerous mission to get weapons for her militia, and was bringing them safely home. Reaching out, she touched Ella's shoulder. "Time to get up. The Nancy Harts are waiting for us."

Both women dressed sensibly for the road. Delia wore a simple brown dress with long sleeves and a fitted bodice. She had a white chemise underneath and one petticoat—no corsets and hoops for the long trip home. Ella buttoned up a white blouse, and pulled a dark gray cotton jumper over it. It was loose-fitting and comfortable for the trip. Each woman wore a gingham bonnet tied with a ribbon under her chin. Their fathers wore plain cotton shirts, cotton pants and homespun coats. No display of wealth on this trip. Thieves and deserters often roamed the countryside, and this group brought enough attention to itself with all their horses and wagons. Horses were disappearing with ever-increasing frequency these days—sometimes purchased—but more often, stolen and forced into service on both sides of the fighting.

They stuck to the main roads where there was more traffic. Hooves created a rhythmic clopping on hard-packed dirt, sounding efficient and purposeful. Today Ella and Dr. Pitman rode the lead wagon with their servant, Cicero, handling the team of horses. With other servants taking up the reins on the middle wagons, Judge Bull and Delia rode at the back of the column with a trusted servant guard. They passed fields of hay and newly-planted rows of corn. Vegetable gardens sprung up almost everywhere as folks had turned more and more to growing food for their families. Leafy lanes, fragrant with honeysuckle and jasmine, stretched out before them and trailed out behind them. Hills turned into valleys—then into hills again, day after day. They nodded politely to travelers along the route, but didn't stop to socialize.

In Columbus, they pulled up to the Rankin House Hotel to inquire about livery services. Several blocks away, the wagon train settled for the night in a large barn with cots in the aisle so servants could keep watch. Meanwhile, the Bulls and Pitmans ate chicken and dumplings for supper, then climbed into rope beds with goose feather mattresses for a quiet night.

The night was also quiet at the barn. At least the horses and servants were undisturbed for now. Yet from a distance, eyes were watching, waiting to see what this caravan might have to offer them. The eyes were hard, mean and patient. The right opportunity was key.

Bud Archer and Jethro Mays had been assessing the travelers and their wagons as soon as they had pulled into town. Hidden from view by a large hedge of boxwood alongside a house, the pair didn't belong here. They belonged to an army that had moved on without them. The battalion was from Georgia, moving three companies towards Virginia in a hard march, sunlight pushing into darkness over endless hours. It was under the cover of night that the pair peeled off into a thicket and lay quietly until the sound of marching dissipated, and they could hear nothing but the crickets and the owls.

Dirty, hungry and on the run, the two scoundrels eyed the arriving party. If they stole a wagon, they would be forced to keep to the roads, but horses under saddle could go on footpaths and backwoods trails. Bud was the smarter of the two, but not by much. "Let's see where these folks and all their loaded wagons go tomorrow morning. Bet we can come up with a plan."

Jethro chuckled. "'Spect so, Buddy Boy."

At noon the next day, Dr. Pitman signaled the wagon drivers to stop. A shallow stream lay just ahead with shade and plenty of room to pull the wagons off the road. A chance to rest, water the horses and people, eat corn cakes and apples, before heading out again. Delia went into the woods, looking for a private place to relieve herself. She spotted one, but before she could lift her skirts, she started to gag. An arm was around her neck, and at the end of a grimy hand, a hunting knife. The man propelled her from the brush and into an opening by the stream, his partner just ahead. With a swagger and a loud voice he announced, "Howdy folks. We're just on our way home and need to borrow two of your horses. Jethro over there is gonna make sure you unhitch 'em, cause he'll unhitch this lovely lady from her head if'n you don't."

Though warned of thieves and deserters, they were stunned. No one spoke. Bud made his way over to one of the wagons and lifted the lid on a crate. "Well, tarnation! You are the *haves* and we are the *have-nots*. Enfield rifles come in mighty handy these days. We are goin' gain plenty this day, and maybe you're going to lose Miss whatsername if'n you don't follow our directions."

Delia was suddenly freed from her fear and infused with a mighty rage. She leaned into the man holding her, forcing him off balance. As he dropped to the ground clutching at her, she fell on top of him and kneed him in the groin. He screamed out, his voice joined by another—Ella's. In the time it had taken for this scene to unfold, she had loaded a cartridge and shouldered an Enfield rifle, which was now aimed at the two men. "You touch that woman and you're dead. Pick which one of you gets the nasty little lead bullet. I dare you to make a move."

No one budged.

"Aw. Ma'am," Bud whined, "I jez wanna go on home. My wife, she wrote old Jeff Davis and tol him she was goin' hungry. Without me to help run the farm, she's gonna die."

Jethro was nearly crying. "We're from the 4th Regiment, Georgia Volunteers. My momma is sick. I just want to see her one more time. If we promise to just walk away now, you won't be shooting us in the back will you?"

Delia struggled to her feet. "That's Gus' Company, Ella. This boy's momma would not be proud of him today."

The deserters turned slowly, uncertain if they should stand or run.

Ella steadied her aim. "I won't shoot you in the back. I'll shoot you in the derriere. I'd just as soon kick your behinds all the way from here to Virginia, but shooting you is easier and I'm in a hurry to get home myself."

Bam! Ella fired off a shot, grazing Bud just below his left buttock. The men lit out, running despite their terror and Bud's pain.

Delia looked at Ella in utter surprise. "How did you do that?"

"I was anxious to get my hands on a real weapon, so when you went into the woods, I pulled an Enfield from the crate and sat admiring it in the carriage. I was studying how to load the cartridge when the scoundrels showed up. Guess I figured it out."

Delia was grateful to her enterprising friend. "Lucky for us, Ella, those dimwits never expected a woman to be armed."

"Guess I've got some work to do before I can claim to be a sharpshooter, though." Ella patted the stock of the rifle.

Ella turned to her father. "I suppose that wasn't very ladylike."

"You are forgiven. You are, however, a constant surprise Ella," said Dr. Pitman. Both fathers were amazed—proud of their daughters in a way they never could have imagined before this very moment. A transformation had taken place in their attitudes, a tiny crack in the cement of their beliefs about women.

"Delia, I always knew you were strong-willed, but I had no idea that quality would be so valuable to so many."

"Thank you, Papa."

Dr. Pitman patted his daughter's hand. "You and Delia are quite a pair. I suppose your militia deserves more respect."

Judge Bull spoke over the clatter of the wagon wheels. "In fact, Elisha, I think you and I should help shine a light on their efforts."

"I completely agree!" nodded Dr. Pitman.

The rest of the trip home was thankfully free of any more drama, making plenty of time to wind down from the stress of their adventure.

Shortly after they arrived safely home, Judge Bull and Dr. Pitman called on Ben Hill, just home from Congress, at his mansion west of the town. Bellevue was a grand home of Greek Revival design, with magnificent Ionic columns supporting a balustrade roof-walk, and a spacious porch around three sides. An intricate iron gate adorned the entrance of the long drive leading up to the house—an exact replica of the gates at the White House in Washington, D.C. They had been forged in 1856, during a more congenial period between North and South, at a cost of $12,000.

Benjamin Harvey Hill was a lawyer by profession, and had become a wealthy and notable statesman prior to the War Between the States. When the Confederacy was formed, Hill had the trust and confidence of President Jefferson Davis, and he soon earned the nickname "The Mouthpiece of

Davis" for his outspoken support. He owned some sixty slaves who tended to the operation of the economically and socially successful plantation—socially successful because his wife, Caroline, was noted for her exquisitely tasteful parties which brought influential people together.

Dr. Pitman and Judge Bull wanted to ask a favor of their friend, Ben Hill. They had started out amused by the young women of the Nancy Hart Militia, viewing the effort as a pastime—a way to forget the hardships of war. Now they knew otherwise: their daughters were standing in for the sons so far away. And for this, their courage and commitment deserved to be recognized. As tea was served in the parlor, Ben listened intently as the men recounted the adventures of their dangerous mission to England.

"These women are tough, and they mean to provide a formidable defense for our town," said Mr. Pitman.

"We should be commending these women for their courage," added Judge Bull. "What do you say? Will you advance a petition to the Governor of Georgia to recognize the Nancy Hart Militia with a formal commission?"

Hill knew of the women's activities; but he, too, had regarded them as just a club from the Methodist Church. "Tell you what, if *The Nancies* are as accomplished as you say, I will personally go to Milledgeville with the number one priority of urging Governor to commission them. But I'd like to see what they can do first."

Judge Bull smiled. "I think the ladies are more than ready to demonstrate their skills."

"Then let's have a troop review right here at Bellevue," said Hill. "Why, Caroline will love the excuse to put on a party here at the house. The Nancy Hart Militia can use the east field for their maneuvers before we plant the hay."

Chapter XIII

Fierce Fighting at Shiloh to Impact LaGrange
D. Bull

LaGrange hospitals are calling on all volunteers to assist with the expected volume of patients following the confrontation at Shiloh.

Reporters at the war front say the Confederate troops were clearly victorious after engaging Union forces on April 6 at Shiloh, Tennessee. During the night however, Union reinforcements arrived to change the balance. At the end of the second day of fighting, Confederate soldiers were given the command to retreat. A preliminary tally of casualties places Union dead at 63,000. Confederate forces lost 11,000. Nearby hospital centers are anticipating a large number of incoming wounded from both the North and the South.

Permission Confederate Press Association-April 1862

Bull Run in July of '61 was bad enough, Delia thought. Even though the Confederate Army was the clear winner, casualties had been high. Now in '62, the Battle of Shiloh wrought a staggering death toll. *This war will not be over quickly,* she told herself. *The Nancies were excited to get the Enfields, but now it's time to get serious about using them. Practice, practice and more practice. That is what we must do now.*

At dinner, Delia asked her sisters to help her plan a new militia regimen. Sallie and Addie enthusiastically agreed that more target practice drills with the Enfields were necessary. There would be a lot of work to do, putting cartridges together with paper and black powder. Each woman armed with an Enfield would prepare forty cartridges, the standard for battlefield readiness. Everything must be by the book. To qualify as a sharpshooter, a soldier had to shoot a ten-inch circle ten times at a minimum distance of three hundred yards. Five of *The Nancies* had already demonstrated this ability. Now, with the superior weapons, they were sure to do better—especially since Ella Pitman had shown such improvement with loading speed and accuracy on the road outside of Columbus. Soldiers in the field were expected to complete all the steps of loading a musket within twenty seconds, and be able to aim and fire three times within one minute. So this was their standard too, and the pre-assembled cartridges would help make it possible. The time-consuming task of measuring the black powder, and carefully guiding it into the musket, was replaced by a pre-measured cartridge which fit quickly into place.

Delia presented a persuasive argument to the women. "Shiloh, Tennessee is too close for comfort. After every battle, there are deserters hopping into freight cars, which could easily put them in LaGrange. And we all know they would be up to no good."

Under this new motivation, drill and target practice were increased from two times a week to four. Everyone wanted an Enfield, and nearly everyone wanted to become a sharpshooter. Captain Morgan decided that the best shots would get the first of the rifles, and that left eighteen to be distributed. First Lt. Heard suggested each woman spend some time training with an Enfield. Those who excelled in target practice during the two weeks prior to troop review would get to keep a gun.

The biggest surprise during that training period turned out to be Addie Bull. She had openly begged to become a regular militiawoman. "I promise to keep playing music for *the Nancies*," she pleaded. "I just want more than anything in the world to try my hand at shooting!"

Delia delighted in her little sister's plight. "I'll braid your hair for a year. I'll give you my ink for your pen," she beseeched.

"Mm…"

"I'll play your favorite songs…even sell my best dresses to buy you ribbons and lace."

"Mm…"

"Wash your feet. Do your chores. Oh, Lordy! I'd even empty your chamber pot to be a real soldier."

"That's it then," said Delia. "You get your chance tomorrow."

When the three sisters stirred from their sleep the next morning, Addie offered her services. "Would you like braids today, Delia?"

"I surely would, Sister, and don't forget the chamber pot." Delia smiled sweetly.

Addie made a face. "I didn't think you'd hold me to that one."

"You're the one who offered, little sister, and the servants will be grateful to you."

Addie reached under Delia's bed, gagging as she picked up the pot in one hand and held her nose with the other. As soon as she was out the door Delia and Sallie began to laugh.

"You are heartless, Sister!" said Sallie.

"Oh, I won't make her do it anymore. I just wanted to see how badly she wanted to become a soldier. I guess we know for sure now."

What Delia and the others *didn't* know was what a surprise they were in for. On the target practice field, Addie was not only good, but getting better each day of the two-week training period. She kept her eye on the target, her hands steady, and for someone who hadn't handled a rifle, her aim was truly amazing. The maximum range of the Enfield was 800 to 1000 yards. Addie was accurate up to 300—well beyond the 200 required of a sharpshooter. She was fast too, pulling off four shots in a minute rather than the standard three. Now, heading into the demonstration at Bellevue, *The Nancies* had, not five sharpshooters, but twelve. The better weapons made a huge difference, and with additional practice, there would clearly be more women joining the ranks of sharpshooters.

Bellevue was resplendent on a warm day in early May, 1862. Caroline Hill's magnolias were in full bloom, and she had adorned the front porch with banners and the Confederate flag. The refreshment tables weren't as spectacular as in years past, but then, everyone had less these days.

Behind the barn, at the far end of the property, the militia women prepared for their demonstration, determined to show their new skills with the Enfields. Addie and Ella Pitman had done this many times in the last weeks, but this was a new challenge.

"I am so nervous," Ella confided to her friend, Delia, as they measured off the distance from firing line to a canvas circle pinned to a stack of straw bales.

Delia was not patient with insecurity. "Don't be such a girl, Ella! You are the best, and don't let me hear you doubting that. No, I take that back. Don't let the pompous men from Milledgeville see you wavering. Not one second of weakness, Ella Pitman! Ya hear me?"

"Lordy, you're tougher than my own mama, Delia."

"Well, I was under the impression you were the tough one when you sent those scoundrels howling and clutching their behinds on the way home from Florida."

"Well, somehow these men today on the revue stand seem more imposing than those stupid barn rats on the highway."

Delia straightened. "Maybe you just need to get riled up again. How about I announce to the crowd how you took your clothes off, running to escape the hornets you blasted out of our tree?."

"Delia, that's a private story just among *the Nancies*!"

"Certainly was funny though."

"You wouldn't dare!" Ella was riled now.

"That's more like it. Now shoot like that target was a hairy behind."

"How 'bout I pretend it's *yours*?" quipped Ella.

"Whatever it takes," Delia replied, satisfied that Ella was back on track.

"Hey, Ella!" Addie shouted, approaching the target area. "It's time to get ready. What are you two fussing over?"

"Nothing to be concerned about, little sister." Delia patted Ella on the shoulder.

"Well, good, because I don't need any more tension in my life today. I'm so nervous!"

"You'd better hold that in, Addie, or your sister will whack you with her secret weapon," Ella said playfully.

"And just what is Delia's secret weapon, Ella?"

"Her mouth. She'll kill you with a tongue-lashing."

Addie started to laugh. "Only one thing wrong with that, Ella. It's not much of a secret."

The humor erased the nervousness. Though Delia would never admit it, she was a little on edge herself. The revue was the one-and-only chance the women would get to show the men from Milledgeville that they had what it took to be a real militia.

The whole town had been invited, including any servants who could be spared to help for a few hours. Hundreds of people—mostly women, children, the men too old to fight—spread blankets on the lawn overlooking the east field. Addie played "Dixie" to open the festivities, and everybody joined in singing.

"Oh, I wish I were in the land of cotton. Old times there are not forgotten. Look away, look away, look away, Dixie Land. In Dixieland I'll make my stand to live and die in Dixie..."

It was a favorite tune of Southerners, and even some Northerners, including President Abraham Lincoln.

Ben Hill had invited some fellow lawmakers from Milledgeville to share the reviewing stand with him. They chatted and chuckled about the young ladies "playing" militia.

"What a fine idea, Ben. The ladies of Georgia have done such a good job entertaining the troops with plays and music festivals. This revue will keep us laughing for weeks to come," said Representative William Collingsworth, clapping Ben on the back.

Ben regarded his colleague. "I don't think the women are putting this on to be funny."

"Well, Sir, it's going to be hard to keep from laughing if their shooting drill is anything like the opening color guard. Take a look." Collingsworth pointed to the south lawn where an unusual equestrian team had assembled. The reviewing stand dignitaries erupted into laughter.

Every fighting unit needed to have a color guard and *The Nancies* had certainly put together a bright and lively team. Horses were in high demand during this war, so the best mounts were not available. But there was Molly, the 11.2 hand pony; Sunny, the 18 hand Belgian plow horse; Picante, the donkey; and Belle, the 25-year-old blind mare. Addie Bull, in the lead position on foot, carried her fife and drum slung over her shoulder, and began the presentation of colors by sounding the traditional reverie on her brother's trumpet. While the four mounted militia women began the opening drill, the rest of *the Nancies* lined up along the perimeter of the field, standing at attention with their weapons at their sides. Molly and Picante rode as a pair with Sunny and Belle behind them. "Bulls-eye Betsy," riding Molly, carried the flag of The Nancy Hart Militia. In a child's side-saddle, Leila Pullen rode Picante, struggling to manage the flag of Georgia and the reins at the same time. This quadrille team was to ride to the center of the field and halt just behind Addie. However, at the hand signal to halt, the donkey kept going, the pony bolted, the Belgian stretched his neck down and started to graze, while the blind mare backed up, wanting to go home. It took the women a few moments to get the equines back under control, but finally they were lined up. Addie saluted to the reviewing stand, now filled with guffawing dignitaries—some holding their sides. She turned to the quadrille and sounded a "ruffle and flourish" with the trumpet, signaling the start of the precision drill. Picante peeled off to the left as Molly trotted to the right. Sunny and Belle followed their rider's cues to do the same.

When they reached the far end of the field, they turned to the center and formed one single line: Sunny in the lead, followed by Belle, then Molly and Picante. When Sunny reached mid-field, he began making a pirouette on his haunches. Belle, next to him, walked in a wider circle. Molly came up on the outside and had to canter to keep up with the rotating Sunny and Belle. Picante took up the outside position of the pinwheel but refused to canter. Instead he trotted so fast to keep up that his little legs were just a blur. It was indeed a precision pattern, but with a completely comical look: from the women in their pretty dresses, to the sidesaddles, and the totally mismatched animals. The women and their mounts carried on, finishing several more patterns, during which Belle bumped into Sunny during the group figure eight movement. Thankfully, no one fell off. Picante, adding that last bit of comic relief when they lined up in reverse, pinned his ears and took a bite out of Sunny's rump. It started a stampede, but all riders stayed mounted, and managed to canter by the reviewing stand with a final salute.

Collingsworth was out of breath, overcome with laugher, as was most of the crowd.

"We should send this militia on the road to entertain our *real* soldiers!" one official exclaimed.

"Except the men might die laughing!"

The Nancies marched in formation to the east field and took up their shooting positions. The crowd settled a bit when Ella walked up to the firing line, but chuckles still rippled through the gathering.

Captain Nancy Morgan had prepared a detailed firing demonstration for the spectators. She would call out commands for the ten steps in firing a musket, and Ella would complete each task slowly so people could follow.

"Load!" Captain Morgan shouted.

Ella took the Enfield from the resting position against her shoulder and placed the butt of the rifle between her feet.

"Handle cartridge!"

Now Ella reached into the ammunition box and brought out one paper cartridge.

"Tear cartridge!"

Ella's teeth ripped the paper along the end of the cartridge.

"Charge cartridge!"

She poured the contents of the cartridge, starting with the black powder and finishing with a small lead ball, into the muzzle of the rifle.

"Draw rammer!"

Deftly, Ella took the ramrod from the channel along the barrel of the gun.

"Ram cartridge!"

Using the ramrod, she pressed the lead ball as far into the barrel as possible.

"Return rammer!"

She replaced the ramrod.

"Prime!"

Ella raised her weapon, half-cocked it, and then placed a percussion cap on the cone of the trigger.

"Ready!"

Ella fully cocked the rifle.

"Aim!"

She placed the butt of the Enfield on her shoulder and took aim on the small target 200 yards away.

"Fire!"

She pulled the trigger.

Crack! Ella's body moved with the kick of the rifle, but she was steady on her feet.

The crowd was hushed as Captain Morgan walked to the target and held up the circle for inspection. The bullet hole was dead center. Great cheers went up from the onlookers.

"Must be a fluke," said Collingsworth, but the next demonstration proved him wrong. The target was reset and Captain Morgan directed Ella to fire at will. This time it was hard to follow all the steps because she was so fast. She got off four shots in one minute, hitting the canvas target every time.

Addie followed with the same stunning accuracy. The next eight shooters hit the target three times within a minute from the 200 yard distance.

Ben Hill turned to his colleague. "I guess it's not funny any more, would you say Collingsworth?"

Collingsworth was bloated and red in the face, but not from laughing. He was flat-out astonished. The crowd was full of people whose mouths had dropped open as the demonstration continued—proving, one woman at a time, that these were indeed proficient marksmen. When *the Nancies* went through their firing line-up three more times with the same results, the spectators clapped wildly, applauding a proven precision military unit.

Dr. Ware nearly burst with pride as he watched from the sidelines with the Bull family. The formation drills on foot were perfect. The muster-to-arms was an exercise in superb organization. Line after line of militia-women moved as ordered, firing in unison, then kneeling as the line behind came forward for the next volley. Their uniforms were their usual pretty dresses. At one time they had talked about designing a uniform, but it had been an intractable meeting. No one could agree on style, color or detail. Dr. Ware remembered suggesting that they each wear something that made them feel good, and that had freed each woman to dress to her individual tastes. Uniforms were for men. These were still ladies, wanting to look their best. But their marksmanship had bested even their lovely attire.

In the end, the review met with great shouts and whoops of laughter—near disbelief at what they had witnessed. The town of LaGrange loved *the Nancies*, and was especially impressed by Ella Pitman and Addie Bull, who as the stars of the day, each had twelve direct hits at two hundred yards—and three each at five hundred yards. Few men could achieve this level of skill.

Ben Hill rose from his chair. "I think we have a militia worthy of a commission, Gentlemen."

The crowd cheered in hearty agreement, including the thoroughly flustered Rep. Collingsworth.

Chapter XIV

Toward the end of May, while the Nancy Hart Militia's application for commission was under review, the Chickahominy River in Virginia was rising. And Gus Bull was in it—drenched, dirty, and splattered with mud. His friend, James Tomlinson, rode beside him as he led his cavalry unit alongside Company B, 4th Regiment, Georgia Volunteer Infantry, Army of Virginia.

Five days of rain normally would have sent everyone in Richmond indoors, but of course, nothing was normal in war. The Peninsular Campaign was underway, and Major General George McClellan had advanced his federal army troops within twelve miles of Richmond. He made a decision to split his troops, and sent three corps to the north of the swollen river and two to the south. Confederate General Joseph E. Johnston received word from his cavalry scouts that McClellan's troops had been divided. This seemed like an opportunity to Joe Johnston. His troops had been marching in the rain towards Richmond. Now encamped about ten miles south of the city, they were headed in the direction of Yankee soldiers—soldiers possibly cut off from the rest of the army by the ever-rising Chickahominy.

Gus' men had ridden and marched four days in the rain without complaint, but they were clearly exhausted. Being tired was just part of army life. So was being hungry and feeling sick. During the time he had been leading the troops, Gus had only lost two men to desertion. It helped that most felt bound to Gus simply by the force of his positive personality. Other units lost more and more men as time went on. Some went home to try to save their families from starvation while others were depressed, scared, or just fed up with war. But Gus and James had lost none of their fervor for the cause. They hadn't seen much major action during their year of service, but felt sure they were on the verge of something very big.

"Can't you just feel it, brother James?" said Gus. "There's a kind of twitching in the air. We'll get our first taste of combat soon."

"The waiting is hard though. Makes me jumpy. Our orders are to pitch tents and try to sleep, but how can we sleep tonight knowing the Yankees are so close?" said James. Was it the chill of the cool night? Or perhaps the rain? Maybe his nerves. His hands were shaking as he dismounted and set about getting his horse settled for the night.

Even with shelter, it was hard to keep the candles lit because everything was so wet. Aides had gone out from General Johnston's tent to find oil lamps because the candle wicks wouldn't hold a flame for more than a few seconds. The General needed some light to make his plans for the next day. Rain or no rain, he intended to strike quickly at dawn, hitting the two McClellan units south of the river. He would map out his strategy and send orders to nearby Confederate troops. Besides the soaked candle wicks, there wasn't a dry piece of paper to be found. Each time he attempted to put pen to paper, the ink smeared with each stroke, blurring the words into nonsensical blots rather than comprehensible instructions. Giving up, he quickly hatched a new plan. "Get me my cavalry scouts! They will have to come here and receive instructions."

When Gus and his cavalrymen were assembled, Johnston gave them each verbal instructions for the battle plan, and then sent them to relay those directives to General Longstreet, Major General D. H. Hill, and General Benjamin Huger—all of whom were nearby, staged for an assault on the Federal troops. But one of the cavalry messengers mixed up one of the details—seemingly a small thing—but with disastrous results. He told General Longstreet that the order was to advance his troops down Williamsburg Road, but General Johnston had said Nine Mile Road. When the units mustered before dawn, Hill and Huger's troops followed the correct orders and marched on Nine Mile Road. The errant unit took Williamsburg Road, and not encountering the other troops there, complicated the mistake by turning the wrong way on Nine Mile Road. Suddenly Confederate soldiers were marching towards fellow soldiers, each briefly thinking the others were Yankees, and thus prepared to fire.

"Hold your fire! We're Longstreet boys."

Gus and James were as confused as everyone else and much shouting back and forth ensued. Finally, the generals gathered together in the middle of the road to figure out what had gone wrong. The miscommunication had shaken everyone's confidence, and after six hours, the commanders still hadn't sorted things out. In fact, they never did.

At 1 pm, an impatient General Hill decided to attack Union troops along the river. Gus and James knew they didn't have the support of the other units yet, but they moved out with the order to advance, hoping the other generals would join in as the engagement began.

Once the battles were underway, it was like a chess game: Advance. Fire. Retreat. Advance. Fire. Advance. Retreat. Gus' company was within firing range now—just 800 yards. Accuracy was poor at this distance, so casualties were few. Both sides were advancing at the same time now. At 500 yards, the chances of hitting something in the direction of one's aim were better. When one side inflicted heavy casualties in a line of fire, the other side would often retreat, but if in the next volley more wounded fell on the advancing side, then they would retreat. The battle went back and forth like this until one side gained the advantage of several advances and gained strategic territory.

The scene looked orderly until the cavalry was sent in. Then the field became chaotic as riders galloped toward the enemy and engaged in close combat. Gus had never killed a man before, and when he fired and someone fell, he imagined it was fire from someone else's gun. Men he had never met and would never know—from places he had never been—were running at him.

"Damnation! Cowards!" shouted Gus as he looked over his shoulder. A few of his cavalrymen were fleeing. Enraged, Gus wanted to go get them and force them back into the fray, but he and his horse pressed on. Valiant proved himself worthy of his name. The horse never bolted, no matter how terrible the noise and commotion. He bravely followed Gus' commands to move forward. Gus fired again, and knew he had killed someone—perhaps someone who at another time or in another place, he would have called a friend. Now the war was more than the adventure of advancing a cause. It was a nightmare of bloody, dispensable men...thousands of them. Gus was no longer a special person, and neither were any of the others. Just bodies—riding, moving, firing, or forever still, lying on ground that was not their home.

Gus heard the order to retreat, and called out to the cavalrymen around him. Some had fallen. Horses were running loose. Soldiers who could retreat fell back 1000 yards. During this run, Gus felt as though he had lost his balance, even though Valiant had remained steady. In the seconds it took for him to reach the ground, Gus thought it odd for an experienced rider like himself to simply fall off. Then he saw the blood. He touched his neck, and his hand was covered with it. Suddenly he was so very tired. All he wanted to do was close his eyes and sleep. The sound of gunfire drifted far away, and he felt peaceful in the embracing darkness.

James shouted to his fallen friend. "Gus, hang on. I'm coming for you!"

Gus had landed on his side. His body sank halfway into the thick mud of saturated soil. An eye, a nostril, half of his mouth now lay hidden in a strange-looking bog. Strange because of its color. It had been brown, but was now turning rusty, and with each passing second, brightening to red. Gus had been hit in the neck, and blood was gushing from the wound, mixing a new palette of colors in the surrounding earth. For a few fleeting seconds, Gus was aware that his friend was coming for him. He felt hands on his face, pulling him out of the blood-stained mud. Just as he lost consciousness, Gus heard a promise he knew could not be kept.

"I'll get you out of this buddy," said James. "You're going on my horse."

As James struggled to pull his childhood friend up to a sitting position, he heard a strident command from behind. "You'll leave him, soldier. We have been ordered to fall back, and you won't make it dragging a body with you." The brigade commander had a rifle aimed at James' head.

"I can't leave him!"

"He's a dead man," said the officer. "He won't live but another few minutes with that wound. We don't take anyone with us except a blown up arm or leg. You stay here and we lose two men 'cause I'll shoot you right now. You're needed to help win this war so let your friend go. He's better off now than we are."

James stumbled backward, gasping at the horror of what he was doing…leaving someone he loved to die. One part of him knew his commander was right. Gus looked like he would soon be dead. But deep inside, James felt like a coward for leaving his best friend to die alone in the mud, the rain, and the brutality of this day.

The Battle of Seven Pines raged on for three more hours. James followed the orders to advance or retreat, but that whole time, tears ran down his cheeks. He wasn't sobbing; in fact, there was little feeling attached to the tears, yet they wouldn't stop. Almost as though part of his brain recognized the unspeakable pain of what had just happened, and the other part denied it. He just kept on, doing what he was told.

During a lull in the fighting, James sat on the ground and stared at the soldier next to him. John Huddleston was writing a letter home. James couldn't imagine having the presence of mind to write a coherent letter in the aftermath of such horror. Huddleston was hunched over the page, intent on his message, perhaps his last.

Dear Brother,

The battle raged desperately and bloody all over the field. The booming cannon, rattling musketry, the glittering bayonets and sabers were all doing their bloody work and such a sight of carnage I never again want to behold.

The loss in our battery is unreasonable to tell, also in our infantry. The Yankees left 1,000 dead and twice as many wounded on the field. I had the brains of my nearest and dearest friend spattered in my face, was knocked twice from my horse by cannon balls, and was twice grazed by musket balls.

I cannot give any further particulars now, as the battle has opened with fearful fury again. I must close my book and use the musket again, and may God be with us and defend us as he has done before.

Yours Devotedly,

John W. Huddlestun

When the fighting finally ended, ambulance crews picked through thousands of bodies on the battlefield. When they came across Gus, he was still breathing, but there was nothing they could do for a serious neck wound. They put a sandbag under his head to keep his face from slipping into the mud, and moved on to the next man.

Chapter XV

June 1862

Just two months since I officially became a sharpshooter and my fingers may be permanently stained from assembling gunpowder cartridges. In addition, the noise of the rifle reports has taken a toll on my hearing. No matter. I am so proud of my shooting skill, and I actually think I'm proud because the Nancies are proud of me. To be esteemed among this remarkable company of women is the greatest accomplishment of all. We have deepened our feelings of friendship, love and loyalty towards one another. I used to have two sisters. Now I have forty-five.

Addie closed her journal and looked out the window. George had brought the carriage around. On the morning of June 2nd, just two days after Gus Bull was left to die on a field of mud and blood in Virginia, his mother and youngest sister were tending to ordinary business in LaGrange. They set out for town in a fine buggy with padded seats and a surrey on top. George took up the reins and clucked to the chestnut mare to move out. Martha was running the plantation while Judge Bull was in Milledgeville for an extended time, involved in the judicial and political affairs of the state. They stopped at the general store for the household supplies they were not able to barter for, make, or grow. Now that Delia had distributed the goods from Liverpool, the general store had salt for the first time in many months. Farmers were beginning to slaughter a few cows, not for immediate consumption, but for beef that would keep for months, using salt to preserve the meat. Beef was once again on the menu in LaGrange households.

At the post office, George pulled up Sallieforth—a horse named for the daughter who learned to ride on her. He helped Addie and her mother down from the buggy and waited outside for his mistresses to collect the mail. This was the high point of everyone's day. Letters from loved ones lifted spirits dulled by casualty lists that were posted outside The LaGrange Reporter office following major battles. Addie was bursting with happiness when she picked up the letter with a postmark from Virginia. It was Gus' handwriting.

"Oh, Mother! More news from Gus."

"That is so exciting, dear, but can you keep the letter a secret until dinner? I think a surprise for the others would be lovely." Addie's mother squeezed her daughter's hand.

Addie held the letter close to her heart. "It will be hard to wait for Gus' news, but it will be such fun to see everyone smile at the table this evening."

"Yes, darling, it will provide us a lovely few moments." The postmaster handed Mrs. Bull two other letters. The first was quite large by comparison to Gus' letter. It was from Milledgeville and addressed to "The Nancy Hart Militia" in care of the Bull Family.

"Could this be a decision on the commission?" asked Addie.

"We are both too curious and excited to wait." Tearing open the envelope, her mother pulled out a parchment proclamation decorated with the emblem of the State of Georgia. It was penned in beautiful calligraphy and signed at the bottom by none other than Governor Joseph Brown. Her mother read:

"On this day of May 16 in the year one thousand eight hundred and sixty two, the Confederate State of Georgia hereby commissions The Nancy Hart Militia to discharge military duties for the protection of the people of LaGrange, Georgia during times of natural disaster, war, or at other times when their services are deemed necessary by this government. May God bless our brave men and women.

Joseph Brown, Governor"

Addie beamed. "We've got happiness to spread today, Mother!"

"And to top it all off, the last letter is from your father. What a delightful evening it will be!"

Addie and her mother chattered excitedly on the way home. "I think a splendid meal would be in order tonight," her mother said gaily

Addie raised her voice over the clatter of the carriage wheels. "Absolutely! We should celebrate."

"I'll have cook prepare a chicken glazed with orange marmalade, a new recipe from Mrs. Hill's cookbook."

At the table that evening, Brussels sprouts and potatoes accompanied the chicken along with a side of cornbread. Addie and her sisters chatted about their world: the incoming wounded on the trains, the conversion of the Presbyterian Church into a hospital, and speculation on how long the colleges would need to serve as hospitals.

When Delia, Sallie, Addie and young Orville finished eating, they sat patiently waiting for their mother to excuse them from the table. Addie tried to stifle a smile. She relished these moments of silence knowing her mother was about to cause quite a commotion with her next words. "Children, we have mail. From Gus, from Father, and from Governor Brown."

Everyone was laughing, shouting, and squirming in their seats. Which to read first? It was a difficult choice, but in the end they voted to hear from Governor Brown. Sallie and Addie were teary when their mother read the proclamation commissioning the militia. Delia shouted and leapt from her chair, grabbing Orville for a silly dance around the table. Mrs. Bull settled the group with the letter from Gus.

Dearest Family,

I am well, if a little tired. James and I are seeing some beautiful countryside we probably wouldn't have seen were it not for this conflict. We try always to find something positive to regard. The rhododendrons seem to have different colors than the ones we see at home, but are not as gigantic as the ones we have seen near Highlands, North Carolina. Sallie will remember those grand bushes from our family vacation there several years ago. They were taller than some of the trees in the mountains.

Addie, there is a beautiful song I have been hearing quite often. Perhaps you have heard it and so can play it. It's called "Lorena." We all get a bit melancholy when we hear it, but it is a beautiful song.

Delia, one of your letters to me, which was so full of patriotism and intelligent political analysis, I felt I had to share with it my Company. The men have asked me to read it time and time again. It makes them stronger in their commitment.

Orville, please help yourself to whatever I have left at the house, whether it is a comb or a set of playing cards. It would comfort me to know you and I were connected if only by having touched the same things. Just don't indulge in the card games that will get you in trouble.

Mother and Father, could you send me my wool shirt and the black leather shoes in the attic trunk? I still have shoes, but they have some holes which allow the soggy ground to keep my feet wet. If you find more socks, send those too, please. It has rained a lot, but we are hopeful it will stop soon. You are the best parents a son could ever have hoped for, and as always, I send you my love.

I love you too Delia, Sallie, Addie, Orville, and wish this war to be over soon so I can come home to you all.

Gus

There was such joy around the table. Everyone held hands while Mrs. Bull said a prayer. "Dearest Lord, we beseech you, keep our beloved Gus safe from harm. Deliver him from all dangers of the body and of the soul. And return him to us blessed by the strength of his brave spirit. Merciful Father, we ask that you stand close to us all for whatever may lie ahead. Amen."

Judge Bull's letter was last to be opened.

Dear Family,

I can't express how proud I am of my daughters and the newly-commissioned Nancy Hart Militia. Ben Hill and other lawmakers met with the Governor, and delivered a round of fine arguments on behalf of the commissioning. At the end, everyone applauded, including the Governor. So many people shook my hand that my fingers were numb. Many of the men remarked that women in the North were making spectacles of themselves over men's issues—things that should not concern them. While in the South, women were making no complaint, but rather putting strength and necessity into action for the good of all. The Nancies have already made quite a name for themselves, at least among the leaders here in Milledgeville. God Bless.

Addie and her sisters rose from their chairs and curtsied to one another. Her mother motioned for them to sit. "That's all very sweet, but it appears the rest of your Father's letter is much more serious." She continued to read to the family.

I am beginning to worry more about Gus. There are signs something major is about to happen, and I fear Gus and his Company might be involved. I do not tell you this so you can worry with me, but rather so you know to increase your prayers.

I cannot leave here for some time, but will write again soon. May God, The Protector, be with us all.

Love, Father

Dinner ended with bowed heads. Addie prayed silently. *Dearest Lord, Please watch over Gus and keep him safe. We need him back home for so many reasons, but the biggest and most important is that we all love him so much. Amen. Oh…James too…please keep him safe. Amen.*

Chapter XVI

Early on the morning of June 2nd, when Martha Bull was picking up her mail in LaGrange, a small contingent of Union soldiers was dispatched to scavenge the muddy and silent battlefield at Seven Pines, Virginia. They poked through the debris and human ruins for useful things. Rifles were the most valuable prizes of war, but shoes were almost as coveted. Long marches and interrupted supply lines led to worn out shoes. Soldiers even marched barefoot sometimes. The horrific scene before them would have stunned and repelled any normal person, but these soldiers were no longer normal. They had walked in the wake of this hell too many times. Twisted bodies. Bones poking out. Eyes wide in never-blinking stares. Mouths open in silent howls. Hands clutching the hands of other frozen bodies in mud red with blood. Flies everywhere, carrion birds circling, landing, then circling again. And the indescribable, but unmistakable smell of death.

Five thousand, seven hundred, and thirty-nine of their own northern brothers had died in this engagement. The Confederates lost more: 7,997 when the body count was tallied. It would have been 7,998 had Col.

Raymund Lee not reached for a pair of boots with a few holes in them. As he pulled them off the poor soul whose head was propped up with a sandbag, he heard a moan. He jumped up, scared senseless. How could a dead man make a sound like that? He bent over the mud-caked face, and the dead man's eyelids fluttered open. Col. Lee shouted. "Oh my God! I've got a live one! What do we do?"

The policy of the Union Army's medical director was to keep the wounded with the troops, rather than evacuate them to hospitals in northern cities. It was an unfortunate decision as the conditions in the field hospitals were deplorable: dirty, crowded, and without adequate rations or staffing. All of which fanned the flames of disease. Malaria, dysentery, and typhoid fever were rampant in hospital camps with one epidemic after another.

Since trauma to head or trunk was deemed untreatable, the majority of the hospitalized suffered from injuries to limbs. With no way to determine the severity of such wounds on the battlefield, many were left to die there. Some did so quickly, while many others suffered horribly before they died—spending long days and longer nights cold, without food, water, or pain medication. And worst of all, leaving this world without the comfort of a kind word or human touch.

This is how Gus Bull would have died had it not been for the scavenger detail. The first medic crews on the battlefield had inadvertently saved his life by placing the sandbag under his head. His jugular had been nicked by a passing minié ball. It was not a direct hit, but neck wounds bleed profusely. The sandbag behind his neck acted to flex his chin forward—that position and the dried mud had shut down the bleeding. Days later, clotting had closed the wound, and Gus' blood flow had begun to improve. He had moved in and out of consciousness for two days until he'd felt a steady pressure on his foot. Startled, he looked up to see a Union soldier tugging at his boot, but was too weak to do anything but moan.

The Union soldiers of the scavenger detail picked up some valuable items from the field, among them more shoes, a few weapons, and a loose horse wandering in the woods at the edge of the battleground, but now they had another task: to build an Indian-style litter for their unexpected patient. Alongside the litter, Col. Lee pulled the horse they had recovered. He tried to go slow and steady, stopping frequently to offer Gus water and some of his hardtack. In the pocket of Gus' pants he had found a worn and dirty piece of paper, folded several times. Sometimes soldiers carried a kind of will with them into battle: instructions regarding their last wishes. But Gus' paper contained a verse. Col. Lee noted the title "Christmas Day 1861" and began to read.

The year's high festival is come
The time of careless mirth.
Of glad reunions in each home
Glad gatherings round each hearth;
But unto us it brings but tears
And painful memories
Of the bright scenes of happier years
Sadly compared with there;
Each household mourns some loved one gone,
The husband, son, or sire;
Now met to talk of friends and home
Around the red campfire...."

It was signed "Sister" and dated Dec. 30, 1861

Col. Lee was moved to tears. This man he was dragging to a prison camp had a family who loved him and missed him terribly. This enemy was like him—a human being with a soul not just some stranger bent on terror. He sat down on the ground beside this silent soldier, remembering his own lonely Christmas nearly six months earlier. Away from his family in Massachusetts for the first time in his life, how he had missed them! How he longed to see his mother's outstretched arms welcoming him back to love and comfort and the beauty of his home. He ached for his father's handshake, his sister's smile, and the sight of his two brothers laughing. It was too much to bear, these longings. He knew his companions would understand his tears, for they had shed their own on other days, but he feared that if he fully opened to these feelings, the floodgates would never close. He folded the paper, stuffed it into his own pocket, and trudged on.

When Col. Lee arrived with Gus in tow at Harrison's Landing on Virginia's James River, he entered a pit of human misery. So many wounded! A few were on cots, but most lay on the ground and few had blankets. There were surgical tables out in the open air—perhaps five across—each with a man being prepped for some kind of amputation. An assistant administered opium to each patient. Sometimes morphine was directly applied to injured tissue. One surgeon moved among the tables, inspecting wounds, his apron dirty and bloody. He swabbed wounds from one patient to the next with the same sponge. Occasionally, the sponge was rinsed in the same bucket until the water itself was red as blood. The assistant readied the patient for amputation by applying a chloroform soaked handkerchief over the mouth and nose. Field hospitals preferred chloroform for controlled hospital use over the highly explosive ether.

There wasn't a lot of screaming among those still alive, as the doctors believed in every form of medication from whiskey to morphine. Truth be told, it was not the amputations that proved to be the real horror, but rather the disease epidemics which doctors were helpless to control.

Most soldiers feared disease more than battle wounds as many died, not from their injuries, but from some infection sweeping the camps. At the beginning of the war, typhoid fever had killed seventeen percent of patients, and the disease rate would only ratchet up as the war progressed. Thousands upon thousands of once able-bodied men survived the battlefield only to meet their end on a cot or dirt floor burning up with fever.

But somehow, Gus appeared to be surmounting the odds. Conscious and steadily gaining strength, he was beginning to believe he might make it home one day. Paperwork was readied to exchange several prisoners, including Gus once he was well enough to be moved. While the men waited to either recover or to die, their faith in God often deepened.

Religion was important to American men on both sides of the conflict. In the camps, morning and evening prayers brought great comfort to the men. Like so many soldiers, Gus carried a small prayer book in his haversack. It fit in his hand and contained only about fifteen pages. Most of the prayers made reference to the rightness of the southern cause, beseeching God to bring the enemy to its senses over their injustice. Gus asked his new Yankee friend, Ray, to read a prayer aloud so that the other wounded might find some small measure of peace. Looking for verses that would be suitable for southern and northern soldiers alike, he found one that spoke to compassion for all. "I think this one speaks to everyone with a mighty wisdom," he said, handing Ray the book.

Dearest Lord, thank you for this day for it is a chance to begin again. O God, we beseech Thee, forgive and pardon our enemies, and give us that measure of Thy grace that, for their hatred, we may love them; for their cursing we may bless them; for their injury we may do them good...

With God's help, they believed they would live through this great trial if only diseases would stay away. But disease had made no such deal with God. Typhoid fever was a scourge for which there was little treatment. No one was sure of its etiology, but a few in the medical community suspected fecal contamination, decaying bodies of animals and humans, and uncontained garbage might be the root cause.

Harrison's Landing did not evacuate soon enough to avoid the next disaster. Typhoid fever went through the assembled wounded like a wave covering the beach at high tide. Those who were not already weakened by wounds or surgery had a chance to ward off the diarrhea and high fevers, but the rest were not so fortunate.

Raymund Lee hurried from the medical commander's tent when word arrived of an imminent prisoner exchange. Gus was still in a weakened state, but Ray felt sure his friend could make the trip home by train. As he made his way through the rows of patients, he caught sight of Gus sitting propped up against a tree and shouted to get his friend's attention. "Gus, you're going home!"

There was no response. Ray knelt down beside his friend and put his hand on Gus' forehead. He was burning with fever. His eyes were closed. His head drooped onto his chest and his breathing was shallow. Ray gently lowered him to the ground, filled a bucket with water, and brought wet cloths to help bring the fever down. There was little else to do when typhoid struck. Now, at least seventy men who might have walked away from Harrison's Landing were felled a second time, not by bullets but by disease. Only a few would survive, and Raymund Lee was determined that Gus would be one of the lucky ones. Why else would God provide such a miracle on the battlefield if not that Gus should live on?

Chapter XVII

Sallie had never worked so hard in her life, but never had she been so excited. When she'd first started, her hospital duties were menial. She wiped fevered brows, emptied bedpans, and kept a notebook on supplies.

50 rolled bandages
5 bottles opium
6 bottles chloroform
3 large jars ether
turpentine
powered charcoal
maggots

Most people were disgusted by maggots, but not Sallie. She had learned from Dr. Ware that these insect larvae cleared dead skin away from wounds, allowing them to heal more quickly.

In a very short time, she was learning a lot about medical care, and allowed to perform duties that involved more skill. Dr. Ware was not only a gifted surgeon, but a gifted teacher as well. With one hand and her help, he had saved many wounded soldiers. She used to think it was horrible to lose an arm or a leg, but after assisting in amputations, the shock had worn off. The prosthetic business was thriving in these terrible times, but at least the amputees would be able to live independently and have lives worth living. She was proud to be part of that effort, and pleased to continue her learning about healing.

"Sallie, see this blackening tissue right here near the bullet wound?" Dr. Ware asked, pointing to the soldier's foot. "That's one clue his leg is infected. Can you think of another?"

"What about the smell?" offered Sallie. "The lower leg has a fetid odor."

"There's my good student! Smell is a very important sense to use when evaluating a patient. The flesh around the wound is rotting and will likely spread."

"Jus' let me die, Doc," the patient said. Private Fred Porter was in a lot of pain and had but one thought: to be released from his suffering.

Dr. Ware sat down next to the patient's bed. "I know you don't want to go on at this moment, but you can live if we amputate the leg."

"No, no! Life is not worth living if I can't walk." Fred began to cry.

"Yes, son, I lost faith too and didn't want to go on, but I promise you, there are many precious moments left for you, and I mean for you to have them. As you can see, I have no right hand, but you can also see the men around you healing because of the work I am able to do—not alone, but with the grace of God and helpers like Sallie."

Sallie stroked the patient's face and wiped away his tears. "We're going to take care of you and make this awful pain go away." She supported his head and offered him a cup with a chalky opium-laced liquid. In a few minutes Fred was quiet, even peaceful.

"Sallie, let's prepare for surgery. Make sure all the instruments have been boiled in water, and have the orderlies get Fred on the operating table while he's still sedated,"

"Do you want to use chloroform or ether for this operation?" asked Sallie.

"Ether. It's still new, but it's much safer for the patient. It also gives us more control over his consciousness during the procedure."

After scrubbing her hands and arms with a strong soap, Sallie prepared the surgical area. This was Dr. Ware's protocol, asserted for all of his surgeries though doctors at other hospitals were not as adamant about cleanliness. Once Sallie cleaned and prepared the surgical instruments, she washed up a second time, side-by-side with Dr. Ware.

"Sallie, I want you to study the suturing procedure today and try a few stitches yourself."

"Yes, doctor. Will you use silk thread or horse hair?"

"Horse hair."

Horse hair, Sallie had learned, became quite soft after boiling, and there were fewer skin infections from it.

She was in awe of Dr. Ware's skill as he cut through bone, then fashioned a flap that would allow an artificial limb to fit more comfortably later on. Here was a surgeon who, despite having only one hand, needed minimal assistance during most operations. She watched carefully as he stitched the ends of the flap over the knee, bracing the tissue with the metal fitting on his right hand, while pulling the horsehair thread with the fingers on his left hand. He had practiced this so many times on fabric that his left hand had developed expertise in making these small, fine movements. To Sallie it was nothing short of astounding that this surgeon could still function so competently without his dominant hand.

"Now you try." Dr. Ware held out the threaded needle to Sallie.

She had done stitches before on a few injured animals, but working on a patient who wasn't in pain was very different. This was much easier, allowing the stitches to be placed with greater care.

When the operation was finished, Sallie dressed the stump with a light gauze bandage and helped settle the young man into the large ward room for the night.

"Good night, Dr. Ware." Was that a smile on the doctor's face as he reached out and touched her hand?

"I couldn't have done it without you, Sallie." He gently squeezed her hand letting the gesture linger.

Sallie was surprised. *Could this be more than praise? That smile...that touch.*

Then she caught herself. *Oh, don't be ridiculous. I'm just tired, imagining something that isn't there.* "Thank you, Dr. Ware. I'll see you tomorrow." Still, the feeling lingered.

Sallie was proud to have learned so much from Dr. Ware. His praise meant a lot to her, but the idea of romance had never occurred to her. She'd have to think about it. *I've always just ignored flirtations from men. I've been so busy and focused on my studies. Is it time to pay closer attention?* She didn't know.

What Sallie did know is that she was in love with learning. She also loved the community of women who had become dedicated to nursing the last two years. Not all the nurses were as skilled as she was, but they were just as committed to the soldiers' healing. Most times, that healing involved fresh air, good food, and human kindness—and the volunteer nurses provided a good measure of that kindness. Young women from all the churches worked shifts, tending to patients. In addition, LaGrange property owners volunteered two hundred of their slaves and house servants for hospital duty. They might dress wounds, apply cold cloths to fevered brows, or simply sit by a soldier's bed holding a hand or telling stories.

Sallie had heard that in the North, attractive women had been banned from nursing. Those in charge felt women were too delicate and had no place in a situation where indelicate things were commonplace. In LaGrange, however, Dr. Ware had urged every woman to get involved in tending to the wounded. He canvassed all the churches in town, pressing the women to get involved. "Ladies, you have the soothing words, compassion, and patience that these men desperately need, if only to help lift their spirits." Privately he communicated to Sallie that he believed this component had a lot to do with healing.

Under Dr. Ware's leadership, LaGrange was beginning to develop an excellent reputation as a hospital center—thanks to the combined skills of local doctors, assigned Confederate Army Surgeons, and the tender care of nurses. Delivered directly by rail, a steady stream of injured men arrived from as far away as Virginia—both Confederate soldiers and Union prisoners. By now all the churches, as well as colleges, had been converted to hospitals. The only thing sorely lacking was another dozen women with Sallie Bull's training and talent. Dispatched by Dr. Ware on a regular basis, Sallie toured the hospitals, assisting the surgeon on duty.

When Sallie lamented to her family about the shortage of skilled nurses, Judge Bull released a house servant to train with Dr. Ware. Accompanying her to the main hospital, Sallie had the pleasure of introducing her to Dr. Ware. "This is Frances. Her mother, Melva, has distinguished herself in our household with her medicinal knowledge," Sallie said proudly. "Melva's performed some real miracles in the slave population. She's a natural healer, and Frances is gaining a reputation for inheriting her mother's gift."

"That's very good to hear," said Dr. Ware. "We could use more miracles." He smiled at his new nurse-in-training. "Please thank your parents for releasing Frances to us."

Frances immediately felt different from the other nurses. It wasn't just that they were white, and therefore treated more deferentially by doctors and patients. But also, she noticed, white parents displayed a lot of concern over their daughters spending so much time with men. Yet no one, not ever her own parents, worried about her tending the wounded men.

One day, Frances overheard Leila Pullen's mother talking about propriety.

"Darling, dressing wounds and holding the hand of a soldier in pain are both noble jobs, but do not forget for a *minute* that these are men and might have other ideas about your healing touch."

"Oh, stop, Mother!" her daughter retorted. "These men are just in need of human kindness."

"Just be careful," her mother warned.

No one would admonish *her* to be careful, Frances thought. Such a double standard was irritating, but was just another fact of being born into slavery. She didn't like it, but what could she do about it? On the other hand, Frances actually found it amusing to watch the southern ladies in action at the hospitals. Romances did develop from time to time, which were not so much grown from the seeds of human kindness, she knew, but from the expert flirting abilities of these young ladies. She also knew Leila Pullen was among the most adept, and her mother, therefore, among the most worried. Frances was aware that Margaret Pullen inspected the troops each morning—going from bed to bed in the hospital that Leila was scheduled to visit, and personally selecting the most unattractive soldier as her daughter's assignment.

Frances could hardly keep from laughing as she watched Leila trying to figure out her misfortune. How did her friends consistently get the best-looking, most charming and intelligent, eligible soldiers in the wards?

"Lizzie Beck, why do you get to nurse that handsome soldier from North Carolina? And Sarah gets the rich officer from the Tennessee Cavalry while I get the unconscious Private with the scraggly beard. Not to mention his hook nose and terrible smell." Leila resented that she was always assigned to the homeliest, and quite frequently, the stupidest man there.

Dr. Ware had told all the nurses that a positive attitude was good for the soldiers' healing. So when Frances saw Leila arrive one morning wearing an especially lovely dress, she imagined Leila was presenting her prettiest self, hoping in the face of mounting odds, that she would finally get to tend an attractive man. *Leila is such an exquisite study in the fine art of flirtatiousness,* Frances thought, *she must feel her talents are being entirely wasted.* Leila wasn't as strikingly beautiful as the three Bull sisters, but she was pretty just the same, and had elevated coquettishness to an art form.

Now, dressed to express that proficiency, Frances could see that Leila fairly floated through the door at the Presbyterian Hospital. The petticoats and hoop skirt beneath her pink dress imitated the sound of fallen leaves rustling in a gentle breeze. A corset pinched her waist to a delicate twenty inches, and the bodice was gathered in tiny pleats adorned with white satin ribbons and rosettes. The same slender ribbons pulled her long brown hair away from her face. She toted a tapestry bag filled with books, writing paper, pen and ink, along with brownies baked from a recipe in Mrs. Hill's latest cookbook. Lining up as usual with the other young ladies, Leila waited her turn to scan the list of assignments. A look of optimism crossed her face when the name *Henry Green* came up next to hers.

"I feel like I'm going to be lucky today. This name just inspires such hope!" Leila said to the others. "Henry Green is a plain name, but could belong to a strong, attractive, and very brave man who is in need of my ministrations this very day."

Frances remembered when Leila had been assigned to a man named Icabod Fernbush. As her finger had scrolled down the list, she had stopped abruptly and a frown had settled on her face. When Frances saw the man later, she thought, *Poor thing! He looks every bit as ridiculous as his name.* There was Leila by his side, reading Bible verses to him. *He probably has a lovely soul, but Leila isn't going to hang around long enough to find out,* she thought.

Frances had already seen Henry Green, so she knew Leila was in for a surprise. He looked like a fifteen-year-old boy, and probably was. Many a teenager, North and South, had joined the war imagining the manly adventure he would be part of. Instead, many grew up far too fast on pain and misery. Many more didn't grow up at all. They died far away from home and a mother who loved them—all for a cause they barely understood.

Frances followed Leila into the ward, and from the expression on her face when she located Henry, Frances could see that she was not only disappointed, but shocked.

"What on earth made you join the Army at your age? What are you, fifteen?" said Leila.

"No Ma'am. I'm fifteen and a *half*. I wanted to be as brave as my Daddy. He joined a cavalry unit that fought at Shiloh, and when he was listed as a casualty, I hurried off to enlist. Lied about my age.

After action at Seven Pines, everybody seemed excited to have General Lee take over for the next push on the Peninsula. We thought we'd win for sure." Henry was injured at Malvern Hill on July 1, when Union forces picked off five thousand men advancing a long slope. They never had a chance against the Union artillery.

Now in LaGrange, Dr. Ware refused to release Henry back to his unit. The teenager was recovering nicely from a wound to his left foot, but Dr. Ware's written instructions were clear, *"permanently disabled and unable to resume duties."*

At least Leila appeared to be tender-hearted towards the boy, but Frances could also hear irritation in her voice. Perhaps Leila felt frustrated that her special effort to lavish feminine charms on someone, were wasted on yet another inappropriate man.

"Well, Henry," Frances heard her say with a sigh, "Let's make the best of this situation. Let's write a letter to your mother, who surely will be delighted to hear you are coming home."

Henry flashed a smile. "I only wish my mother cared as much for me as your mother cares for you. She came by very early this morning to make sure you were assigned the right patient. She said I would be a perfect charge for her precious daughter and I thanked her for selecting my name."

Leila rolled her eyes with sudden insight. "I should have known. My mother, Henry, will *always* be there for me. Let's start this letter, young man.

"Dearest Mother,

I am in the presence of one of the most beautiful ladies in the entire South...."

"How's that for a start, Henry?" Leila gave him her most dazzling smile.

Frances let out a snort and hurried down the aisle, stifling her laughter. *At least in the middle of so much misery we have Leila to thank for some relief. She thinks her life is full of drama, but it is more like a rousing comedy.*

As the day wore on, the mirth Frances had enjoyed became a distant memory. A dozen badly injured soldiers were unloaded from the train and triaged at the hospital. Well into the night, she assisted Dr. Ware in surgery after surgery. Finally, about 3 a.m., Dr. Ware sent the last of the cases to the ward.

Frances walked from bed to bed, making sure her patients were as comfortable as possible, and administering additional pain medication if necessary. Satisfied that the ward was quiet for the time being, she headed for the lobby to stretch out on the sofa. *Maybe I can sleep for a couple of hours before hell serves up more mangled men tomorrow.*

"Get me out! Help! Help! Something's got me! Get it off my leg!"

Frances bolted upright. Had she slept minutes...or was it hours? She ran along the row of beds until she found the screaming patient writhing on the floor. He was bleeding profusely from his amputated limb, having torn out the stitches in the flap trying to throw off his imagined attacker. Frances knew the only attacker was pain.

Frances roused an orderly from his badly needed sleep, and together, they struggled to get the soldier into his hospital bed. He was incoherent now, and Frances knew she wouldn't be able to get him to drink anything to ease the pain. She ran to the medicine supply cabinet and removed a small vial of chloroform and a sponge—then located some boiled horse hair and a clean needle, hurrying back to her frenzied patient. The orderly held him down while he continued to scream for help.

"I'm going to help you. Take a deep breath now." Frances placed the sponge over the man's mouth and placed a few drops of chloroform on top. While it soaked into the sponge, she pinched his nose. As the patient gasped for breath, he began to relax. Apparently the monster and the pain were receding.

Frances repaired the torn blood vessels and re-stitched the flap over the stump of the knee. When she was finished, she cleaned up the bloody scene with the help of the orderly. Frances was wide awake now—the adrenaline surging through her bloodstream. The patient could so easily have bled to death. She didn't dare take the time to find Dr. Ware or another doctor. Somehow, she had found the wherewithal to deal with this emergency on her own. Throughout the night, she checked on her patient every two hours, administering enough pain medication to keep the monster away.

At 9 a.m., Dr. Ware made his rounds, calling Frances to his side.

"This patient looks like he's had some additional trauma. There are new tears in this tissue and new sutures. Did you re-stitch this flap?"

"Yes, Doctor. The patient tore the first ones out, delirious that something had hold of his leg. He was losing so much blood I had do something quick."

"It was the right decision. I'm sure he would have died. And these stitches are the smallest, straightest, and tightest I've ever seen. Impressive! You've given our young man another chance."

While Sallie was assigned to other hospitals, Dr. Ware and Frances worked side by side, day after day throughout the summer. In the aftermath of the Peninsular Campaign, however, they often labored all night— hardly noticing whether the moon was out or the sun was up. Both doctor and staff only had time for short naps and hurried meals. By Friday, exhaustion had set in and Dr. Ware ordered most of his help to go home and get some rest. Frances and he would stay on to finish a surgery and keep watch over the patients. Just as the last stitch was placed, Frances saw Dr. Ware go limp, as if his knees were about to buckle. He didn't seem to notice when Frances took the needle from him and finished the stitches herself. Then she led the nearly catatonic doctor down the hall, and into his makeshift office, settling him onto the cot by his desk. He made not a sound either in protest or resignation, and was asleep before she could pull a blanket over him. Returning to the surgery area, she finished with the patient and tucked him into a bed on the ward. When all was quiet, she let herself back into Dr. Ware's office to check on him. Sitting next to the cot, she watched the rhythmic rise and fall of his chest. Soon her own exhaustion crept over her like a winding river surrendering to a waterfall.

The first thing Dr. Ware noticed when he became conscious again was the weight of someone leaning on him. Then he noticed a scent. He didn't know how long he had been sleeping, but he knew his work awaited him, so he must rouse himself. With his eyes still closed, but his wakefulness returning, he drank in this aroma. It almost brought tears to his eyes. *This is how a woman smells. Not perfume and powder, but a natural blend from skin and hair…and from moist, hidden parts.* How he missed that fragrance and the feel of a woman in his arms! He rarely thought about it because his days overflowed with work, but now it wouldn't let go of his senses.

Opening his eyes, he saw a hand on his shoulder. Without thought, he traced the hand and arm with his own, all the way up to her face. Frances was an attractive woman with high cheekbones, deep-set brown eyes and a figure that offered graceful curves on an otherwise slim frame. Her arm on his shoulder expressed such tenderness. As she sat sleeping soundlessly, Dr. Ware moved his hand to her lips and traced their fullness with his fingertips. Her eyes opened slowly, and her lips parted slightly, but no sound came from them. They gazed silently at each other, their weary, but longing eyes mirroring a thought that needed no words. Dr. Ware made love to Frances, weeping from the exquisite touch he thought was lost forever. Feeling broken because of his disability, and undesirable as a man, he hadn't dared to hope for a moment like this.

Frances brought healing, and in return, she began to understand her own sexuality. This was not the first time a man had touched her, but in past encounters, she had been expected only to lie still. Dr. Ware, however, was not only a skilled surgeon, but a tender and proficient lover. With his slow, deliberate touch, Frances experienced a whole-body quaking. She didn't know what was happening, but it was more pleasurable than anything she had ever felt before. And unlike the others, Dr. Ware kissed and caressed her as he rhythmically moved inside her. When he moaned and became very still, he held her gently, kissing her eyes, then her mouth. Frances stroked his back and sank into feelings of warmth and release. She didn't think for a moment there was a future for this relationship. Certainly they shared special feelings for one another because they worked together so closely, but romance was out of the question.

Dr. Ware took in a sharp breath. "I'm so sorry..."

"Shhh...don't..."

"I didn't mean to..."

"It's jus' this one time...it's all right..." She was not unhappy about this unexpected event, but knew any more trysts would be unwise—opening herself up to hospital gossip or gossip at home for that matter. The Bull sisters were dear to her, but they did tend to talk too much. She didn't want word of this to become public. Whatever this burst of passion meant to either of them, she hoped it would remain their own secret.

Dr. Ware managed to compartmentalize his affair with Frances. There was nothing to be gained by continuing a physical relationship with his surgical nurse—and besides, he was too preoccupied with saving lives to get involved. He would not lapse from his mission as a doctor. Frances, he felt assured, understood the impossibility of a love relationship between them.

Chapter XVIII

There was something Dr. Ware wanted more than sex or romance: to be a seeker of medical advances. And he was aware that his nurse's expertise with patients was valuable to him, freeing him to think like a researcher and not just a technician.

He began to study disease transmission, believing that there might be something unseen at work in the spread of illness from person to person. He thought strong cleansing agents might somehow impede this mysterious process. Everyone on his medical teams washed their hands with lye soap before working on patients. Carbolic acid was used to clean equipment and instruments. Fresh water, cleaned cotton, and boiled sponges were used as a matter of standard practice. As a result, LaGrange hospital mortality rates were among the lowest in the country.

Attitude may also have played a large part in those survival statistics as Dr. Ware certainly made lifting the men's spirits a priority. At least once a day, every wounded or sick soldier was visited by a nurse who read to them. Poetry was popular, as was reading from the Bible, but it was stories of every kind that released the men from battlefield memories. Bulwer-Litton, Hugo, and Dickens were the favorites. Sometimes the young ladies would write letters for their patients or simply chat at bedside about happier times.

"Tell me, Fred, what's your best memory of home?" Addie asked the young amputee.

"I 'spect that'd be riding my horse, Mystic, up in the mountains of North Carolina. I kin almost see the trail snakin' up and around, surrounded by woods. Air smellin' so clean. We're coming 'round a curve, can't see nothing up ahead but begin to hear a rushing kind of sound. Gits louder and louder 'til you're almost scared...and then you see it! Wow! This big, ole waterfall up ahead."

"What did Mystic do? Was the horse frightened?"

"Naw, he loved the trail and seemed to accept whatever came along. You could always trust him to take care of you. Miss that horse, yes, I do."

"What happened to him?" Addie asked cautiously

"He got shot out from under me two fights ago. Landed on top of me, but juz managed to move hisself off before he took his last breath. That wuz *some* brave friend."

"I bet you are so sad when you think about him." Addie patted his hand.

"I 'spect he's in a better place. Juz before my surgery, that's where I wanted to be more 'n anything—in heaven with Mystic, but nurse Sallie and that Dr. Ware, they talked me into stayin' alive."

"And we're all glad you're still here, Fred. There is so much still to enjoy. Why, the Electa Club will be coming be this evening to put on a musical play. I know they will make you smile."

"You've already made me smile, Addie, juz sittin' by my bed listening to me and my memories."

In the early days of the fighting, families were asked to take the wounded into their homes because the hospitals were not yet organized. Now the hospitals were established, but often overwhelmed by the numbers of wounded men so convalescent hospitals had been hastily set up in the local colleges. LaGrange was not just getting Confederate soldiers, but a number of Union soldiers who were sent to prisons upon recovery. A special ward was set up for wounded prisoners in the largest college building, which sat on a hill at the end of Broad Street. Sgt. Major Oscar Hugh La Grange of the Union army spent his recovery time in the company of prisoners of war there. The great coincidence of his name struck everyone, but nonetheless, they were happy he would be moving on once his wounds were healed. Dr. Ware wisely assigned Delia to tend to him. He knew her no-nonsense approach would keep the work strictly professional.

The Union officer had suffered burns to hands and arms, fleeing a barn on the outskirts of West Point, Georgia. It had been deliberately torched by a contingent of Confederate soldiers chasing Sgt. La Grange and his cohorts—a way to force the Yankees from their hiding place. They were there as spies on a mission to scout key rail stations in Tennessee and North Georgia. The small Rebel unit from Chattanooga had organized patrols around the clock as they closed in on the Yankees. Night patrol yielded the clues that led to the capture. Amid the rustlings of a light breeze and the scurrying of nocturnal critters, came the sound of human voices in tones hushed but urgent. The night patrol barn-burning was successful. Of the five reconnoitering Yankees, one escaped, three died in the fire and Sgt. La Grange was captured. Now it was Delia's turn to deal with him.

Dr. Ware, feeling that the medical community was completely out of touch with disease transmission, was trying new approaches to the treatment of burns. He had a hunch there might be something that grew and advanced through the body, particularly when there were open wounds or burns. Instead of lard and bandages, he preferred to wash a burn site with water and leave it open to the air. Many of his patients treated in this way avoided fevers and recovered, even if scarring and disability were the end result.

Dr. Ware instructed Delia in his new treatment plan for burns: water, fresh air and drugs for pain. Though Delia detested this enemy soldier, she nevertheless, provided compassionate care. "Let's wheel you out into the sunshine today. It is *such* a beautiful morning." Delia pushed the wheelchair onto the broad front porch of what used to be the college's administrative office. Whether inside or out, she sat by the prisoner's side for hours, reading to him and distracting him from the pain until another dose of morphine could be administered. She talked to the officer about family, not war. She spoke of the gardens of LaGrange, and chatted about the people who made up such a fine community. "We have quite a few doctors, lawyers, and educators here. It's unusual to have this concentration of professionals who also run plantations."

When she ran out of non-war local history and current events to talk about, she spoke of her childhood—all the silly things she liked to remember. Like the time her sister, Addie, had called her to come see all the snow that had fallen during the night. LaGrange received a good snowfall only once in a great while, so Delia dashed excitedly to the front door in her nightclothes. Her little sister quickly pushed her outside, and in an instant, her brother, Gus, dumped a bucketful of heavy snow from the balcony which, of course, landed right on Delia's head. She screamed and squealed and dashed back inside while her siblings howled, doubled over with laughter. However, by sundown, she had found a way to get even. As Addie pulled on fur-lined slippers to warm her chilly feet, they met with the snow Delia had packed into the toes. How she had delighted in the sound of Addie's shrieking!

Delia wasn't sure if Sgt. La Grange heard anything she said as he was often bleary from pain medication. In his lucid moments, he spoke often of returning to his unit. She supposed he had collected valuable information during his foray into Georgia—scouting railroad towns for their strategic importance should the Army ever advance through this territory.

The patient's burns eventually healed. He was left with scars, but could still move his fingers and hands. When Delia followed the doctor's orders to ease up on morphine, Sgt. La Grange found his voice.

"Why do you tell me family stories and keep up pleasant conversation?" he asked Delia. "Why not take this opportunity to indoctrinate me with talk of States Rights and southern loyalty to the Confederacy?"

"I don't fool myself that you would understand our way of thinking about government," Delia replied. "But I believe there's a chance you have a human soul. I suppose I want to put a face on your enemy so the next time you are called to battle, you will think about the sameness between us, whether North or South. We each have brothers and sisters, mothers and fathers, husbands and friends that we love and cherish."

Delia had seen the orders for her patient to be exchanged as a prisoner of war. She was glad he would be leaving soon. The town would be rid of one La Grange, who in her opinion, brought no honor to the name bestowed on the town.

Chapter XIX

L uella Biggs hadn't seen a bar of soap in two years. She kept herself as clean as she could given her situation—which meant a quick dip in an ice cold creek during winter, and a dangerous swim during the summer months. Dangerous because that's when people were more likely to be about in the countryside. Luella had been a creature of the woods for two years now, living on roots and berries and what small animals she could trap in snares or camouflaged pits. She lived in a cave during the winter, and in summer, her dwelling was a stick lean-to she had fashioned from debris in the thick woods.

A person could get lost here, and that's just what she had counted on when she ran away. She figured her only other choice was to kill herself, but she wasn't a person without hope—just a person in a hopeless situation. She had lost her status as a house servant taking care of the mistress' young children when she was but a child herself. One of her young charges had falsely accused her of slapping the baby, and the mistress had her promptly sold off. Under the new owner, she was a field hand slave where long hours and backbreaking work were expected of men and women alike. She would have submitted to this life without complaint had it not been for the overseer of the plantation—a man of infinite cruelty. Terence Lange beat his charges over the smallest infraction. That was bad enough, but what he did to the women was worse. He would single out a black woman to serve his sexual desires for as long as he fancied her. Some just submitted. Others resisted and were beaten into compliance.

Lange threatened to sell a woman's babies if she didn't go along with his tactics. Luella remembered when Lange argued with a young slave who carried her two-month old baby in a sling around her body. The woman kept saying, "No, no, please Mistuh Lange! No!" In one swift motion, the overseer swept a big hand into the sling, pulling the infant out by its feet and dumping it head first into the horse trough full of water. The woman screamed and screamed all the while Lange kept the baby's head under water. She fell to Lange's feet, grabbed hold of his trousers, yelling, "Yes, anything, anything. Give me my baby, please Mistuh Lange!" Lange removed the child from the trough and casually dumped it into the wailing mother's lap. It wasn't clear whether the baby had survived. The slave woman cradled the wet body in her arms as she followed the overseer into the workshop.

When Luella imagined what went on behind those closed doors, she shuddered. She knew some slave women actually killed their own children so they couldn't be used in this kind of extortion. The added benefit was that these children wouldn't grow up in slavery. But Luella knew she could never do that. She believed her two children belonged in God's hands, with His plan for their lives, not hers.

Mae was two years old and Daniel was three. These precious little ones did not yet know they were valued as property rather than human souls. They smiled, laughed and hugged their mama, who dreaded the day this particular understanding would dim the light that danced in their eyes. Would they ever long for the father they never knew? It didn't matter now. They were too young to comprehend, and besides, so many black children grew up with no daddy. Her own children had plenty of company in that regard.

She and Sam had been teenage lovers when, at fifteen, she turned up pregnant with Daniel. Then Mae was born five months after Sam was sold to a new master in North Carolina. In many ways, her children transformed her because through them, she discovered the power of love. But time with her little ones was always short since, after they were born, she was considered part of the adult workforce again. Picking cotton since she was twelve years old was hard, but not as hard as watching the terrible beatings the overseer meted out to discipline the workers.

She always knew she would join their ranks when she was considered old enough for such harsh punishment—and one day, it happened. After years of work in the fields, Mr. Lange had whipped her for not saying "Yes, Sir" when he told her to hurry up. He used words she didn't know—like "insolent" and "obstinate," as well as words she did understand: "lazy," "nigger," "whore." He had not yet demanded sex with her, but she was sure it would happen. To Luella, having sex with Mr. Lange would be worse than enduring a beating because of the damage it would do to her soul. She decided she would resist, and hoped her children would be safe with her sister, Bess. In resisting, she would probably die. But there was another possibility, and that thought strengthened her resolve. So she was not surprised when the advance came, but she was afraid.

"You, girl. Your break time is with me today. I know you've been missing your man so I'm going to stand in for him," Lange leered.

Luella was sitting with the other slaves under the canopy of a big oak tree, trying to eat something and get relief from the sun. She sat motionless, unresponsive.

"Girl, get up off your ass! I said you were going with me."

Slowly, Luella stood.

"Now! Get moving!"

"No, Sir."

"You sorry nigger. You're going to give me a pot of pleasure willingly or not. But if you put up a fight, I'm gonna beat your ugly face so's even your chillin' don't know you. Understand?"

Luella stood tall, glaring at the devil before her, hate coursing through her veins.

"Looks like you want a beating, girl." Mr. Lange stroked the whip he always carried and closed in on Luella.

No one moved. This kind of thing had happened before, and if you moved to help you were included in the punishment. Lange repeatedly struck Luella until her clothes were in shreds. She whimpered, but did not cry out. He walked up close to her body and with one quick motion, ripped off what was left of her blouse. He pressed the tip of his finger to her lips and asked her if she was ready to feel something else. Luella knew what she was about to do might cost her life, but she might lose it anyway. She bit down hard on Lange's finger. She heard the crunch of bones as his blood filled her mouth and a fist landed squarely between her eyes. Luella hit the ground with a thud while Lange screamed obscenities, kicking her in the side with a booted foot. She didn't move or make a sound, losing consciousness briefly.

"You tell this nigger bitch that when she comes to, there'll be more of this. Now somebody get me a bandage quick, or I'll kick me some more black asses today."

A couple of the slaves picked Luella up off the ground and took her into the sleeping cabin. Inside, she opened her eyes and whispered to her friends. "You juz' keep tellin' Lange I'm out cold. When night comes, I'm running away to the woods. Bess gonna love my chillin' fo' me, and maybe one day I'll see 'em again 'dis side of heaven."

The other slaves knew getting to heaven would be easier than seeing her children. The overseer would send out bloodhounds in the morning if she didn't die from the beating she just took. And even if the dogs didn't get to her, food would be hard to find, and the winter harsh without warm clothes or a roof over her head.

Luella was clear about what mattered and what didn't. "Better to die out there with them dogs chewing on me than with that devil Lange."

This is what Luella had planned: to head for the woods if she got any kind of chance. And now was her chance. Other slaves had run for the dense cover of the Georgia woods, and most were brought back within a day because of the expertise of the hounds. Some lasted longer with cleverness, luck, and the help of other slaves who occasionally brought supplies. But overseers were clever too. They watched patiently and followed those who tried to sneak supplies into the woods. The runaways were almost always caught, punished, or killed—and those who had helped them often met the same fate. Rare runaways became legends because they were never caught—most likely because they died from hunger or cold. But working slaves preferred to believe these brave souls had made their way north and were now free.

Luella had been gone two years, considered dead by many. She was both lucky and clever, but she was often hungry. In this time, two important events had occurred—things that went beyond the realm of mere good luck. She figured God had a hand in both. The first happened during those early weeks, when she could still hear the hounds howling for her blood. She had done her best to erase her scent by crossing as many creeks as possible, but the dogs kept her relentlessly on the run. Finally, all seemed lost. The dogs were closing in fast, and she was cornered on a cliff with nowhere to go. But something had made her look down. She spied a small ledge about six feet below, and summoning all of her courage, jumped. She heard a faint echoing noise as she landed on the narrow patch of dirt, a hollow sound just behind her. She turned around, assuming she would see a wall of rock; but instead, hidden under the cliff's edge, was a cave. Stooping to get inside, she edged her way along until she was completely hidden. The dogs and men converged on top of the cliff just overhead. The animals were wild with barking and grunting, but the men could only see a sheer drop from cliff to river. "The dogs must be picking up the spot where she jumped to her death in desperation," a voice said. "All right, fellas, nobody's going to survive a fall like that—and even if she's down there somewhere, she'd be useless. Let her die."

Luella listened as they left—the dogs still yelping wildly over the scent. Luella had found her home, and for that, profusely thanked God. She was used to being cold since there were never enough blankets in the slave cabins, but she truly didn't know if she could survive a whole winter without warmer clothes.

About the time of the first frost, the good Lord had provided again. Out in the thick forest collecting edible roots, she had spotted a wool coat on the ground. It was gray with blue trim, and on further observation, she realized that it cloaked a body. She was frightened to see another person, especially someone not moving so she watched quietly from a distance. She stayed for hours just observing, but the body never moved. *He might be sleeping or sick or injured*, she told herself. But long into the darkness, a bobcat began tugging at the flesh on the still arms, and at the first light of morning, buzzards confidently perched on the man's head. He was undeniably dead. Luella picked up a branch from the dirt and began swinging it at the birds until they abandoned their picking and perched in a nearby tree making their own observations. The whole lot of them watched as Luella pulled off the man's coat and shirt. Thinking she should leave him wearing something, she left his pants alone, but took his shoes and his cap. Then about to hurry off with her new winter clothes, she decided those pants might deserve a second look—in the pockets. *God is so good to me,* she thought as her hands closed on a flint and a sheathed knife in the dead man's pocket. She would survive this winter and the next.

Luella improved her hunting skills, trapping small animals with snares. And she was good at digging and covering holes as though nothing had been disturbed. When wild pigs, and sometimes turkeys, wandered into her traps, she now had a knife to butcher the meat and flint to build a cooking fire. Though she was grateful for the means to survive, it was a meager and incredibly difficult existence. She constantly searched for food and continually waited. She didn't know what she was waiting for, except that God had helped her stay alive so far, and she wanted to see what He had in store for her. Through her determination and patience, Luella had become a legend.

As fall turned to winter, bringing new challenges to Luella, another slave woman wondered what God had in store for her as well. Frances was pregnant. Dr. Ware was the father, but she didn't know if she should tell him. What purpose would it serve? Plenty of black women gave birth to mulatto babies. They were merely absorbed into the property of the plantation owner, even if he was the one creating this variation in his family. This situation was so common it hardly raised any eyebrows. For the most part, people accepted that this was just what white men did and black women had to endure.

Frances imagined that her parents, Melva and George, would welcome this baby into the household of plantation help. The Bulls were generous people, and would give her time to tend the newborn. Primarily her situation was different from most only because she didn't despise the man who had impregnated her. In fact, she felt affection for Dr. Ware because of the devotion he showed to his patients day after long, difficult day. Frances knew he was a good man, but she had no idea if he would admit or deny his fatherhood, welcome or reject this baby. Perhaps there was some slight chance he would acknowledge the child, but what would that mean? She didn't know.

Frances had heard a lot of war talk and much of it made no sense to her—like Judge Bull telling his friends that the war was about states rights, not slavery. Frances couldn't read, but she wasn't stupid. Her own family knew very well that slavery was the underpinning of the South's economy. If slaves were set free, so many things would change, and the confusing possibilities were frightening.

She had no false illusions about a future with Dr. Ware. There simply was no future other than what already existed. And there were risks in revealing the truth to anyone. She would undoubtedly cause the doctor great social discomfort if this situation were made public. It was one thing for white women to hear whispered talk of these black/white sexual liaisons—even if it involved their own husbands—but quite another to have it confirmed and talked about openly. At some point, her condition would be obvious and then what would she do? Again, she didn't know.

Frances was confused and tired most of the time these days. Biding her time in silence seemed the best for now—along with prayer. She would have preferred to stay at home to avoid prying eyes while her body was changing, but she couldn't. She had hospital duties and social responsibilities. Her parents would have been far more distressed by a refusal to attend church services than by the sight of her swelling belly. Attending church was not only a time to celebrate God, but a time-off period. Most slaves in LaGrange enjoyed being regular churchgoers, attending services with their master's family.

The Methodist and Presbyterian churches were still in use for the sick and wounded, but the Baptist church was once again available for worship services, and thus was shared by all. Because of the large memberships in the three denominations, it would have been impossible to conduct just one Sunday service. Besides, people in LaGrange took their own religion very seriously, privately feeling that theirs was more righteous than the others. Therefore, with three services to house, the Sunday schedule in the Baptist church was a long and complicated one.

The Bull family along with Melva, George, and Frances waited under the church portico as the Baptist congregation exited after their early service.

"I wonder how many Methodists will turn out today." Judge Bull chatted with his wife.

"It is an odd feeling to attend the Baptist church. I feel like I'll be expected to shout 'Amen' as the spirit moves me," chuckled Mrs. Bull.

"Don't you do it, Mother! You'll embarrass us all," said Addie.

Frances thought her family would probably like to shout out "Amen" or "Hallelujah!" What could be embarrassing about praising the Lord? But she knew attending church with the Bull family required restraint. Not only did the Negroes have to sit separately in the balcony, they had to sit quietly. Frances overheard Delia whispering to Sallie.

"There's that prissy, two-faced parlor decoration, Mary Susan, with her little friends."

Then Addie leaned in, covering the side of her mouth with a gloved hand. "You mean the fluffy-head always asking about The Nancy Harts?"

"The one with the smarmy smile and a giggle," added Sallie, and the three women imitated Mary Susan giggling.

"Morning, Ladies. Are you trilling together about the latest exploits of the Nancy Hart Militia?" Mary Susan managed to combine a smile with a sneer—a dubious talent. The sisters paused for the giggle sure to follow. Mary Susan turned to her circle of friends and…giggled.

Delia started. "God…."

"…Bless you, Mary Susan!" Sallie added quickly.

"Same to you," she called back, waving with false gaiety. The sisters headed into the church, Sallie and Addie on either side of Delia, pushing her along.

Frances could see that Delia was fuming. *These girls don't know nothin' 'bout life and hard times…nothin' 'bout suffering.*

Now a long line of Methodists were streaming into the Baptist church, among them, Dr. Ware. Just a few steps ahead of him, Frances paused with the other slaves waiting their turn to go up the staircase.

"Morning, Frances. Hope you got some sleep after such a hard week at the hospital." Dr. Ware took off his hat, smiling warmly at one of his best nurses.

"Well, I'm still a little tired, but don't worry. I'll be there for surgery come Monday. Nice day, Doctor."

"May I escort you to your seats?" asked Dr. Ware.

Frances was astonished until she realized that Dr. Ware was speaking to the Bull sisters, not her. Things were as they were supposed to be, of course, though for an instant, her heart had fluttered.

"We'd be delighted," answered Delia.

Dr. Ware offered his arm to Sallie, and led the way down the center aisle. Addie and Delia exchanged a quick glance of surprise.

Frances had noted the implications of the subtle flirtation between Dr. Ware and Sallie. Now seeing this, she felt more strongly than ever that the identity of her baby's father should remain unknown. She turned with the other slaves and headed upstairs to the balcony—to her place in the Negro section.

Chapter XX

Ray Lee wrapped his arms around his friend, hoping that Gus, in his confused state, would feel it was his mother comforting him. He had sat beside Gus for many hours in his feverish delirium—exhausted by typhoid fever. For a time, he appeared to have slipped into a coma, and it seemed his chances for coming out of it were little to none. So Ray startled when all of a sudden, Gus spoke in a clear, strong voice.

"Ray, will you tell Delia to keep writing her beautiful verses? Sallie, how needed you are by so many! I can feel your compassion and love at this very moment. Orville, you are a fine boy. Addie, my beautiful baby sister, never let go of the music. I hear it right now. So lovely. Mother and Father, thank you for giving me life. It was a good one except for the war. And, Ray, you have been a good friend. Perhaps we will meet again one day in a better place."

Ray was stunned Gus could speak with such strength and clarity. As he waited, breathlessly, for him to say more, the enduring silence spoke instead. Gus had gone home, but not to LaGrange. Another prisoner would take his place on the transfer list and get to see his loved ones again.

At camp headquarters, the news of Gus' death meant little more than a secretarial chore. His name was crossed off the prisoner exchange document and Jesse Hobbs' name was added. Lee was assigned to lead the detail for this particular exchange that was to take place in two days on a bridge near Richmond. There a Confederate detail would return a prisoner named Oscar Hugh La Grange. There would be some fanfare over this event because the North and the South both wanted to show a measure of benevolence. Officers would wear dress uniforms, some on horseback, others on foot, and the units would proceed to the middle of the bridge, with a bugle signaling the beginning of the exchange. Lastly, a war photographer would take pictures so that newspapers all across the country, and even over the world, could see an act of generosity.

But before this charitable ceremony took place, Raymund Lee had one of his own rituals to undertake. He was angry with God for letting Gus come so close to being reunited with his family, but found he couldn't sustain the anger because the war, and this particular tragedy, had drained his emotional energy. Still, there was one more thing he was determined to do simply because it was the right thing. The terrible toll of typhoid fever involved one more denigration: those it killed were thrown into a big ditch and buried in a mass grave, left unmarked. Ray could not bear the thought of his friend being treated so casually, so callously in death. He would bury the fallen soldier in a place of honor.

So once again, Ray put Gus on a litter and pulled his body along the same trail they had traveled together just a month before. This time, he would be returning to the battlefield. Now the scene was desolate, but no longer so gruesome. Trees had been cut for the making of embattlements—spears of wood tied together and set in the path of the enemy to discourage advancing against strategic positions. The tangle of wood on the otherwise barren field might have looked like gigantic toothpicks if you didn't know their terrible purpose. To Ray, these pickets were a monument to terror. The dying and the dead were gone from this field now, except for Gus. Ray did his best to find the spot where he had first come upon this soldier, and there, he dug a grave. When he had placed the last shovel-full of dirt on top of Gus, he knelt and prayed.

"Dear God. I believe you to be a loving father. I know we, not you, make war. We bring such terrible cruelties upon each other, but you are there to pick up the pieces. You love us no matter who or what we are. Thank you for your miracles. For a brief moment I thought they should last forever, but I realize now they are fleeting, and blessed are those of us who get to see them. People probably witness a lot of miracles, but don't see them for what they are…your wondrous touch in this fragile world. Thank you for Gus' miracle. I know now it wasn't just that he survived his wounds—it was that he brought us closer to you in this dreadful thing called war. Through Gus, we feel the power of your perfect love. I will remember him always."

The officers in charge at Harrison's Landing welcomed the opportunity of the upcoming prisoner exchange. From it, they hoped the camp might attract a bit of positive publicity, since conditions here were all but devoid of human comfort. It would provide the public a glimpse of kindness, however small the gesture. The exchange of captured soldiers would soon end, but for a time, both sides thought the practice was good for boosting public opinion. In reality it was merely a bit of propaganda—a manipulation of the press that might briefly ease the repugnance of war.

In nearby Richmond, the Army of Virginia received the prisoner to be exchanged: one Sgt. Major Oscar Hugh La Grange, transferred from his stay in LaGrange, Georgia. His hands had been bound despite the pain that the rope caused to his still-tender burns. There were limits to compassion in wartime. The sergeant was still a prisoner until the moment he was released to Union forces. This event was to be photographed, with a wood block etching of the image sent to newspapers all over the country. The officer in charge assigned James Tomlinson as artist and photographer, and told the weary, troubled soldier that in return, he would receive a short furlough. Desertion was becoming such a problem that whenever possible, furloughs were granted to help keep morale intact. James' mental and physical state was fragile. Grief, fright, hunger and fatigue had taken a mighty toll. The idea of going home was now bittersweet. He longed to stay there, but knew he could not. He ached to see Delia smile, but guessed he never would because of what happened at Seven Pines. His life was once full of possibilities, now only fettered with duty and heartache.

James arrived at the designated exchange point early in the morning as setting up the camera and necessary equipment took a great deal of time.

At noon, he could see soldiers approaching from both sides. He was ready, though still needed to instruct the participants on posing for the camera. Jesse Hobbs' hands were bound just as the other prisoner's were, but Jesse, unlike Hugh, had a smile on his face. La Grange, appearing neither happy nor sad, repeatedly tapped his foot with impatience.

Ray Lee rode his horse in front of Jesse, leading him to the center of the bridge as Hugh was being escorted to the same spot. James, looking up from his camera was stunned by what he saw.

"Where did you get that horse?" he shouted at the Union cavalryman.

Everyone stopped. What was this outburst? Why was a photographer rudely interrupting this historic moment? Ray Lee was as surprised as the rest of them. "I came across him after Seven Pines," the man shouted back.

"That horse belonged to my friend, Gus Bull, who died at Seven Pines."

"Your friend didn't die there."

Col. Lee then explained what had happened to Gus, and how they had become good friends, if only for a short time.

"I'm sorry he's not here on this bridge with us today," he told James. He was set to be exchanged when typhoid took him."

The implications of this news stung James as if a bullwhip snapped with great fury, had found its target. "He almost got to come home?"

Lee stared at the ground. "Almost doesn't count."

James couldn't imagine yet another tragedy for poor Gus. First, his best friend betrays him, leaving him for dead. Then he is nearly released from the hell of life as a prisoner, only to be plucked from this earth by a fever. James hadn't known it would be possible for his grief over Gus to deepen, but with this news, it plunged him even lower. If emotional pain could kill, this blow would have done the job.

"Soldier, I can see how much you are hurting. I imagine his family is hurting too. There is precious little compassion in this war. The prisoner exchanges were supposed to help fill that void. Since Gus is not returning, please take his horse back home. I get no pleasure knowing this horse was supposed to bring his master home safe."

James did his jobs, both the one assigned by his commanders and the one this sensitive Union cavalryman had given him. When he'd taken the photographs of the prisoner exchange, he then took the reins of Gus' horse, Valiant.

Hundreds of newspapers printed the etching James made from the photograph of the two soldiers, waiting with hands bound, while the paperwork for their freedom was exchanged. Though it was a small moment, it represented something the people of the nation had precious little of these days: hope. The *LaGrange Reporter* included a reference to the recent hospital residency of one Oscar Hugh La Grange. His departure and Jesse Hobbs' return to Georgia were both reasons for the people of LaGrange to take heart.

The processing of the prisoner exchange and then the furloughs took some time to complete. When so many newspapers printed the sketch of Jesse and Hugh on the bridge, Confederate Army officials felt pressure to send Jesse home. Perhaps additional sketches could be done in Atlanta, showing the brave soldier reuniting with his family. No harm in taking advantage of this positive thread and continuing to influence public opinion. Since James was being released for a furlough at the same time, it seemed reasonable that he be charged with escorting Jesse home. Valiant would make the journey too, aboard a freight car, creating a very different kind of reunion for Gus' family.

The clattering of the train on the tracks provided an underscore for a symphony of thoughts. For Jesse Hobbs, it was a rhapsody. For James Tomlinson, a dirge. The trip would take several days, and he knew the mournful moment of reckoning would come at its end. Seeing Jesse safely home was of little comfort when he knew that, once there, he faced a monumental task—one that would shatter a family he dearly loved. In his pocket, he carried a letter from Col. Lee addressed to the Bull family, a letter he had promised to deliver in person. This encounter would be hard, but nothing could be as horrific as leaving his best friend on a bloody battlefield so far away from home. His sadness and guilt engulfed him. He questioned whether his commanding officer was right in ordering him to put Gus down, especially in light of the fact that Gus recovered from his wound. The officer had no way of knowing if Gus' wound was fatal, but it was battlefield practice to leave soldiers with wounds to the head, chest or pelvis. The only thing James knew for sure is that he would have been shot if he failed to obey the order. Oh, how he wished he had made that choice! It could have been over right then and there. He just couldn't bear any more of this endless horror—around him and within him. Still, he had a duty, not just to the Confederate Army, but to his people in LaGrange.

Chapter XXI

A dreadful routine had developed in LaGrange and all over the south: folks greeting each new day with the anxiety that horrifying news would descend upon them. Perhaps news of a dead son? A wounded father? A dying husband? Word didn't always travel fast during the war. The telegraph brought some news very quickly, but the laborious task of tallying the dead and wounded took many weeks, even months, in the aftermath of a battle.

As a columnist for the LaGrange Reporter, Delia made frequent trips to the office. Casualty reports were delivered there and then posted outside the building. She dreaded each new accounting of the dead and wounded, but forced herself to check if Gus or James was listed. Every day she felt relief when her loved ones' names were absent from the list. But not this day. New information came in just as the office was closing. Delia ran her finger down the long list from the Seven Pines' battle. There it was: the name she had hoped never to see: Gus Bull. She held her breath and closed her eyes, hoping to open them and find she was mistaken; but no, his name was there. The notation beside it was odd though. Instead of being listed as dead, wounded, or captured, it said "presumed dead." *What did that mean? Was there still hope?*

At home, Delia went out to the garden to be alone. Pacing back and forth, she cried, wringing her hands when she wasn't using them to wipe away the tears. She would give up her life if she could make this nightmare vanish. If she didn't tell her family, maybe they would never find out, never have to be plunged into pain and have their world dumped upside down. She knew this wasn't rational, but the mighty Delia Bull, whose personal force had altered the course of so many things, now felt weak and powerless. She had just met a mountain she could not move. She could not change what she had seen nor what had happened to Gus.

The burden of telling her family felt crushing—not just emotionally, but physically. Stumbling to a garden bench, she collapsed on it, her knees weak with the blow of such news. She needed a compromise—some kind of bargain with God. Perhaps if she just told her father and no one else, he could make sense of the "presumed death." She clung to the only thought that allowed her to walk into his study: this was all a mistake and her daddy would make it all right.

Judge Bull struggled to control the shaking of his body as Delia told him the news. It was barely perceptible to his daughter; but to him, it felt like an earthquake in his bones. In a way, it *was* just that, and there would be damage. When he finally found his voice, he forced himself to sound strong. "Let's not tell anyone else just yet. I want to telegraph Ben Hill. He will be able to get us some definitive word."

If anyone could verify quickly whether Gus was, in fact, dead or missing, it was the well-connected politician from LaGrange. Mistakes had been known to happen in the difficult job of accounting for casualties. The Judge and Delia would soon have an answer, and they prayed it would come before the townspeople started to call on the family, offering their condolences. After the casualty reports were posted, such visits would surely begin.

The evening was long and agonizing for Delia and Judge Bull. They feared that any peace they managed to hold onto could be instantly shattered. Yet they did their best to pretend everything was normal, hoping to keep the rest of the family from alarm. A restless night followed, and in the morning, they had George drive them to the newspaper office before it opened. Delia rushed up to the editor as he was unlocking the door. "We are in desperate need of a favor, Mister Willingham."

Once inside, she offered her plea. "Sir, I found Gus' name on the casualty lists that arrived yesterday at closing time." Her voice was shaking despite her efforts to control it. "I know the list is to be posted this morning, but could you please delay for just twenty-four hours, Mister Willingham? We need time to send a telegram to Ben Hill, asking him to verify whether Gus is dead, or if there could be some mistake. You see, he was listed as, "presumed dead.""

Judge Bull took up the plea, "We would like to spare our family and friends unnecessary grief if this turns out to be false."

"Well, all the news on these lists is sad, so I don't see the harm in people having another day to hope for happier times."

Expressing gratitude for his help, Delia and her father composed the message. Then Mister Willingham tapped out the Morse code sending the urgent communication to their friend, Benjamin Hill. Afterward, they reluctantly went about their normal activities. The Judge had some banking business in town, and in the afternoon, a meeting with his lawyers. He wanted to sell off a piece of the plantation to ease the increasing financial hardship, though finding anyone with money to spend on investments would not be easy. But on this day, money was the least of his worries. *What had happened to Gus?* The tension of waiting, of not knowing, left Judge Bull wondering if his heart would give out—and Delia worrying that she would faint. In the offices of The LaGrange Reporter, she tried to write something coherent for the newspaper, finally penning a curious piece about the overuse of alcohol among the troops. Evidently it was a problem for armies on both sides, but Delia hadn't given it a thought until now.

That's what she wanted—a drink! Something strong. She had never had this thought in her life, but her anxiety over Gus made her feel like she was jumping out of her skin. It wasn't just that she wanted to relax, exactly. She just wanted to forget. Suddenly Dr. Ware's descent into alcoholic oblivion seemed not only understandable, but appealing. Yet writing the editorial instead seemed to help revive her strength. She sat back and re-read her column.

Spirits Dull Spirits

It is not difficult to argue that the images of war are so horrendous that they ought to be erased from a soldier's memory. Many of our men are turning to alcohol to cope, but heavy drinking among our fighting men is killing their will. Our armies are reporting difficulty in maintaining the military discipline necessary to meet and overcome our enemy.

Senator William Lowndes Yancey of Alabama, addressed our legislators in Milledgeville recently with the dire message that the Confederate cause was "suffering morally due to the disorganization of the army because of liquor."

Let us support a law which Yancey favors, to punish officers for being drunk. Under the proposed "Act to Punish Drunkenness in the Army" Yancey demands those found guilty be "cashiered or suspended from the service of the Confederate State, or be publicly reprimanded, according to the aggravation of the offense."

Self-control and clear-headed thinking make us strong. With that sober strength and resolve, along with the grace of God, we will prevail."

D. Bull

Delia made a few changes and checked the time. Her father would be arriving any minute to walk back to the telegraph office. She still wished for a stiff brandy, but thoughts of her father's disapproving eyes quickly quelled the notion.

When he offered his arm to Delia upon arrival, she held it more tightly than usual as they crossed the street without speaking. Once inside, Judge Bull inquired about a return message.

"Yes, Sir. It came in a short while ago," said the operator.

Delia and Judge Bull stared at the message that could forever change their lives.

"Investigation not clear. Some record Gus held prisoner. Will continue inquiry. Be strong. Pray. Your friend, Ben Hill"

It was strange that such terrible news would bring happiness. Delia and her father hugged each other, rejoicing that perhaps Gus was still alive.

"Delia, my darling, you are not to breathe a word of this to anyone, especially your mother. We have to wait this out and discover the truth. There is still so much uncertainty. Agreed?"

"Agreed, Father."

At home they once again got through dinner, trying hard not to show their angst. Later, the family gathered around the piano to listen to Addie play, and at nine o'clock, the Judge announced he was retiring to his study to look over some Milledgeville business. Mrs. Bull went to bed, as did young Orville and his sisters, Sallie and Addie. Delia lingered in the parlor, then knocked on the door of the study. "Father, are you all right?"

"Come in, Delia."

He was sitting in the big leather chair at his desk, sipping brandy from an elegant snifter. She pulled up a chair and sat beside him. The Judge shifted his worried gaze from the brandy glass to his daughter. They didn't have to speak to transmit the intensity of what they were feeling at the end of this day—one of the longest of their lives. The Judge reached for another snifter from the cabinet beside his desk and poured a generous amount of brandy from the crystal decanter. Then extending the glass to his daughter, he put his index finger to his lips. "Shh."

Delia nodded. Of course, she would never tell. She wrapped her fingers around the snifter, lifted it to her lips, and inhaled deeply. Then, in one great gulp, she swallowed it all. After hugging her father, she walked, heavy-hearted, to the bedroom she shared with her sisters. That one drink wasn't enough to make her drunk, but it pierced her armor of self-control as she lay in bed, unable to sleep. There in the quiet and dark, she turned her body to the wall and began to weep. *Where was Gus at this moment? Was he suffering in some miserable prison camp? Was he in pain from a battle wound? Or was he dead?*

Sallie woke to the sound of the crying and stumbled over to her sister's bed. Slipping in beside her, she put a hand on Delia's cheek. "Why are you crying? What could be so bad?"

In the other bed, Addie stirred too, sensing the drama in the room. She listened as Delia revealed the news. "I'm not supposed to tell you this, but something has happened to Gus. He's either dead or in prison and Father expects to hear which very soon."

Delia continued to weep quietly as Sallie hugged her. Addie crossed the cold room and joined the warmth of her own body with that of her sisters'. The three of them huddled together against the darkest of possibilities: the loss of Gus.

Early in the morning, as another message was coming into the telegraph office, the train from Richmond pulled into the depot, delivering two native sons. One was full of joy—the other, grief. James felt obligated to face the Bull family and deliver the news that weighed like an anvil on his heart. He couldn't let a stranger, or an impersonal list, notify them of Gus' death. He'd decided they should know the whole story even if they hated him for it—and he suspected they would. But nothing could be worse than what he had already experienced, he told himself. So facing this onerous task, he set out for the Bull family home, leading Valiant behind him. It was the only honorable thing to do.

Sunshine streamed through the windows as Martha Bull walked down the hall, pausing to admire her new fall plantings along the path to the front door. A soldier on foot was coming down the walkway. Martha's hands flew up into the air and she hurried to open the door. "Oh, Glory! What a sight you are, my dear James!"

Hugging James, she called out to the Judge. "Come see what blessings have arrived on our doorstep this beautiful morning!"

When she turned to smile again at James, she gaped in horror instead. Just beyond the gate at the hitching post stood Gus' horse, Valiant.

In their bedroom, the Bull sisters were getting ready for another day. With all they had on their minds, there was still a pressing obligation to manage hospital rounds and comfort the sick and wounded. Addie thought she heard a thud downstairs, and the next moment, Melva was clattering up the staircase, yelling for Sallie. "Miss Sallie! Your Momma fell down. Come quick! Oh, this is mighty awful!"

Sallie scrambled down the stairs with one shoe on, and both sisters trailing close behind—buttoning and tucking clothes as they flew into the front room. The ghastly scene and its ungodly meaning registered in seconds. Their father sat in the big wing chair by the fire, holding his head in his hands. Servant George was kneeling over their mother, cradling her gently, urging her to wake up. James Tomlinson stood quietly with his cap in his hands, head bowed, silent and somber.

"Oh, no! It's about Gus." Delia cried out. The impact of her worst fears gripped her body mercilessly. She flew to her father's side. They had feared this confirmation, but had no idea it would come from James. Sallie rummaged through her medical bag and brought smelling salts while Addie took her mother's hands in her own and started to cry. Mrs. Bull began to stir from the ammonia vapor under her nose. "George, Melva," Sally said, looking toward the servants, "Take Mother to her room and put her to bed."

Delia looked over at James. "He's gone isn't he?"

"Yes."

Young Orville came into the room.

"Perhaps he shouldn't hear this," Sallie said.

"I don't think any of us can be shielded from the realities of this terrible war any longer," said James. "I want you all to know what happened to Gus."

James proceeded to tell the story of Gus' brave last day and his own wrenching act, whether it be viewed as cowardly or courageous. "I saw him go down. There was a lot of close fighting, and then an order to fall back. I got to Gus, told him to hang on, and started to lift him up. Before I knew it, my commander was standing over us, ordering me to put him down. Said he'd shoot me if I didn't, and put his gun to my head. Said Gus wasn't going to survive—that he had a neck wound, and had lost too much blood. So I put him down." James' voice broke with emotion. "He never made a sound."

Delia broke the silence. "So that's how he came to be listed on the casualty report as 'presumed dead.'"

Judge Bull reached out and took Delia's hand. "Delia and I were hoping this was a mistake, and that we could spare the rest of you worrying. It could still be a mistake."

"No, Gus is dead," said James. "I was asked to return his horse and bring you a letter from the person who can tell you the whole story. Here it is."

James handed the letter from Raymund Lee to the Judge and he read it aloud.

To the Honorable O.A. Bull and family,

I have struggled so with this task, but know it is what my parents would want from a friend upon my death. I am a friend of your son, Gus Bull. I know it is odd to call myself his friend when I was sent out to be his enemy as part of the Union forces. He was duty-bound to be my enemy and split one nation into two. But what happened to us in war brought us both peace when we thought that impossible. I want you to know about my time with Gus so you will be comforted, if possible, by the incredible impact this courageous man had on those around him.

I thought your son was dead when I first saw him. He was pale and still with no rise and fall of his chest to suggest he was still breathing. Sandbags had been placed under his head like pillows. I am embarrassed to say I was in the process of taking his boots, but had I not been tugging on him, he might not have responded. He returned to consciousness quite abruptly and my small contingent of soldiers took him to the field hospital at Harrison's Landing not far away.

There were more Union wounded than Confederate there, but the misery was just the same. I tended to Gus and many others, but Gus became my friend. We spoke often of our families and our agreement on the terrible cost we were all paying for trying to work out our political differences on battlefields.

Gus also shared his deep faith in God with me. This is often a topic men brush over very quickly rather than delve into, but Gus was moved to share and to motivate others at the camp. As his health improved, he led morning and evening prayers for all those who wished to have a stronger connection with the Lord. The men took great comfort in Gus' words. I knew he was special when he came back from the brink after the Battle of Seven Pines. At camp, my awe and respect for him grew. He was fearless in the face of death. He had no anger towards those of us who were supposed to be his enemies. When he got back some small measure of strength, he spent himself helping his fellow wounded no matter Blue or Gray. He read them stories, sang songs, and held hands that needed human warmth.

When he died from typhoid fever, I was shocked—not that the disease isn't rampant at the camps, but I was so convinced by his survival of a great injury that God had other plans for him. Now I think Gus' mission must have been to spread a little spiritual light among those feeling such darkness. He was a light among us. If that can comfort you, I'm glad to have told you about his last days. His last words were about all of you. I have tried to remember them exactly as he spoke them so that you can be lifted up by his voice. This is what he said:

"Tell Delia to keep writing her beautiful verses. Sallie, how needed you are by so many. I can feel your compassion and love at this very moment. Orville, you are a fine boy. Addie, my beautiful baby sister, never let go of the music. I hear it now. Mother and Father, thank you for giving me life. I had a good one except for the war. And you have been a good friend, Ray. Perhaps we will meet again one day in a better place."

I buried Gus back on the battlefield where I first saw him. He was a brave soldier, a fine man, and an exceptional friend. Whatever happens to the country, I want you to know there is someone in the North who will never forget the strength and courage of Gus Bull.

His horse had lingered near the battlefield instead of running off, as so many do. I think he meant to stay with his master. He should at least be with his master's family, so I return him to you.

May God bless us all and have mercy on our souls.

Yours truly,
Col. Raymund Lee

Judge Bull was not shaking anymore. The letter brought a measure of relief. To be sure, it was not happy relief, but it freed him from the torture of not knowing how his son's life had ended. The truth was difficult: Gus lying alone and dying on a battlefield, surviving his wounds and being imprisoned, set to come home, and then taken by a dreadful scourge. But in the midst of that hideousness, at least there was peace now. It seemed incredible to contemplate feeling peace upon the death of a loved one. Now with the truth known, Judge Bull felt honored to have given Gus life and love. Nothing else seemed the slightest bit important—not the war, nor everyday events and challenges.

Delia turned and fixed her stare on James. She began speaking quietly, but the volume increased with her fury. "I want you out of this house now! I never want to see your face, hear your voice, or remember your miserable soul. The Bull family, however, will *never* forget your betrayal."

Judge Bull was quick to intervene. "Dearest Delia, though it's hard not to lash out at the one who delivers such devastating news, this is not James' fault." He continued, struggling through his tears. "James, I respect you for the integrity it took to come here. I know you are in a great deal of pain over Gus' death."

"Well, *I* have *no* respect for this coward," hissed Delia. "If I can't speak for the family then I speak for myself. You deserve nothing from me, James, but my scorn and you *certainly* have that. How could you just leave him there to die?!"

Judge Bull stood. "Best go now, James."

He heard no wailing as the door closed behind him, only silence. As he neared the end of the walkway, he turned back for a last look. The house seemed to sag from the weight of unspeakable loss inside its walls. Then suddenly, the front door flew open. It was Addie nearly stumbling down the path. "James, wait! You can't leave like this."

"Addie..." The words wouldn't come.

"You don't have to say anything. I am the one who needs to speak." Though choking back tears, she forged ahead. "You loved Gus like a brother, and that's all that matters. We are all broken-hearted, but we don't all hate you. I know you are the same loyal friend we have always held dear. Please consider me a friend as well."

"Thank you, dear Addie, for your kindness in the middle of such sorrow. I'm not sure I deserve it."

The terrible truth had the audacity to come to the Bull household a second time that day. An hour later, a telegram from Ben Hill arrived, confirming Gus' death. In the days that followed, streams of people came to call on the Bull family, certainly everyone in LaGrange, and many more from as far away as Columbus, Macon, Milledgeville and Atlanta. Swags of black crepe hung from the front porch, marking this house as one touched by death. The family members were all devastated—that much they had in common—but each reacted differently to the loss of dearest Gus. Martha took to her bed, physically disabled by grief. She couldn't trust her knees not to buckle under her weight when she tried to walk. Her sorrow was a crushing emotional blow that translated itself directly to the body. Delia's grief brought anger. She hated James specifically, but almost everyone else too, just because they were alive and her brother wasn't. Judge Bull was in shock, mostly numb, as he greeted the callers who came to offer condolences. Sallie's heartache took the form of busyness, which some might have construed as disrespectful. Nothing could have been further from the truth. Feeling on the verge of panic when she opened to the assault of emotions, she found she could stave off her helplessness by working almost non-stop at the hospital. Familiar routines and the ever-present urgency of other people's care, kept her away from herself.

But to Addie, Gus' death and what happened in LaGrange afterward, were simply unfathomable. People simply went on doing what they had always done! How could anyone enjoy a cup of tea ever again? Why did the sun come up in the morning, ushering in a new day of possibilities? Why were people still getting into buggies going to town, doing their errands, making social calls? She wanted to shout at everyone to *stop*. Didn't they know how the world had changed? Gus was no more, and therefore, a part of her was no more. The world was no longer the place she had believed it to be. How could she ever play a lively tune or smile again? How could love hurt so much? Her church-going family always said everything was part of God's plan. But if God's plan was for Gus to die, how could she worship a deity that ordained such cruel wreckage? In a continuous state of anguish, she mostly sat in the parlor staring in disbelief at those who came and went from her house.

No one in the family knew what Orville was going through. He shut himself up in the room he had shared with his big brother—refusing to eat and unwilling to talk. His father thought it might help for him to stay with neighbors for a while, and when the idea was suggested, Orville didn't protest.

The evenings were warm, pleasantly full of the sounds of summer slowly turning to fall: crickets, bullfrogs, and a dog barking in the distance now and then. Shocking how ordinary life could be on the outside when such stunning changes had taken place inside. Every member of the Bull family was different now and forever. Judge Bull, laden with grief, forced himself to make arrangements for a memorial service, but first took a few moments to write a letter.

Dear Ben,

Thank you for your friendship and kind attention to my family.

I dream of those moments when I clung to the hope someone had made a mistake. They were fleeting, but allowed me to imagine my children's smiles and laughter, my wife radiant and alive with joy. In an instant, those images disappeared and were replaced with anguish.

Gus was a remarkable young man. Sadly, there are many thousands of remarkable young men who have also given up their potential for some words that spelled out a cause. I pray God it is a cause worthy enough to have cost so much.

I sit at my desk this evening with sad tasks before me. I must change my will and plan a memorial service. I think the town square would be a good place to hold the service since there will be so many people to accommodate.

I wish I could say I look forward to seeing you and your family, but those sound like happy words. If sadness were fatal, my household of lost souls would surely die. We need your support. In that way, all of us in the Bull family look forward to your presence next Saturday.

Your devoted friend,

O.A. Bull

A day of pouring rain would have matched the gloom felt by the entire town during memorial services for Gus Bull. The Square was jammed with people dressed in black, eyes red-rimmed from crying, faces full of sadness. A dreary cloud of silence hung low over the crowd. Even the children were quiet, sensing the weight of their parents' grief. But in contrast to all that darkness, the sun was out in all its bright summer glory. Only a few appreciated the symbolism. Judge Bull was one, as well as Addie and Sallie. All of them knew how fitting it was that Gus be remembered on a brilliant, sunlit day—a day replete with LaGrange garden fragrances and overflowing love. Delia, however, remained bitter, her heart firmly closed. She still blamed James for what had happened to Gus, and refused to recognize any good coming from this dreadful situation.

The Reverend Caleb Witt Key of the Methodist church delivered a speech to the crowd that none would ever forget. The minister had written a beautiful tribute to a courageous fallen son and friend to all in LaGrange.

Dear People,

We have both lost and found our hope in Gus Bull. We had such high expectations of Judge Bull's oldest son. Many among us thought he would be Governor one day, and there were others who thought he might even lead the Confederacy when the war was over. How can God take such brightness from our midst? Is it not cruel and unfair?

Remember that it is not God who declared war. But it is God who stands beside us in all times, both those that result from man's good judgments and bad judgments. Whether we are happy or sad, at peace, or in pain, God is always ready with a comforting hand on our shoulder. Look for that hand today. God knows how sad we are that Gus has been taken from us. God also knows what a legacy of love and courage he left behind. Gus, by his example in battle and in enemy hands, shows us what faith is all about.

He never lost his trust in God. He helped those around him who were overcome with pain and fear to find their own spiritual peace. Perhaps that is the greatest form of leadership Gus, or any man, can achieve. So, while we mourn that his time was too short, God exalts the time he spent, for his last work was the greatest of all his achievements. "Love thy neighbor as thyself"— this is what God commands us to do. In his last days, Gus' neighbors were called enemies, but he called them friends. Gus did not fall short of our expectations; he exceeded them and brings us new hope for the future. Thank you, God. Amen.

The Bulls had chosen not to share the complete story of Gus' survival from battlefield wounds—only to die weeks later from disease. The family even kept the details from Martha, as Judge Bull thought his wife would suffer even more—and unnecessarily so—with the whole truth. He feared she might not even survive if she knew how close Gus had come to making it home. Needing someone to talk to, the three sisters confided in the family's close friend, Mrs. Robert Ridley. Mary Elizabeth bore her husband

Dr. "RAT" Ridley seven children, four sons and three daughters. The oldest son, Charles, had been close to Gus. Delia, Sallie and Addie thought of Mrs. Ridley as a second mother, and since they couldn't tell their own mother the truth of Gus' demise, they poured out their hearts to the compassionate surrogate of Mary Elizabeth. When she came calling after the memorial service, she sat down with Addie's memory album for quite some time, penning a verse dedicated to the honorable G.A. Bull.

> *A prisoner, wounded and alone,*
> *Thy proud spirit chafing at thy bonds,*
> *Pining for liberty.*
> *We thought of thee suffering alone,*
> *Thy bright eye dim, thy strength all gone,*
> *Muttering in fevered dreams,*
> *Of far off spurting streams*
> *In boyhood known;*
> *Calling a household word,*
> *Whispering a name endeared;*
> *And in delirium striving to trace*
> *A look familiar in a stranger's face.*
> *But thou wert freer then than we,*
> *Who sat in dust and wept for thee.*

Chapter XXII

Sallie knew more death would come. Through the winter, there would be relative calm at the hospitals, but that would change as soon as the weather made it easier to engage in massive campaigns. So no wonder that in April of 1863, signs of spring—usually so welcome—brought renewed anxiety instead.

The hospital staff was gearing up, readying beds and supplies for a new season of the wounded. Everyone was busy, but not bone-tired the way they would be in a few months when the never-ending stream of maimed soldiers started to arrive. But Sallie could see that Frances was already having a difficult time. Months ago Sallie began to suspect Frances was pregnant because her belly filled out her dress as never before. Now the bulge was so large, Frances' condition was obvious to everyone.

"Frances, you look pale. You must be pretty far along with this baby because you are waddling. And look at those ankles! They are so swollen. I'm worried about you."

"I'm about eight months along. I surely am tired and my back aches somethin' terrible."

It would have been an ordinary pregnancy if Frances lived in the world of gentrified white women. They suffered from fatigue, swollen ankles, and backache too, but they didn't have to work. Frances, however, was expected to stay on her feet for as long as the work demanded.

Sallie did the same, but doing this work was her choice, and she wasn't pregnant. Though surprised and a little curious about Frances' pregnancy, she felt it wouldn't be polite to ask too many questions. Generally people didn't raise an eyebrow over the out-of-wedlock pregnancies of slave women, and slave men weren't socially or culturally compelled to stand by a woman or protect children. Neither were they permitted to legally marry as slaves belonged to their white masters, and therefore, children were part of a property management structure. Sallie had heard the whispers about slave women being sexually used by masters and overseers. She wondered if slaves wanted monogamous relationships. But even if they did, it would be near impossible with the difficult circumstances imposed on them—being sold and separated time and time again. Perhaps Negro mothers weren't always sure who fathered their children, and it looked to her like Negro babies were born and cared for in a communal kind of way.

Frances had not volunteered any information about the father of her unborn child, and Sallie knew it wasn't any of her business. Once she had overheard Melva and George asking Frances who the daddy was, but Frances said she didn't want to talk about it. Childbirth carried considerable risk for women under the best of circumstances, but Frances was burdened with an extra measure of stress from the demands of her work. The added tension of continual life and death situations had worn Frances down unmercifully since last summer.

Melva had tried to prepare her daughter for childbirth, telling her what to expect throughout the stages of labor and birth. Frances was still so young, just twenty, and living with her parents in a cabin on the plantation grounds. Since her parents were house servants, her station in life was somewhat better than that of field hands, who aged early from a life of picking cotton. Since she acted as midwife for most births on the plantation, Melva expected to attend the birth of her grandchild. She had seen plenty of complicated births, and had intervened to save mother, baby or both. But sometimes, nothing could be done. She had come to accept that women had more misery in life because of the birthing of babies, but believed they also had more joy from loving the souls they'd brought forth. Frances didn't look good though. Nearing the birthing time, her daughter's face was puffy, and her ankles had been swollen for a long while. This worried Melva, but she told herself that was from standing on her feet all those long hours at the hospital. Now her hands had begun to swell too, and Dr. Ware had told her to go home and rest.

"Mama, I'm feeling poorly," Frances told her mother. "My head hurts, and I can't keep any food down. Is this what happens when the baby comes?"

"Darlin', that baby gon' come soon, but you jez need to stay in bed with those feet up." Melva knew her daughter's symptoms were not part of a normal pregnancy, but she didn't want to worry her. Nothing much to do but get her to rest—and pray. That night Melva woke to the sound of her daughter vomiting. She quickly found Frances' hand which was clammy and cool to the touch. She felt for a pulse. It was fast but not very strong.

"Oh Lordy, we got trouble," she muttered to herself.

Frightened by what she saw, Melva shook her husband George awake.

"Get to the big house quick and call for Miss Sallie. I'm gon' need help. Frances is in real bad shape."

When Sallie threw open the cabin door, she could see Frances stretched out on the rope bed in the corner. Her large belly and swollen extremities had swallowed up the Frances she knew, making her look grotesque. Suddenly her entire body stiffened and began to shake violently. Melva bent over Frances, turning her daughter's head to the side and opening her mouth to keep her tongue from blocking the breathing passage. "She's having a seizure, Sallie."

Melva forced some softness into her voice so her husband might think the situation was under her control. "George, you leave us women to this. Go on now."

George's eyes flashed with fear as he quietly closed the cabin door on his way out. If anybody could make things right it was Melva. *God help them*, he prayed.

Sallie sat down on the floor next to Melva. "I've never seen anything like this. What can I do?"

"Frances is in God's hands now, Miss Sallie. We wait and see. If He gon' call her on home, you and I might need to take this baby. Go to the kitchen and boil some water. Put a couple of sharp knives in it along with some big spoons, wooden ones. We could use some linens too if you can spare em."

"How much time do we have?"

"Don't know. Best be quick as you can."

George joined Sallie in the cooking kitchen between the cabin and the big house He stirred the cook fire while she put some water on to boil and then went to gather up some linens. Sallie thought a ball of twine might be needed, and perhaps a needle and thread. When the water was roiling, she put in two paring knives and two wooden spoons along with the needle and spool of thread. At the sight of the knives, George's eyes grew large with fear.

"Try not to worry, George. You know Melva knows what she's doing."

"Yessum, I do. I reckon you're a blessing as well."

"Thank you, George. Praying might help too."

Sallie made her way back down the dark path toward the cabin. The night air was cool with a faint lingering of spring's budding fragrances. She prayed that this night would yield new life, but death seemed to be hovering near.

Inside the cabin, Melva had changed from her night clothes into a work dress. The one-room dwelling was bathed in the glow of candles, and Melva had cleared the small dining table. She directed Sallie to set the pot of water on top.

"Been my experience, babies do better if everything's clean and ain't nothing better than some real hot water."

"How's our girl?" Sallie asked.

"She bad. Those shakes have quit, but feel like she ain't with us by much."

Sallie moved to the bed. Frances' breathing was shallow, and her pulse felt weak. She wasn't moving or making any sounds. Neither did she respond to pain when Sallie pressed a needle into the back of her hand. "She's unconscious, Melva. Have you ever seen someone recover from something like this?"

"No," Melva said quietly. "I reckon it's time to make a decision. Do we want to try and save this baby or jes let 'em both go?"

They both knew it wasn't much of a question. They would take the baby now, praying that the little one had some life left. Melva had done this procedure before, but always when the mother had already died. She didn't think her daughter had much of a chance, but told Sallie, "Let's keep the trauma to a minimum in case God wants Frances to have one last chance." The two made a quick agreement. Melva would use the knives to cut through skin, then the uterine muscle. Sallie would use the spoons to hold the incision open. Then Melva would reach in and pull the baby out, giving all her attention to the newborn while Sallie looked after Frances.

Melva kissed her daughter. "We gonna bring you your little one now, darlin."

Frances neither flinched nor moaned as the first incision was made. Melva then made a careful, shallow cut in the uterus so as not to injure the baby, and directed Sallie to insert the wooden spoons and pull back the tissue. Clear fluid gushed from the opening, but when it slowed to a trickle, the two women could clearly see hair on the top of the head. Now Melva gently reached a hand in and under the tiny head. She felt for a chin, found it, and lifted. Easing the head through the surgical incision, she gave another gentle pull, and the entire body slid out.

"It's a boy. Now lez see if we can git him breathing." Melva placed the infant face down on a towel over her knees. She let his little head hang down while she rubbed his back. Fluid drained from the baby's mouth and nose, but still no breathing. She picked him up by his feet, hoping to encourage more drainage. Still nothing. In a last attempt, she put him back on her lap and slapped the soles on his tiny feet. Suddenly, a gurgling, a gasp, and a wail!

Sallie realized she had been holding her breath, which now came out all at once. "Praise God! Melva, take him to the kitchen. George has it all warmed up from the cook fire."

The baby's crying had begun to ease, so Melva carried him over to his mother's side. Gently, she placed Frances' hand on the infant's head. "Be proud, Mama. He's a fine baby," Melva whispered to her daughter. Then she wrapped him tightly in linens and a blanket, leaving Sallie to work over Frances.

"Thank you, Miss Sallie," Melva said as she turned to leave.

Both women's tears glistened in the candlelight.

Sallie had stitched up hundreds of wounds in her work at the hospital and knew that infection was a constant enemy. But as she threaded a needle, she wished infection were the biggest worry in this case. She was fairly certain Frances' greatest risk came from whatever had stricken her in the last days of her pregnancy. After closing the incisions, she sat down next to her patient, holding Frances' hand. Then shutting her own weary eyes, silently asked, *Dear God, we have one miracle tonight, may we have one more?*

In the kitchen, Melva carefully unwrapped the infant and cleaned him up. George sat nearby wishing he could be useful, but realizing the women were doing all that could be done. He had never felt such an odd mixture of relief and anxiety. He didn't want to ask about Frances just yet for fear of what the answer might be, so he sat quietly by, watching as his wife dried the baby's hair. When Melva finished toweling his head, they both let out a little gasp of surprise. His hair was not black and curly. This little bronze-colored baby had a head of wispy, straight, honey-colored hair.

Just then Sallie opened the kitchen door. She felt as though she were dragging a thousand-pound bale of cotton behind her, forcing one foot in front of the other. When you thought life couldn't get any harder, sometimes it did just that. She stopped when she reached George, but she couldn't look at him. Or at Melva either. Her gaze was drawn to a baby who didn't look at all like Frances.

"I reckon we know who the Daddy is now. There's only one white man she been around on account of working so much," Melva said.

Sallie sagged against the wall for support. *Did they think Dr. Ware was the father? Was that possible?* She'd been paralyzed with deep grief, and now abject fear. She had to speak, but *could* she? First gulping, then sputtering, she forced the two dreaded words out of her mouth. "She's gone."

Melva and George stared wordlessly at Sallie, the weight of her pronouncement crushing their spirits. Melva's tears spilled onto the baby's swaddled body.

By the end of the day, everyone in the Bull household was crying. Effie, the Bull's cook, was devastated as were her children, who had always considered Frances a sister. Martha and Judge Bull had great affection for the young woman who had cared for their daughters with such devotion. And as for Delia, Sallie and Addie, they had grown up with Frances helping them with everything from gathering up clothes to be laundered to braiding hair, and in more recent years, lacing up corsets. In fact, when they were young children, Frances had played "house" with them, dressing up in their mother's old dresses and shoes, and serving tea in little cups with matching saucers. Sometimes she had persuaded Effie to make tiny scones for the sweet little rose-patterned china plates that had been imported from Europe for children's play. So much giggling! That had always been their strongest memory of Frances: the connection with laughter and joy.

Sallie had another sad mission on this heartbreaking day. As Dr. Ware was making his evening rounds at the Presbyterian Church, she showed up much to his surprise.

"Sallie, you're not scheduled for hospital duty tonight. Did you forget?"

"No, Dr. Ware. I'm here because I have some sad news and need a private moment with you.

"It's hard to find a private place these days. Perhaps we could just sit up near the altar.

As Sallie recounted the story of Frances's death in childbirth, Dr. Ware put his head in his hands. He waited until she had finished to respond. "I'm so terribly sorry. Frances brought the world some remarkable gifts. We are all blessed to have known her. Did the baby survive?"

"We came close to losing him as well, but, yes, he is alive."

"I'm sure his survival had everything to do with the skills of two amazing women, you and Melva."

"Thank you, but there is something else. This baby has straight, honey-colored hair, not at all unlike your own."

Dr. Ware stared at the floor. "I believe I am the father," he said quietly.

Sallie felt rage seep into her pores.

A tear began to wend its way down Dr. Ware's face. "I'm so sorry, Sallie. Frances' death is so hard for all of us."

Her cheeks flushed with anger, Sallie rushed down the church aisle, shoulders heaving, with one hand over her mouth to stifle the sobs.

Two days later, in the early morning, the Bull family led a procession to Hill View Cemetery on the north side of town. Martha and Judge Bull rode with their children and Thomas followed in the wagon—carrying Frances' body in a simple wood coffin. Melva and George were next, with the other Negroes of the household trailing after them. Effie stayed behind to care for the baby, but all of her children joined the heavy-hearted trek to the gravesite. The prominent white families of LaGrange all had plots at Hill View Cemetery. The headstones were large, ornate pieces of marble decorated with carved stone garlands and engraved with poignant verse. Martha Bull's little baby girl, Martha, was here. She had been the first of the Bulls to occupy this reserved space. Frances' coffin passed by her grave where the headstone read: *"Little Martha, so precious, so loved, so young. Too soon to say goodbye."*

The group continued on to a section of the cemetery set aside by some families for their Negro servants. The Rev. Patrick Arminius Wright offered the funeral service by the grave. He knew Frances and her family from church, sitting quietly in the gallery with the other Negroes.

But the Negro spiritual tradition was only quiet and restrained in the white folks' churches. On their own, the Negroes let their emotions loose. Here in this place Melva and the others brought their faith, unshaken, to this solemn moment as they sent a loved one on to glory. Dr. Ware joined the group and stood next to Judge and Martha Bull. The servants glanced in his direction, but the only one to nod in acknowledgment was George. Rev. Wright began with a prayer.

"O, eternal Lord God, who holds all souls in life, we beseech Thee to give to Thy whole Church, in paradise and on earth, Thy light and Thy peace; and grant that we, following the good examples of those who have served Thee here and are now at rest, may at the last, enter with them into Thy unending joy. Through Jesus Christ our Lord, who liveth and reigneth with Thee, in the unity of the Holy Spirit, one God, now and forever. Amen."

Shouts of "Hallelujah!" "Praise God!" and "Thank you, Jesus!" rippled throughout the Negro assembly—quietly, fervently, earnestly. Mutterings as offerings.

Delia was stricken. She hadn't realized her grief would feel like a tunnel with no exit. She closed her eyes and traveled back to a memory that was once filled with laughter.

She was giggling all the way home on her pony, then fighting for self-control as she entered the stable and turned Molly over to one of the servants. She headed to the main house, her underclothes covered with dirt. Not daring to draw any attention to herself, she slipped back into the house and tiptoed into her bedroom. The fun would be over if any of the adults found out she had ridden a horse like a boy—and in her pantaloons yet! She stole into her room as quietly as she could, with one hand on the doorknob, and the other over her mouth, stifling a new fit of giggles. She would have to get rid of the dirt-covered pantaloons as no explanation would be acceptable. Thankfully, the room she shared with her sisters was empty. She didn't know where her sisters were at the moment, but hoped they were out for the afternoon with her mother, perhaps calling on friends. As Delia peeled off her underclothes, the creaking of the door caught her ear.

"Don't come in! I'm dressing."

"Is jez me, missy. Suppose' to hep ya change after your ride." It was Frances, the daughter of the main servants and housemaid to Delia and the other children. Delia thought Frances had been a wonderful replacement to Luella who seemed so often irritated with the children and her duties. Delia never saw anything but kindness from Frances. She attentively laid out their clothes, helped them dress, fixed their hair, picked up their toys and tidied their rooms. Delia never tired of the stories Frances told them when they were restless or the songs she sang just for some fun. She loved the calming effect of a hug from Frances when she was sad or angry about something, and appreciated that Frances tried to head off trouble when she saw the children beginning to stir things up. Delia and the others could count on Frances to come to their rescue when mischief went too far.

"Lordy! What done happened to ya underthings?"

"You've got to promise you won't tell, Frances."

"Yessum."

"We had a horse race and I rode like a boy with my dress tucked into my underclothes. I know I was a little naughty. Oh, Frances, it was the most fun I've ever had! That is until I fell off and landed in the dirt!"

Frances stood there for a while, not moving, until a smile slowly formed on her face. The corners of Delia's mouth began to turn upward too. Both girls peered into one another's eyes as the smiles continued to widen. Then mouths opened, teeth showed, and bodies began to shake. The giggling was quiet at first, then so raucous the girls fell to the floor clutching at each other. Irrepressible snorting and gasping, shaking and sputtering ensued. It wasn't even about the pantaloons anymore. This was the pure pleasure of a mighty giggling fit—because if there was something young girls did better than anyone else, it was giggling. Despite their efforts to stop, all it took was one look at each other, and it started all over again. When they were finally spent, Delia had the hiccups.

"Can you... hic...help me...hic...with the clothes?"

"Gimme da' dress and da' underthings. I'll take 'em to Momma's house and wash dem mysef so's nobody sees what you been up ta'."

"You are my best friend, Frances."

"Yessum, less I tell on you…which I *won't*."

Delia took off the dress and handed it, along with the dirty pantaloons, to her trusted house servant and pal.

Frances turned to leave the room. "Did ya win?"

"No, but it didn't matter."

The giggling threatened to start all over again, but Frances bit her lip, bundled up the clothes, headed out of the room, and through the dining room toward the back door. Delia watched through her window, hoping Francis could sneak into the servants' cabin without being seen. But Delia's mother was on her way down the path from the opposite direction, carrying an armload of flowers from the garden.

"Whatever are you doing Frances, dear? Aren't those Delia's clothes?"

"Uh, yessum, but Delia done gave em ta' me on account dey' don't fit no more."

"Well, I don't know about that. Let me have a look."

Frances extended the dress, but let the pantaloons trail on the path. Appearing to stumble on the white fabric, she became so tangled in it that she fell to the ground rolling in the dirt.

Through the open window Delia heard her mother shout, "Oh, my goodness, girl. Are you all right?"

Frances stood up, breathing hard. She held out the underthings. "Yessum. I just tripped."

"Well, those pantaloons are ruined now. You just throw them away. And, Frances, the next time Delia gives you her old dresses, please check with me first to see if they are truly ready to pass on to you."

"Yessum."

And with that, Frances had clearly proven that she could be counted on to keep a confidence within the family.

A little giggle escaped from Delia's lips. Then as she opened her eyes, returning to the funeral, she felt a sob emerging as well. Forcing it into her throat, the lump of grief burned there even as her tears refused to obey her orders. Delia cried softly, not just for Frances, but for Gus, and for so many losses: of innocence, optimism, hope, happiness. The devil was keeping the list and it just kept getting longer.

When it was time for the eulogy, Delia was glad Sallie was speaking. She, herself, had no words of comfort in her. Sallie spoke with great tenderness about the many special talents of her lifelong friend: how she had given so much, including great joy to three little girls…what a distinguished student she had been of her mother's gifts in natural medicine…and what a tireless nurse and surgical assistant in this bitter war. And, finally, such a brave mother, who gave up her life for a new soul to enter this world.

Afterward, Addie led the mourners in reading Frances' favorite verse: the Twenty-third Psalm.

"The Lord is my shepherd.

I shall not want.

He maketh me to lie down in green pastures.

He leadeth me beside the still waters

He restoreth my soul…."

Effie's children followed the reading with a gospel choir rendition of *The Lord Is My Shepherd*. Their exquisite voices blended with their passion for the Lord, and with their love for Frances. There was not a dry eye among those gathered to see this sweet soul home. Melva walked to her daughter's coffin and knelt. With her eyes lifted up to the heavens she began a song and the children joined in.

"Lord, I want Jesus to walk with me.

In my sorrow, Lord, walk with me

In my sorrows, Lord, walk with me

When my heart is aching

Lord, I want Jesus to walk with me…"

Some of the servants were on the ground now, sobbing, and pounding their fists. Others raised their hands to the sky, swaying, almost swooning. Raw grief mixed with the raw joy of devotion to their God—almost physically painful to watch. The Bull family held hands and hugged one another. Dr. Ware walked over to George and embraced the sad old man.

"George, not so long ago you saw me in the deepest anguish of my pitiful life. Now I see you in this moment of unfathomable pain. I am so sorry for your loss. I believe I am the father of Frances' baby. She was a good woman. I will miss her."

Dr. Ware paused but there was no response from George.

"I have spoken with Judge Bull about the child. The boy will be free according to our agreement, but I cannot raise him. I have medical duties that give me scant time even for sleep. I know you and Melva will be better parents in any case. I will see that this child has what he needs."

The doctor extended his hand, but George did not shake it. The black man's face was heavy with grief, his cheeks wet with tears. He met Dr. Ware's eyes with a hard gaze, then tilted his gray-haired head slightly, slowly dropped his chin, and closed his eyes.

Dr Ware could feel the old man's bitterness. "I understand," he said. As he turned and walked to his buggy, deeply stricken in his heart, he wondered, *Could there be any more sadness in this time and place within the universe?*

Chapter XXIII

The Bettencourt brothers were known as "the two S.O.B's" in their community of Wedowee, Alabama and around Randolph County. The older one, Simon Oren, was a world-class bully who mercilessly tormented his little brother, Seth Otto. They were both ugly and mean, but because the younger S.O.B was afraid of the older S.O.B, he just went along with whatever Simon wanted as a means of survival. As teenagers they liked to stir up trouble.

"Les us go on over to that darky Leroy's chicken house and grab us some eggs, maybe kill us some chickens, Seth. What you say brother?"

"Aw, Simon, Leroy catches us half the time and he's gone kick our asses—likely mine cause you run faster."

"Hey, stupid, I'm gonna kick your butt if you don't start moving. I've got a taste for some fried chicken tonight." Simon picked up a stick from the ground and started poking Seth in the ribs.

Seth knew if he didn't go along, Simon would beat him worse than Leroy. "What you have a taste for, Simon, is trouble, pure and simple. I'm going! I'm going! Don't poke me no more."

The two had grown up in poverty and without anybody to care for them. They must have had parents at some point because they had a last name, but neither brother remembered anything about them. Living in a shanty on the drearier side of Wedowee, they mostly stole things and pushed people around to make their way in life. As the boys grew into adults they found work occasionally in the local tannery, but when war broke out, they joined the Confederate Armed Forces just for the hell of it...literally. They didn't sign up on a whim, but rather because Simon thirsted for legalized mayhem. He couldn't wait to mix it up on a meaner, grander scale. Even in peacetime he was always looking for some action. In fact, he and his brother liked to travel from Wedowee a few miles south to Roanoke, where "fight nights" were held on a regular basis.

"Come on brother Seth," Simon would say, "Roanoke is were the action is. I'm gonna get in some licks tonight. They gonna declare me champion."

"And that'll win us a couple of beers, which you'll drink it all as usual, then jump back in the ring swinging at anything that moves. Don't you get tired of fightin all the time?"

"Naw, gets my blood pumping! Fight night's real livin'. Come on Seth, let's git on down there."

"Can't say as I want to, but I will jus to enjoy somebody other than me gittin' beat on." Seth pulled on his shoes with a sigh.

"Hey, les see if we can kind of borrow somebody's horse on the other side of town so's we don't have to walk all the way," said Simon

"Aw, shit, Simon. You're gonna git us in trouble before we have a chance to find trouble." Seth shook his head and followed his brother down the dirt road on their way out of town.

Bullies showed up from all over the county on Saturday nights. In a roped-off area, two men at a time went at each other, fighting until one of them hollered "Enough!" Most of the men required some whiskey to lubricate the fighting spirit, but not Simon. And since he was sober, his reflexes were usually superior to those of his opponents. Therefore Simon was something of a legend for his Roanoke "fight night" victories.

When it came to signing on for war, Seth resisted as usual. "I don't want to leave Wedowee and join the Army, Simon!" In response, his brother beat him senseless—that is, if he had any sense in him to begin with. "There's more where that came from!" Simon threatened him. The next day, they joined the Army.

Unsurprisingly, the pair won no popularity contests in the service, creating such trouble that they were often shipped out to other units. Now, Braxton Bragg's Army of the Mississippi had to deal with the two S.O.B.'s. They were good at skirmishing, but unfortunately, the fighting was usually against men in their own unit. Simon was having the time of his life until they left for Bardstown. They marched day in and day out, and for two of those days, they had little food. But Bragg forced them all to keep marching.

Simon's mood was flagging with each passing hour. He told Seth, "I'm so dang bored, tired and hungry, I feel like I jus want to kill somebody."

Seth knew Simon was as likely to take his foul mood out on him as any of the other soldiers. "Simon, jus keep walkin' and keep your trap shut."

In response, Simon tripped his brother who fell and got trampled on by the remaining soldiers in formation. Now *Seth* was ready to kill somebody. Finally, they stopped for a short rest near a farm. The men thought this would be a chance to get supplies, or at least something to eat from the farm. But after about fifteen minutes, Bragg ordered the unit to get ready to move out. Seth was hungrier and madder than he'd ever been in his life—at his brother, at Braxton Bragg, at the whole stinking world. He fell into the rear of his unit when they moved out. Passing the farmyard, something inside him snapped. He turned with his Enfield and aimed at the chickens. *Damn, if he wouldn't kill one and have something to eat tonight.* Bang! On hearing the shot ring out, the commander stopped his troops, and then walked slowly to the rear of the column. Seth was preparing to fire again because he'd missed the chicken. The bullet, however, had hit a Negro worker who had been collecting eggs. The man was dead, and immediately people from the farm ran from sheds and barns, scurrying about with cries of terror and disbelief.

After he had disarmed Seth and handcuffed him, General Bragg approached the owner of the farm, offering his apologies to the family. He promised to restore order in his unit, and with that, Bragg wasted no time in assembling a firing squad. Seth protested mightily, as did Simon, but in the end, the young S.O.B. was relieved of his duties with a volley of bullets. Simon wasn't so much sad as outraged. How could they shoot a man just for killing some black bastard stupid enough to take a bullet for a chicken? The thrill was over.

Damn, he thought, *I don't have Seth no more and that means I ain't got nobody.* He was alone in the world, and this particular world was about marching and going hungry, not kicking butt. He'd had enough. The next day's march was the same—almost no food and men weak from hunger, some almost passing out. When he got his chance, Simon peeled off the line and faded into the woods. He'd take his chances, find some adventure, and if he had a mind to, make his way back to Alabama. Even if Wedowee was a lousy place, it was better than this. *I'll shoot anybody who comes after me,* he told himself. It was a thought that perked him up.

The summer of Simon's desertion would have cheered him up had he stuck around for the action. In May of 1863, General Lee launched a successful surprise attack on the Union forces under the command of General Hooker at Chancellorsville. Later that same month, Confederate General John Pemberton surrendered at Vicksburg, Mississippi. Port Hudson, Louisiana, fell into Yankee hands a short time later. In July, at the Battle of Gettysburg, Union General Meade prevailed as Lee retreated back to Virginia. And in September, not far from where Simon mustered himself out of the military, the terrible battle of Chickamauga got underway at the point where Georgia, Tennessee and Alabama intersect. General Braxton Bragg set his troops up in the mountains around the city of Chattanooga, and a siege there cut off vital rail lines. A month later, Ulysses S. Grant distinguished himself in a series of brilliant attacks which broke Bragg's blockade, setting up Chattanooga for the base of General Sherman's Atlanta campaign the following year. The toll of dead and wounded on both sides just kept mounting. Had Simon survived the battles, he would have gotten the war experience he hoped for, but instead his life took a different turn. He was a fugitive, threading his way back through mountains and underbrush, stealing what he needed to survive, and always looking over his shoulder for bounty hunters.

There were the cowards and scoundrels like Simon, and there were the brave and upright like James Tomlinson. James continued to honor his commitment to the South. Whenever he got the chance, he captured images of the war, determined to show the world the truth. He couldn't undo the tragedy that he'd helped bring down upon the Bull family. And though many might absolve him of any responsibility for Gus' death, he himself could not. He longed to reach out to the grieving family that meant so much to him. The love Delia once felt for him was gone. Only Addie had given him some comfort during his brief stay at home. He wanted so much to thank her, and tell her what her compassion meant to him. Someday the war would be over and he desperately hoped she would welcome him back as a friend. He had always been so impressed by her musical talent, feeling that gift was every bit as much an art form as the painting of portraits or the taking of photographs. He was affected by her in so many ways, and found himself longing to hear her play the piano or the harpsichord. To honor her somehow became his greatest desire.

James pulled a small box from the breast pocket inside his coat. He opened it and there, in a locket-like case, was a photo of himself with his best friend, Gus—both in full uniform. How brave and stoic they looked. The picture had been taken long before Seven Pines. Now an inspiration suddenly came to him. He would paint a large canvas portrait of Gus from this photograph and send it to Addie. Perhaps it would bring her comfort.

The photography crew with his unit traveled to Richmond for supplies and brought James the materials he needed for his project. They also agreed to pack the canvas in their wagon along with all of their own bulky equipment as they moved from place to place. Most bivouacked soldiers complained bitterly of boredom, but not James. He spent every available moment painting and wished he didn't have to limit his work to intervals between battles.

He finished the painting early in December of 1863. Granted a furlough at Christmas time, he crated up the portrait himself and took it with him on the train back to LaGrange.

Christmas was cheerless for nearly everyone in the country. There was no longer a spirited debate between opposing philosophies. In its place was a bottomless pit of emotional pain. The men at the front expressed it with high rates of alcoholism and a malaise of spirit. Families and friends expressed it with sadness, anger, withdrawal, and uncharacteristic aggression. When the ambulance wagons were allowed onto the battlefield to collect those who might be saved, James had taken photographs of the grisly reality of battle. It was appalling to him now how willingly, even ardently, young men volunteered to be killed or mutilated—realizing that he had been one of the eager ones in the beginning. But after Seven Pines, he had little stomach for it. He hoped his images would horrify the public. Then they might sicken of this business of killing and demand that it come to an end, both sides agreeing to disagree. The sacrifice of war was enormous, and Gus had paid the ultimate price. So it was with this spirit, as well as his deepening feelings for Addie, that James ventured home to honor the memory of Lt. Gustavus Adolphus Bull.

It was difficult for James to even look at the finished painting. Seeing Gus standing upright in his full dress uniform, looking dignified and brave, was bittersweet. He loved this man, and the reminders of what happened to him, and his own part in that fate, continued to be painful. He loaded the crated portrait onto the train and sat beside it, protectively guarding it throughout the two-day trip home. Rumbling along in the night, he dreamed about Delia.

She looked more beautiful than he remembered, her black hair pulled away from her face with a silk ribbon. Smiling and laughing, she gathered two young boys and a little girl about her skirt as though to read them a story. The boys were dressed as if they were going to church, with good linen pants, white shirts and neat caps on their heads. The girl had on a blue dress with a pinafore over it, her hair in braids, and her sweet face hugged by a ruffled bonnet. These were his children—his and Delia's. She spoke to the children and they stood up, excited to go outside and play in the warm Georgia sunshine. Delia led them through the front door of the fine Southern home, and out into the yard. She lined each one up, side-by-side against the brick wall that ringed the garden. While they faced the wall, their mother turned around and signaled to a line of soldiers. Their commander shouted, "Ready," and the men dropped to one knee. "Aim," he called out, and they brought their rifles up to their shoulders. "Fire!" They shot the three little ones who crumpled to the ground, their bodies twitching with the sudden ebb of life…then stillness, as blood slowly puddled and then sank into the earth. The commander turned to face Delia and saluted. It was James, himself.

The screaming woke him—his heart pounding in utter desperation to undo what had happened. The soldier on the seat behind him shook his shoulder. "It's going to be all right. You're just having one helluva nightmare, buddy. I get them too. A lot of us do."

"Thanks," James mumbled, barely able to get the word out. He was breathing hard, as if he had run a five-mile race. He imagined that the three children in the dream represented him, Delia and Gus and their close childhood friendship. He couldn't banish these feelings of guilt during his waking hours, and now it appeared he couldn't escape them during sleep either.

Addie abruptly stopped playing the piano. She thought she heard the sound of a horse and buggy on the street in front of her house. Looking out the front window, she couldn't suppress her elation. *James!* She threw open the front door, running headlong to meet him at the gate.

"Tell me you're home for good, James," Addie said, grinning as she touched his hand even as he climbed from the buggy.

"If I'd known that smile was waiting for me, I might have had thoughts of deserting. But no, my sweet friend, I am on a short holiday furlough."

Addie's face reddened. *Was he flirting? Oh, no! What about Delia?* She was flushed with embarrassment and intrigued at the same time.

"Addie, I brought something for your family." He heaved the portrait from the carriage and began to uncrate it. "Mostly I thought of you as I worked on this because I couldn't find the words to thank you for your compassion." Removing the final covering, he stepped back. "I hope this portrait bestows the honor I feel for having known Gus."

Tears came instantly, followed by Addie's sobbing. "Don't misunderstand, James," she said when she could catch her breath. "My tears are mingled with something I haven't felt for a year: joy. Not only is it an incredible likeness that perfectly captures the spirit of my brother, but your gesture of painting it for us melts my heart. I am so grateful to you for this moment."

"You are a good girl, Addie."

"And I know you are a good man."

Now tears sprang to James' eyes as he turned to leave. "Please tell Delia my heart aches for our ruined friendship." James pulled a lace handkerchief from his breast pocket. "This belongs to Delia. Would you give it back to her for me? I know she hates me, but she should know that I hate myself too. If I'm killed in battle, it could not possibly be more painful than the hurt I bear today. Dying would bring some relief."

"Please, James, don't talk that way. My family knows you are not responsible for Gus' death. Maybe Delia's strong feelings are the result of her deep friendship with you; and if so, perhaps she'll sort them out one day. Please don't go until I have a chance to talk with her."

Addie rushed inside and found her sister staring out the front widow. "Sister, James has brought us something. Won't you come look?"

"I know what he has brought: grief. I can't stand the sight of him. Tell him that."

"We're all still hurting, Delia. But maybe it's time to think about forgiveness."

"No! Never!"

"You might feel differently if you would come see the extraordinary portrait of Gus that he painted. Oh, and he asked me to give you this." Addie held out the delicate lace handkerchief. "James says this belongs to you. You must have given it to him as a gesture of love and affection."

"Here's my gesture now." Delia threw the handkerchief into the fireplace. The flames curled the edges brown and in an instant the lace had turned to ashes. "And if you hang that painting in this house, I'll hang myself."

"But you haven't even seen it," objected Addie.

"And I don't want to! I will always see that betrayer bringing it to the gate as though delivering up Gus' dead body."

Addie returned to the front gate where James was standing, his cap in his hand, looking somber. "I'm sorry, James. Delia won't budge."

"No, she won't, and I won't likely forgive myself either. You have shown me such tenderness and I will treasure it always."

"For me, there is nothing to forgive. You loved my brother. Please, won't you try to forgive yourself, James? I would like to write to you. Perhaps my friendship will help you find peace."

"Bless you for your generous spirit, Addie." Receiving letters again would feel good he realized, and any measure of peace would be welcomed too. James climbed into the buggy, and snapping the reins, urged the horse into a trot. As he slowly made his way down the tree-lined, shadowed lane, he wrestled with his muddled feelings. He could not escape the darkness of his life, yet he felt a fleeting glimmer of light where there had been none—light that came from Addie.

"God, be with you, James," Addie called out as he disappeared down the road. Her own feelings clashed inside her as she watched him go. She had tried to help reconcile James and Delia today—sincerely tried. But now she felt a small stirring of excitement. Delia had turned her back on James, which meant that she was now free to muse about a deeper friendship with him—starting with prayers for his safe return.

Chapter XXIV

The Christmas holidays only served to remind Delia of the news delivered a year ago: Gus, dead. After all these months, her feelings were still raw. *How did people survive this kind of pain?* Melva and George seemed to bear their grief with dignity and grace. Though Sallie was clearly damaged. She kept up with her work, but her eyes were listless and she kept to herself most of the time.

Delia gazed through the window at the stark winter garden and watched Sallie. Sitting on the bench under the barren arbor, her shoulders heaving, sobs shaking her delicate frame. Delia put on a thick wool shawl and stepped outside.

"Why are you out here crying in the freezing cold?" Delia asked upon approach.

"Leave me alone," Sallie responded ruefully.

"It might help to talk about things,"

"That won't change anything."

Delia knew what was wrong, and it was more than just the war, Gus, and Frances. Sallie's heart was broken too. She still worked as a nurse, but had resigned her position as Dr. Ware's assistant.

"Don't you think you're being too judgmental? Isn't it time to forgive him? He's just a man and don't we all have human failings?"

"I can't believe what I'm hearing, Delia! *You* of all people."

Delia could see that anger and disappointment were scouring the sweetness from her tenderhearted sister. It was harder to see what anger was doing to her own soul.

"Some things are just not forgivable," she replied in defense of her own vendetta. Sallie didn't respond except to continue her weeping. In the face of her sister's silence, Delia plunged into her own thoughts. To her, anger made her strong. Without it, she would have no defense against the utter hopelessness of her life. She opted for anger over emptiness, and her writing was an outlet for all the strong feelings cinched up inside her. She could express her opinions on a variety of important topics, which had become her greatest comfort. True, the women of the town didn't always appreciate her views. She knew the kinds of things some of them whispered behind her back: *Bossy. Brassy. Big-headed. Or was it pig-headed?* Either way, Delia didn't care. Save for *The Nancies*, she thought many of them to be small-minded and prone to silly gossip. The fact was that certain things needed to be said in these desperate times—and if she was the only one with the guts to say them, then so be it.

Delia's recent essay, *Finish What You Start,* was a forceful argument for gathering resolve at a time of great emotional vulnerability. So many families, like hers, had lost loved ones, and the toll of the injured and incapacitated brought an ever-rising sorrow. It would be so easy to let flagging spirits deplete the energy needed to carry on.

Delia knew from her news gathering that an increasing number of voices in the South were speaking what would have been treasonous in 1861: the end of slavery. Now on the brink of 1863, she was reading editorial pieces from members of the Confederate Congress arguing that slavery was obstructing victory for the South. In the North, black men had joined the fight against the South. Manpower was a critical issue on both sides, and black soldiers could help turn the odds in favor of the North. In one of the latest editorials from the Jackson Mississippian, The LaGrange Reporter reprinted, *"Although slavery is one of the principles that we started to fight for, if it proves an insurmountable obstacle to the achievement of our liberty and separate nationality, away with it!"*

Delia pushed *The LaGrange Reporter* even further into the growing debate with some thoughts of her own:

Change is certain. That is the only thing we can count on. If we honor our slaves, they will honor us. In granting them freedom in exchange for joining the Confederate forces, we allow them to invest in the homelands they love. No longer will they be just a piece of what we own, but part of the human structure that allows all of us, white or black, to strengthen the spirit of the South we hold dear.

She concluded her essay with an urgent plea.

We cannot go back to life as we knew it. It is gone. But we can build something new and of our own making here in the South. That will be possible if we win this war. Losing is unthinkable because the cost will have been too high. We must finish what has been started, and we must do it together—not as slave and owner but as neighbor to neighbor."

Delia knew her words would create a stir in LaGrange, but the town had not shrunk back from controversy at the beginning of the war, and it would not back away now.

Delia suddenly came back to her senses and back to her sister's plight.

"Sallie, let me distract you from your misery. George is taking me into town. Why don't you come along?"

"I told you, Delia. I want to be alone."

"The only one you are hurting with your anger is you. Promise me you'll think about what I've said?"

"I promise," said Sallie. "It's one thing to understand something intellectually, and quite another to reconcile it emotionally."

"But you'll work on it?" Delia queried, staying with her point.

"Yes, sister. I'll try."

Delia headed to the barn where George was readying the buggy. Her first stop would be the newspaper office to deliver her latest column. In the editor's office, she scoffed at his concerns about reactions to her editorial, "Finish What You Start."

"Why, Mr. Willingham, think of all the newspapers you will sell."

His thought process didn't take long. Charles H. C. Willingham began to smile as he contemplated the increased income. "Keep up the good work, Delia."

Out on the street Delia nodded to George. "Let's go over to the bank. I have to check our accounts." George dutifully steered the rig down the street.

"I'll only be a few moments," she told him as he helped her out of the buggy.

As soon as she came through the door of the bank, she saw Nancy Morgan waving.

"Good to see you today, Mrs. Morgan."

"Same to you, Delia. Will I see you at *The Nancies* drill on the Square this Friday?"

"You certainly will. The Bull sisters have not missed one practice since this militia began. Neither cold nor rain would keep us away."

"Well, bundle up. It might be chilly."

"Oh my Lord!" Delia cried out, staggering, and then slumping to the floor in a faint.

Tellers and customers rushed toward her as Nancy hovered, fanning Delia's face.

Nancy let out a sigh as Delia began to stir. "What happened? You suddenly looked stricken and pale as a ghost."

Delia's voice was uncharacteristically shaky. "As we were talking, I gazed at the row of tellers and just over their heads, on the wall, I saw Gus."

"What ever are you talking about, Delia?" Nancy shooed the whispering group of people away. "Everything's fine now, people. You can go back to your business."

When the crowd thinned, Delia pointed to the rear wall. "The portrait—that damned portrait! The one I never wanted to see. My family agreed to discreetly display it somewhere other than our home."

"Ah, the portrait! You didn't know it was here in the bank," said Nancy. "Well, it's a wonderful painting of Gus, isn't it? I look forward to coming to the bank these days just to see it."

"It's just such a shock, suddenly seeing him there. I believe I need to sit down for a spell."

Nancy led Delia to a corner with a few empty chairs and a desk. She took a couple of deep breaths, then slowly lifted her gaze and stared at the painting. *Gus looks so handsome.* Indeed, this portrait was a beautiful piece of work, capturing the essence of her beloved brother. *So many men have been sacrificed. And it's not over yet—this damn war! Somehow we have to finish it!*

And what about us? The Nancies? Are we finishing what we started? Have we done enough?

Now on the verge of tears, Delia pleaded with Nancy. "We've got to do something more! Everyone is enjoying the drills and target practice, but we *have* to instill more seriousness. We didn't organize this militia to amuse ourselves!"

Nancy was concerned about Delia. "This isn't like you to fall apart. You've been under a great deal of stress. And now this shock today."

"No, that's not it. Something is not finished in our training, and we need to find it and fix it," she said definitively.

"Any ideas?" asked Nancy.

"Well, I've been thinking about that scoundrel Col. La Grange. He and the other Yankee spies were caught during a night patrol. The Confederate unit knew that darkness would provide the best cover, so they waited, listened, and smoked them out. I would guess that's not the first night patrol those men experienced."

"Night patrol! What a daring thought for our militia." Nancy clapped her hands.

"I've always loved the word 'daring.' " Delia suddenly felt alive with excitement.

"Yes, I know, dear. That word is the very foundation of the Nancy Hart Militia!" And with that declaration, Nancy Morgan squeezed her friend's hand.

Chapter XXV

S omewhere in the woods east of LaGrange, Luella Biggs was skinning a squirrel and weighing the dangers of building a small cook fire.

To the north, just over the Tennessee border, Simon Bettencourt was surveying a place in the brush to bed down. He felt meaner than ever this particular night. Hunger had brought out the worst in him, and there hadn't been a farmhouse or cabin to rob in two days.

In LaGrange, *the Nancies* galvanized their resolve to finish what they started. A higher level of training was in order. Word of the commencing night patrols had spread, and predictably, the Electa Club and members of the Ladies' Home Society whispered behind gloved hands, snickering about the Methodist ladies and their latest lark. Delightfully scandalous! But others in the town were not so judgmental.

There were plenty of stories lately about Yankee raiding parties in the South. They had all heard shocking accounts of homes burned to the ground, families routed to dirt roads with only the clothes on their backs and nowhere to go. The Nancy Hart Militia was an active military unit, its members proven to be excellent shots with both rifles and handguns. If *the Nancies* wanted to get more serious about their protection of the town, it was time to put away silly, outdated social constructs designed to protect a woman's virtue. And most of the townspeople agreed. Besides, the outing they had planned would not be so different from the old "gypsy night" campouts where large groups of ladies would tent at a rural churchyard for an evening of singing and telling stories. Night patrol would be more solemn of course, but no one could deny that *the Nancies* were more capable of looking after themselves than anyone else in town.

This would be a training session, lasting from early Friday morning until Sunday morning. The women were to spend two nights just on the outskirts of town, adhering to a strict schedule. "We will end our night patrol session on Sunday morning," announced Captain Nancy Morgan. "I expect to see the four patrol units in formation at the town square promptly at 9:30 a.m. From there, we will march together over to the Baptist church for our usual 10 o'clock Methodist service."

Delia directed the women to build a latrine at each post. "There are four shovels for each unit, so four of you will dig at a time. The trench needs to be two feet wide by four feet deep. Six feet long will do for this small group and short stay."

"You can't be serious?!" Leila Pullen was visibly pale.

Talking about a latrine was distressing enough—much less *building* the dreadful thing. Delia tried to convince the women that since men had to dig latrines at the army camps, they should do it too. "This is how it's done, ladies. Are you going to be wilted flowers or tough soldiers?"

"Well, I suppose we should follow military standards," said Leila, "but you don't expect us to actually *use* the latrines?"

Delia was shocked. "Of course not! We'll just dig a trench to prove we can do it. When nature calls I, for one, will walk to the nearest neighbor's home and use the outhouse."

Thus ended the controversy over latrines. So *the Nancies* dug ditches, set up a kitchen at each post, and were given supplies of candles, blankets, buckets, mess kits and rations. And finally, each unit organized its own night sentry shift. Addie had been assigned to the group charged with setting up camp to the north of town—out Cameron Mill Road about a mile from LaGrange Female College. First Corporal Leila Pullen and First Sergeant Augusta Hill were the unit officers in charge. Elizabeth Haralson,

Mary Ann Parham, Martha Wimbish, Margaret Cox, Isabel Reid, Ella Pitman, and Anne Elizabeth Whitfield completed the patrol.

At about 3 p.m., Addie's group gathered in the clearing they had created that morning. Sitting on logs that surrounded a fire pit, they anticipated their first evening meal. "We're lucky to have warm days and comfortably cool nights this July weekend," one of them said. The women nodded in agreement. "Unlike what the Confederate troops had to endure, we won't suffer terrible storms and fields of mud," another added.

Neither would the women suffer through indigestible meals as did the men at the front. Addie had heard many a story from a hospitalized soldier about rancid salt pork or salt beef. She'd also heard the soldiers refer to hardtack made with flour and lard as "worm castles" because of the maggots and weevils that infested the rock-like cakes. What passed for coffee, some said, was merely an herbal concoction that resembled dirty water. Though *the Nancies* wanted their camp experience to be authentic, they drew the line when it came to rations. There would be no worm castles and salt pork.

"Ladies, the menu tonight is warm ham biscuits, butter beans, peaches, lemonade and real coffee." Addie reported.

The cooks for the evening readied the campfire and oiled the cast iron skillet while the rest of the women inspected and cleaned their weapons, preparing for their patrols. The watch was assigned at two-and-a-half hour intervals throughout the night, with two women on duty at all times.

Out in the woods, a pair of eyes had been following the activities of the north patrol *Nancies* throughout the day. In fact, Luella, silent as an Indian scout, sat within twenty-five feet of the camp at this very moment. She was utterly shocked to see a group of white ladies outfitted with rifles playing like they were men. She had no idea what was going on, but felt certain this was not a new search party sent to capture her. She nearly swooned from the smells wafting towards her—ham and beans! And she barely held back a small shriek at the sight of these women feasting on such a banquet. There must be more food in that tent of theirs. She would wait and watch for a chance to steal some of it.

If his brother hadn't already been shot by his commanding officer, Simon Bettencourt would have shot Seth himself in exchange for an insect-infested "worm castle." He had been traveling a long time, raiding homesteads to provide food and water. On one of them, he'd made a lady who was running the family farm alone, pack up a bunch of stuff in a basket all nice and pretty. That had lasted awhile...eggs, bread, some carrots, and apples. But for the last few days, he had kept away from the roads when he got close to a town. He didn't want to increase his danger of being captured—and either be sent to a military prison or set before a firing squad. He was hungry, and tired of sleeping lightly so as to hear if somebody snuck up on him in the dark. He had always thought of his home life in Alabama as decidedly disadvantaged, but in light of his experience with the army, and now on the run, he saw that there had been good times. He and Seth even bullied the slaves living in shanties along the river. They would beat them unless they were paid. The poor Negroes had no money, but paid in whatever food they could scrounge so the pair would leave them alone. Those collards and pork bones provided a pleasant memory. So did the fishing in Lake Wedowee. And, of course, "fight night" in Roanoke. Walking home was the hard way for sure. Listening for a train whistle as his cue, he planned to follow the sound and try to hop aboard a freight car.

Some miles away in LaGrange, the night was peaceful, but full of unusual activity. The north unit of The Nancy Hart Militia was fully engaged in their night patrol mission. Leila and Augusta had an uneventful shift. All they'd heard were the crickets and bull frogs down by the river. Occasionally, a branch crackled in the dark, but the women assumed it was some nocturnal animal—hopefully minding its own business.

Luella was used to staying up at night since she considered it the safest time for her. Not many people went out in the dark with search parties; and by now, it had been so long since she'd run away that the sound of baying hounds was a distant memory. But she was worried about what these ladies were up to. They had weapons, and seemed to be on some kind of patrol. She would just follow them through the night, keeping her own curious watch.

The *Nancies* kept to their rounds. "All's well at 8:30," Leila reported to her replacement. Mary Ann and Martha shouldered their Enfields and began the long march on the silent roads.

Mary Ann checked in with Ella at the end of their rounds. "All's well at 11."

Now Ella and Annie would take the watch until 1:30 in the morning. Back at camp, Betsy and Elizabeth stood guard while the others slept. They were energized by this training exercise and serious about doing the job right, though just a little nervous about being out in the eerie dark.

Luella watched as two ladies handed off the patrol duties, yet again, to another pair. Would this be the last before daylight? No, there was one more watch with two women who seemed to make more noise than the others, whispering and giggling every now and then. And next thing she knew, Luella smelled coffee again.

As night gave way to morning, militiawomen Leila and Margaret reached the campfire just as Augusta was pouring coffee and setting out biscuits with jam. Leila smiled. "Nothing to it. Night patrol's easier than changing bandages at the hospital."

"But not as fun as flirting with the patients, that right, Leila?" joked Isabel.

"Oh, I can't help it if I like to cheer up our boys," said Leila, her voice hinting of both petulance and mischief.

It was time for Luella to sleep. She figured the ladies would stick close to camp during the day and repeat their mysterious patrolling again tonight. But now she had a plan to get her hands on some fine Southern vittles once she was rested and at her best. When she reached her familiar cliff top, she dropped down to the landing and pulled herself into her cave dwelling. Luella was used to falling asleep in stressful circumstances, so she had not the slightest trouble now.

Simon hadn't figured on sleeping much during his furtive southward trek, skirting Atlanta; and by now, he was mighty weary. But his body was suddenly energized with the sound of a distant train whistle. Sure enough, he had at last come across a town where the train stopped to unload cargo. It was the middle of the night, so the depot was barely lit—a single oil lamp hanging in the entrance didn't cast enough light to see the name above the depot door. He slipped to the far side of the train, walking alongside as it began its slow pull, and then gradual acceleration out of town. Waiting until most of the cars had rounded the bend and were just beyond the houses, he swung himself up onto a freight car. Inside, there were barrels and boxes marked with numbers and letters, mostly hardware he discovered when he broke them open. The only edible thing he found was onions, bag after bag, stacked in one corner of the car. He ravenously downed three of them before his stomach started protesting. Better to feel queasy than be wild with hunger.

Settling himself behind some boxes, he leaned against a bag of onions, and quickly fell asleep. When the train whistle startled him out of unconsciousness, and back into his all too uncomfortable life, sun was streaking through the slats in the freight car. In an instant, he realized what that whistle meant: he was coming into a town, and would be ushered to the pokey if he were discovered hiding behind the onions. It would be clear from his gray uniform that he was going in the opposite direction of the war—and tellingly, all alone. He didn't care if he was a deserter, but plenty of other people would. He jumped from the freight car just as the depot sign came into view: "LaGrange." So he was somewhere near the border of Alabama. He could make his way on foot to Wedowee from here, he thought, as he tumbled to the ground. The train had not slowed enough to make for an easy fall. As he hit the dirt, everything went black.

On Saturday, *the Nancies* settled into a routine of guarding the roads just outside LaGrange. Eating was the highlight of this excursion though some of the ladies made it clear they would have preferred more variety. Leila and Augusta had kitchen duty for this second, and final, day of *the Nancies* inaugural patrol.

"Ham biscuits and butter beans again, Augusta?' Leila whined.

"My mother prepared the menu for the ladies, and felt it would be ostentatious to lay out a sumptuous feast in light of the hardships our men are facing at the battlefront. Honey-cured ham and buttermilk biscuits seemed appropriate without being excessive, especially if we ate leftovers the second night."

"Well, I just would have preferred...."

"Leila, you poor thing! Maybe Addie or Ella can go shoot a squirrel so we can slip something different into your biscuits this evening," Augusta said, clearly annoyed.

"Lordy, no! Ham will be just fine, thank you."

With that, Leila and Augusta went about the business of starting the cook fire and hanging the kettle of butter beans from an iron rod that was held in place by a rod forked at either end. The ham was placed in an iron skillet that sat on top of the flames—and hopefully could be pulled out before it burned. But the biscuits had been baked in advance, needing only to be warmed on a plate that also served as a lid for the pot of simmering beans.

Luella watched a distance away, hidden by trees and scrub brush. She drooled as her hungry gaze fixed on a woman slicing juicy peaches into a bowl. If these ladies followed last night's pattern, they would all eat around the campfire at the same time, which meant that no one would be in the cook tent where the food was stored. Her plan was to slip under a tent flap while the women were distracted with their meal, and steal whatever she could get her hands on. She had brought the haversack she'd found along-side the dead soldier back at the start of her life as a fugitive. She would pack as much as she could inside it, then ease her way back under the tent flap and be on her way. She didn't fool herself. These women would have no mercy on her if they caught her. No doubt they would tie her up and march her back to that monster Terence Lange. Slaves were valuable property, and runaways were not tolerated. She would have to be stealthier than she had ever been in her three years out here in the Georgia woods.

The Nancies served up their plates, found their places, and waited for Augusta to say grace.

Dearest Lord, watch over our brave men far from home this night. Give us strength to persevere in this courageous fight for control of our own destiny as the Confederate States of America. We pray thee to watch over us this night as we guard our families while our men fight on for the South. We thank you for many things, including the food we are about to eat, and the uncommonly strong friendships we have forged as members of the Nancy Hart Militia. Amen.

Now Luella understood quite a bit all at once. She had figured there was a war going on, what with finding the dead soldier. But now she knew it was a war between the South and the big government up North. The dead man was likely a soldier running away from the fighting. He'd had no injuries, so Luella thought he must have died from hunger, cold or sickness. These women—as hard as it was to imagine—had evidently formed a homeland defense force. *Lord, hep 'em if they ever have to shoot those guns! They probly can't hit the side of a barn. But they sure can cook!* The food smelled so delicious that it was almost more than she could bear just watching them eat. Holding her breath, and waiting for just the right moment, she seized it when it came.

"Addie, you know what we really need to make this an authentic camp experience?" asked Martha Wimbish. "We need some music, and you are the only one who can provide it tonight."

The rest of *the Nancies* hollered and clapped in agreement, but Addie hadn't brought anything to play. After Gus' death, she had put music aside.

"Sorry, ladies. I didn't come prepared to entertain."

To everyone's surprise, Martha pulled a banjo out from under her blanket. "I thought you might need some coaxing, so I brought this along."

She extended the banjo to Addie while the women cheered. As soon as her fingers touched the instrument, a spark of something touched her soul…something she'd almost forgotten. Was it joy? As she began to play, she felt the spark quicken in her heart. Yes, it *was* joy! Her fingers flew across the fret and a smile stole across her face in the flickering light. For the next hour, Addie played, and *The Nancies* sang. Southern tunes filled the air in a rare, lighthearted blink of time, making them forget the misery of a war that had gone on way too long.

It was just the opportunity Luella had prayed for. The women were making so much noise they wouldn't possibly notice any of hers. Flattening herself onto the ground, she inched her way to the far side of the cook tent. No time to pick and choose—she would just grab whatever looked edible. First she scooped up three peaches, and then plunging her hand into a sack, came up with a fistful of biscuits. Next she spied a ham butt, and swept it up into her pack. How she longed for those butter beans, but there were none in sight, and rooting around for them might alert the ladies. She would get out now, while the music and singing still camouflaged her presence. Scurrying out of the tent, Luella disappeared back into the woods as the music played on.

"That's all ladies. It's time for the first watch," said Augusta.

Addie's grin almost glowed in the dark. *What a healing force! Music was good medicine!* She felt happy for the first time in so very long.

Nearby, Simon stumbled on a knobby root rudely poking up on the path. The light was fading quickly, and he wasn't sure he was heading in the right direction. "Damn!" he howled, grabbing his injured toe. When he'd come to after the blackout, he'd found himself in a ditch, his head throbbing. It still ached, and now his toe hurt too! Moments ago, he thought he heard voices—maybe women's voices—which seemed very strange. Human voices anyway to be sure, so he best keep moving—even though it was hard to find the way at night. Hours later, Simon was back where he started. He was sure of that because he stubbed his toe again on that same damn root! Maybe better just rest awhile and try to figure out where he was going wrong.

Betsy and Isabel took the kitchen clean-up after supper, and quickly noticed the sack of biscuits was wide open. On inspection, they found quite a few missing, and then saw that the bag of coffee was gone! Bolting from the tent, they reported the missing food to the officers in charge.

"Oh, probably just a raccoon," one of them said.

"But what about the coffee?" Betsy asked. "Raccoons don't like coffee."

Addie glanced around the group. None of them seemed spooked, but she had gooseflesh.

Luella was ravenous and the peaches overtook her senses. She was nearly faint with their scent, their ripe plumpness, and the thought of how sweet they would taste on her tongue. After the limited fare of the past few years, a peach was more treasured than a pair of new shoes, although that thought set her to aching as well. How she would love real shoes—not worn out soldier's boots. But she could do something about the peach. As soon as she felt she was a safe distance from the camp, she ate two of them, letting the juice run down her arms and drip from her chin—savoring every bite. They tasted even better than she remembered.

Simon thought he must be dreaming—either that or he had gone plum crazy. Coffee…he smelled coffee! And where there was coffee there might be food. He hadn't had food for days, but he hadn't had coffee in years. *Was his mind playing tricks? No, that was most certainly coffee.* He decided to follow the scent even if it turned out to be an imaginary trail, but instead, this intoxicating aroma led him, trance-like, to a small clearing. *Was he seeing things too?* A soldier was hunched over a small fire surrounded by a circle of rocks. The man's back was to him, but he could easily see the gray jacket and Confederate cap. Great slurping noises filled the air and that strong coffee smell wafted upon it. No weapon in sight. Plainly another deserter, someone who might have what Simon wanted most—food.

"Don't move soldier! Simon leveled his rifle at the chap's head. "Whatcha got there, Sonny?"

The figure turned around, slowly offering up a sack.

"Don't be reaching into that sack," Simon warned. "Just throw it over here."

The sack landed at Simon's feet with a thump. Without taking his eyes off the soldier, Simon reached down and into the bag.

"Biscuits! Lordy, I've forgotten what they taste like without worms." He jammed one in his mouth. "Now you swing around here so's I can see you straight on and then sit still."

Luella swung her feet to the other side of the log she'd been comfortably sitting on, savoring a meal she never expected to have in her life as a fugitive. Maybe now it would be her last meal.

"What the hell? You're no soldier boy!"

Simon could see by the dim light of the flames that his dining companion had long hair and breasts, but no beard—not a man, but a *woman*; and not white, but black.

"Well, fancy that. A runaway slave I'd bet. But you surely do have what I want. Soon's I finish these fine fixins, I'm gone have me a serving of something else I been missing. Bet you been missing a man way out here by yourself."

Luella's skin crawled. This was just the kind of brute she had run away from! Only this one was genuine white trash, and holding a gun on her.

"Take all the food, mistuh and jez go on." Luella threw the other bags of food in the man's direction.

"I don't think so, though I'm mighty grateful for your generosity." Simon poked through the bags, stuffing ham and peaches and biscuits all together in his mouth.

Nearing the end of their patrol shift, Addie caught a whiff of something as they made their way towards camp. *Coffee. But that couldn't be!* Coffee and breakfast were many hours away.

"Do you smell that?" she asked Isabel

"Do you suppose we ought to go take a look?" Isabel's tone sounded quite tentative.

The aroma didn't seem to be coming from the direction of the camp and that was worrisome.

"Yes, I think we need to investigate."

"Why don't we just get back to camp quick and tell the next shift about it? Maybe it's just our imagination 'cause we're tired. You think?" Isabel said hopefully.

Then they heard a scream. It wasn't that loud—more like a shriek, but it was unmistakably a woman in trouble. Who else could it be but one of their own? Addie and Isabel ran hard, trying not to collide with trees or roots or who-knew-what in the darkness. Thud! Addie looked back. Isabel had vanished.

"I'm down here in some kind of pit, maybe a hunting trap. I'll be all right—just keep running."

Addie could hear some kind of scuffle just ahead. Muffled exclamations from a male and a female, but none intelligible. Suddenly, she could make out a struggle, a man on top of the woman: a skirt flying up, a fist hitting a head. Addie's thoughts were firing rapidly. *Must be Leila or Margaret. Some man attacking. A rifle set by a tree nearby. Rape. Murder. Do something! Act!*

She took steady aim at the man pummeling the woman on the ground. He was beating her senseless all the while trying to get her skirt up and her legs apart.

Crack! The Enfield fired. Addie barely moved from the kick that followed. She was riveted on her target, and that target lay still. Maybe she had shot both of them.

Oh dear God, how can this be happening? She stepped over to the still figure on the ground, pushing him with her foot until he rolled off the person underneath. The shot had gone clean through the base of his skull, and there was no doubt that he was dead. But the woman lying on the ground was a great surprise. Not one of their own, but the face of a young black woman, staring up at her shaking and sobbing.

"Who are you?"

"Name's Luella Biggs"

Addie's hand flew to her mouth.

Back at the north patrol camp, *the Nancies* were scrambling to their feet, pulling on shoes, and grabbing their rifles. Not one of them had slept through the loud report of the Enfield. They recognized that sound and knew that two of their sisters were in trouble. Augusta kept them in check, reminding them of their training and discipline. Following her orders, they pushed through the forest in two lines—four in front, four behind.

"Help! Help!"

It was Isabel's voice, but she was nowhere in sight.

"Over here in a pit! In the ground."

Margaret and Mary Ann cleared away debris to reveal a cross-hatching of branches framing a hole. About six feet below, lay a crumpled Isabel clutching her ankle. They dismantled the animal trap, leaned in, and pulled her out.

"Addie's up ahead. We smelled some coffee, then heard a scream. We took off running, but when I fell, I told her to keep going."

"Fan out!" Augusta ordered. "Circle around in the direction where we heard the shot ring out." When they reached the small clearing, they found Addie sitting on a log, crying, her arms around a young Negro woman. Not far from them, a man lay flat out on the ground in a Confederate uniform—staring up into the sky, blood oozing from a hole in his face and spittle mixed with buttermilk biscuit dripping from his mouth.

Startled by the scene, Augusta spoke for everyone. "God in heaven! What happened here?"

Addie slowly lifted her gaze to the women gathered around her. "I killed a man."

"Ain't no man you killed," the black woman said. "That was a piece of yellow-bellied white trash, vermin running the wrong way from his own soldiers."

"A deserter." Isabel voiced what the others were realizing. But what none of them understood was the presence of this Negro.

"Who is *she?*" Augusta asked, gesturing in the woman's direction.

"Her name is Luella Biggs. She used to take care of me when I was a little girl," Addie said, trying to stifle her tears.

"I done ran away after being moved around a bit. Picked cotton some 'til a bad boss-man tried to rape me. Been in the woods a long time, and now here come a 'nother bad man."

Addie had lost the battle with her tears, which were freely coursing down her cheeks. She remembered that moment so long ago when she'd lied about who slapped the baby. She had told her mother Luella did it. Now she was stricken with shame. Every terrible thing that happened to Luella since then was her fault!

"What I did was wrong, Luella," she murmured. "I caused you all this hardship."

"Thas childish thinking. Put the past aside." Luella winked at Addie. "What you did today came from a grown-up woman. You done saved my life, missy, and I thank you wid everthin in me. That buzzard wuz nothin but evil."

Turning to the other women, Luella made an apology of her own. "And I'm sorry I done stole dem biscuits wid da ham. They mighty good, though. And oh, yeah, them peaches and coffee, too." I couldn't hep mysef. Thought I'd faint from the smell. Then that no-good weasel, he done pointed his rifle at me and took my food. Had his fill then wuz all over me."

Leila suddenly burst out in excitement. "My gracious! Don't you know, this sounds just like the real Nancy Hart! Those Tory soldiers came barging into her house with their muskets and ordered her to kill the best pig and serve them up a feast. She did alright, then blasted a big hole in one of their heads while they sat eating."

"One of their own guns too!" Mary Ann added.

Addie had proved something to all of *the Nancies*—especially those who may have harbored private fears about facing danger. They weren't going to go out looking for a battle, but if war came to LaGrange, they were ready to respond!

After some discussion, the group decided to bury the body and leave Luella to her own wily survival skills. Horrified by Luella's description of her life in the plantation fields with that brutal boss, they had no wish to return her to such misery. Relieved and grateful, Luella helped drag the man's body back to the pit Isabel had fallen into. She had dug it herself two years ago to trap animals, but thought this was a much better use for it. Before they rolled the body into the hole, they helped Luella look through the man's pockets for useful things. They found a knife, more flint, and though his shoes and socks were shabby and worn, they were nonetheless useful for wilderness living. His haversack revealed eating utensils, a tin cup, and powder cartridges for the rifle. "'Spect I won't need cartridges or a rifle cause if'n I go shootin somethin, somebody's gonna hear it and come after me. And likely won't be the good Nancies." She held out the ammunition to Ella. The women filled in the grave with dirt and forest debris until it looked just as it had when Isabel dropped into it an hour before.

"Do you suppose we should say a prayer or something?" Addie asked.

"Let me." Luella answered. "Dear God in heaven, bless *the Nancies* for their good hearts. Keep them safe and strong. I thank you for lookin' after me out here all this time. Keep lookin' after my chillin and my sister. Thank you, Lord, for bringing these ladies to my rescue. We all done what we had to do. We return this soul to you now and trust you'll know what to do with the SOB. Amen"

Augusta took the runaway slave's hand and squeezed it. "Thank you, Luella. When we break camp we're not going to take any leftover food with us. You'll know what to do with it."

Addie felt a stormy brew of emotions: shame, pride, relief, horror. It was one thing to be confronted with a split-second decision, but quite another to live with the decision once it has been made. She had never imagined she would kill another person—whether they deserved it or not. But another part of her was comforted by rescuing Luella. Perhaps in this way she had atoned for her sin.

The other *Nancies* rallied around her with words of comfort and support.

"You proved your metal, Addie" said Augusta, patting her shoulder.

Leila hugged her. "I'm so proud of you."

But it was Ella who summed up the feelings of the others. "I've being feeling so low these days about the war and all, and I wasn't sure if *the Nancies*, myself included, had what it really took to fight. But you've lifted me up, Addie. Because of you, and what you did, I know we are up to the job of defending our homes and families if we have to."

Together they pledged to keep the events of the night to themselves. It would be their secret forever. It was best that way. Unsure of what trouble might come from telling, they did know that trouble would be big. No one wanted new search parties launched for Luella, and neither did they want the news they had killed a Confederate soldier to get out. He certainly acted and looked like a deserter, but who knew for sure?

After cleaning up their camp, Addie was glad they were headed for church. She was feeling in need of reassurance that a more comfortable and predictable life still existed. The familiar hymn books, the well-worn pews, the pastor's sermon, and trusty neighbors—all the rituals that told her life was well-ordered. The unit marched single file until they neared the town square where they were joined by the rest of their sisters, coming into view from all directions: south, east and west.

As Addie led *the Nancies* north patrol, Ella reached up behind her and tenderly placed her right hand on her friend's shoulder. Then Augusta, behind Ella, did the same. Mary Ann, Martha, Annie, Isabel, Leila and Margaret all followed suit, marching single file, rifles over their left shoulders and right arms extended in a gesture of sisterhood and solidarity.

Chapter XXVI

Sept. 1864

S ummer night patrols were full of the warmth of friendship and sisterhood, and I was embraced with love and support following that dreadful night I killed a man. Those good feelings from my sisters have now taken a back seat to the horror of a war we thought could not get worse. The fighting is brutal, and close. Will it ever end—this death and destruction, the grief and unrelenting joyless days? Atlanta is lost and Sherman marches on.

Addie wondered if hopelessness was contagious. If it were, that would explain why most of the people in Georgia—indeed everywhere in the South—seemed lost in the wake of Sherman's rampage. The destruction of Atlanta had brought the war so close to LaGrange that *the Nancies* stepped up their drills, target practice, and night patrols in an effort to increase their military readiness. Other states were reeling from the wreckage of Sherman's advance too, and newspaper accounts confirmed that the Confederate Army was shrinking in both number and spirit.

The despair Sherman brought to the South continued into the winter. Judge Bull assembled his slaves, both household and field workers, telling them he would take care of them until the conflict was over and would then give them their freedom. They could stay and work for wages, or they could leave to follow a destiny of their own choosing. Fear and uncertainty reigned about what would happen when, and if, the war was finally over— making the slaves on the Bull plantation feel it was best to stay put for now.

When spring came, Addie wondered why Mother Nature ignored the scourge of hopelessness and allowed the crocuses to bloom. Other forms of optimism had all but vanished, and still, Sherman was not done with the South. Through Delia's skill in gathering the news, the people of LaGrange learned that small towns along railroad routes were his current targets.

A group of Union soldiers received new orders. They were called "Wilson's Raiders," charged with the destruction of military industries in Alabama and Georgia. Chasing Confederate units, they were bent on destruction of the industrial heartland of the South. General James H. Wilson commanded these 14,000 men, and when they rode into Alabama, he split them up into smaller units, instructing them to find and destroy Confederate war support industries including railroads.

Delia reported the raids as telegraph wires clicked out the news—until the lines were cut. April 2, 1865, Selma, Alabama fell to Wilson's Raiders. April 3, Tuscaloosa. April 12, Montgomery was lost. In Opelika, Alabama a terrified telegraph operator sent a message: the Raiders were headed to West Point, Georgia, just over the border from Alabama.

As with most southern towns, West Point had only a few old men left to watch over their town but war-wounded General Robert C. Tyler presided over the fort. He had lost a leg in an earlier battle but vowed to continue the cause. A telegraph message came from West Point, asking for help from anyone in the next town who could come to their aid. That town was LaGrange, Georgia. On the 15th of April, LaGrange Mayor, Henry Long, received the urgent call for help. He immediately went to the hospital to ask Dr. Ware for advice. "Do we have any soldiers who are well enough to go to West Point?"

"Just a very few," the doctor replied, "but I'll go through the wards and see who might be able and willing to volunteer."

A few convalescing soldiers quickly agreed to join the force, along with two others, just arriving home on furlough: Col. James H. Fannin and Lt. James Tomlinson.

James had hoped to visit Addie when the train stopped in LaGrange, but he was met at the station by a crowd shouting for him to stay onboard. Some twenty young boys, old men, and wounded soldiers climbed aboard as the train moved out to West Point.

On Easter Sunday Addie held onto a thin strand of hope that somehow Wilson's Raiders could be stopped at West Point. Anxiety was rampant in LaGrange. There was no longer a working telegraph to bring them news, and no locomotive delivering their few precious men. The families had gone to church in the morning to celebrate the resurrection of Jesus Christ, all the while praying not just that their own souls would be saved, but that the people of West Point would be spared. In the afternoon of a day that should have been filled with celebration, three men on horseback came galloping through the center of town. They shouted to anyone who could hear.

"The Yankees are coming! The Yankees are coming!"

Addie saw people running in every direction. She called out to one of the fleeing soldiers. "What happened?"

He slowed his horse. "West Point is gone. General Tyler was killed along with another twenty or so. Our ammunition ran out in the afternoon, and anybody left was taken prisoner. A couple of us made a break. LaGrange is next!" He spurred his horse into a gallop and shouted over his shoulder, "Run for your life!"

As word of the impending invasion spread, some families buried valuables in their yards and scurried out of town, even as many slaves fled into the woods. But Addie knew her family would stay. They had spent several hours deciding what was worth trying to save, and then burying it on the land. The silver service found a home about four feet from the smokehouse. Addie used her bare hands to dig in the red Georgia clay, committing to the earth her two most treasured possessions: her memory album and the trumpet Gus had given her so long ago. As she hollowed out a spot beneath the azaleas that ran along the front porch, she thought about her life. Perhaps tomorrow would be her last noble act: the honor of dying for James and for Gus. She settled the disturbed roots of the plant around her treasures, filled the soil back in, and smoothed the top. Then after pulling some of the pink blossoms from the bush, and scattering them to hide evidence of fresh digging, she stood and smoothed her dirt-streaked skirt.

She heard a carriage pull to a stop at the front gate. Looking down the path, she saw Nancy Morgan waving and shouting. "Addie, it's time to send out the call!"

"Yes, Captain Morgan. Right away!" Addie knew just what to do. Quickly, she ran to the town square and sounded her bugle—the signal for *the Nancies* to meet at the church. Suddenly there was a voice behind her, "Hey, hey, hey!"

Addie wheeled at the sound. There in the faint light of dusk, she saw someone she had never expected to see again: Luella Biggs.

"Why aren't you hiding in the woods, Luella? We're all in more danger than ever before."

"Thas' what I come to tell you bout. Theys a big mess of Yankees in the woods. They done settled in a spot besides the West Point Road, 'bout half way between here and there. I 'spect they'll bed down for the night. Ya got to go tell *the Nancies*."

"How many Yankees?"

Luella wasn't sure how to describe the number of soldiers she had seen.

"Luella, are there more than a 100 soldiers?" Addie prompted.

"Yessum."

"More than 500?"

"Yessum."

"More than 1000?"

"I reckon so."

Addie felt her stomach seize up with fear. Could forty-six *Nancies* gather the courage to face more than a thousand Yankees? "Get on out of here, Luella. You've been a better friend than I deserve. Stay safe."

"Y'all, too Miss Addie." And with that, Luella disappeared into the shadows of the alley. Now Addie knew the fear that Luella had lived with for years.

By 6 p.m., all the members of the Nancy Hart Militia were seated in the pews of the Methodist Church. Addie sat at the piano and waited for the signal to begin. Her tension eased as her fingers found the right keys to the familiar hymn. She hoped "A Mighty Fortress Is My God" would somehow inspire courage.

Capt. Nancy Morgan delivered a passionate message to her militia about commitment, duty and honor. She pledged to stand and fight—alone if necessary. "West Point is lost. Wilson's Raiders are perhaps busy at this very hour burning and pillaging there. They will most likely sleep there and pull out in the morning. The only questions remaining are when they will arrive in LaGrange and from what direction."

Addie stood up. "Capt. Morgan, I believe I have some vital information in that regard."

"Please tell us, Addie."

"A good soldier coming through town just now told me that Wilson's Raiders had already moved out of West Point. They are camped about half way between here and there along the West Point Road, and appear to have settled in for the night."

"Do we know how many soldiers?"

Addie thought about the ramifications of being too precise. "Uh…I was just told 'a big mess of them.' "

"Thank you, Addie. We'll muster at the Heard House on Broad Street, then march out to the west end and draw a line of defense across the road. Remember, we are soldiers who have spent four years preparing for this moment. Go home, get ready, and reflect on the importance of this mission. In the morning, we will face the enemy with unwavering strength. That, and the grace of God, will see us through."

They filed out of the church silently, steeped in a swirl of emotions. Some had been lifted up by Captain Morgan's speech, some wrestled with fear, and still others, left cloaked in dread. How many would muster in the morning? First light would reveal the answer.

At midnight, Addie joined her sisters in their bedroom, checking their rifles and ammunition. Everything was ready. "Can I really kill someone?" Sallie touched her rifle. "I've seen men die, but I don't know what it would feel like to actually kill someone."

Delia shivered. "I've been angry enough to kill, but to really do it? That has to be awful."

"It is," said Addie softly.

"What do you mean, 'It *is?*' " Sallie gasped.

"Addie, what are you saying?" Delia leaned in close with a piercing stare.

"I killed a man, and, yes, it was awful." Addie recounted the fateful events of the North night patrol. "We made a pledge not to tell anyone because we were afraid of what might happen to Luella if word got out that she was still on the loose."

"Good Lord, Addie. What a burden to keep all this inside." Sallie hugged her sister.

Delia suddenly brightened. "I guess you've shown us all what courage is, so we must trust that it runs in the family."

The sisters fell quiet in the gravity of the moment, each deep in her own thoughts.

"But what should we *wear?*" Sallie blurted out suddenly.

At this moment of unbearable stress, it was such an absurd question—contemplating what might be fashionable for the shooting of Yankees! The women collapsed on the floor laughing hysterically, though their laughter was mixed with tears. Still, it broke the tension and filled them with gratitude that at least they had each other. With hugs and tender kisses, each sister retreated to her own bed. Unable to sleep, Addie wrote in her journal by candlelight, glancing up now and then at the clock over the fireplace.

The clock ticks away my life. Every second, a dream vanishing and a memory grieved for its fleeting presence. Eighteen years is not all that I want. I have never yearned to be an old woman until now. To be fifty with a family of my own and to have grandchildren—that is what I want. How I ache to know that happiness. How stricken I feel over the real possibility my years will be too short. I'm not ready to die.

Damn, I guess all those boys who went off to war didn't want to die either. The day they all left LaGrange, I thought they were so noble and brave. They were smiling and cheering about going off to fight. How could they do that? I don't feel like cheering tonight. I feel like throwing up when I think of facing the Yankees tomorrow, especially those Sherman soldiers who kill innocent civilians—rape, torture, take what they want and burn everything to the ground. Do men find pleasure in violence? The officers give orders not to hurt innocent people, but in the primitive frenzy that overcomes fighting men, it happens anyway. I can't fathom men behaving this way, but I also can't find a single sane reason to be happy going off to war. Are they insane? Is it possible for a government and a culture to twist their minds? Maybe none of the men really believed they would get killed. Perhaps they fooled themselves. If I didn't love my brother, Gus, so much and miss him so desperately, I suppose I could wave the Confederate flag, sing Dixie and pray for glory. All I want to pray for now is an end to this misery called The War Between the States. I don't care about the slaves or the South or government tariffs or General Lee or Abraham Lincoln. I just want this nightmare to end.

At 5 a.m., Addie woke her sisters. Sallie went over to the trunk next to the wing chair and pulled out her prettiest silk gown: daffodil yellow with white satin buttons down the bodice.

"Are you really going to dress for this battle?" Addie was puzzled now.

"Well, dear sister, I just figure if the Bluecoats burn the house down, I want to at least have one nice dress for whatever lies ahead. But two would be better, so I'm going to put another one over it."

Addie and Delia both thought this was a very sensible idea, so each selected a dress from the trunk, put it on, then slipped another dress over it. In the foyer, Martha Bull waited trembling, offering cups of steaming tea for her daughters. Judge Bull had forbidden his young son, Orville, from joining the rag-tag group that had left to defend West Point, but now he offered his only surviving son the chance to get involved. The two had left the house before sunrise, headed to the square hoping to help save the courthouse.

Martha's hands shook as she handed out the tea cups. "Are you sure about this, my dearest girls?"

"Mother, I have never been more sure about anything in my life." Delia kissed her mother, and the other girls wrapped themselves around her, praying it would not be the last time.

Out in the street, they shouldered their weapons and began walking towards the square. As they turned west to the Heard Mansion, the other *Nancies* joined them in the semi-darkness, all silently making their way to the muster location. Even in the dim light, the grand Greek revival antebellum Heard Home stood out with its huge Doric columns across the front and around the sides. The boxwood that lined the long walk from the street to the porch had been planted in 1861, and was still so graceful, softening the outlines of the long, angular porch.

When Captain Morgan came out the front door of the house, Addie caught a look of surprise as the commander looked out over her troops. Every member of the Nancy Hart militia stood shoulder-to-shoulder on the front lawn. But it wasn't just that all the women had shown up, but *how* they had shown up. Most looked like they had gained ten to fifty pounds overnight.

"Leila, how many dresses do you have on?"

"Captain, Ma'am, I have on six."

"And you, Augusta?"

"Four, Captain."

"Can you walk in those?"

Leila, fully-layered in her best dresses, took several steps and curtsied awkwardly.

"May God be with us," Capt. Morgan muttered. "At least this militia will look imposing." She saluted her troops. "All right, soldiers, form your lines. It's time to move out."

Chapter XXVII

The Nancy Hart Militia marched across the lawn and onto Broad Street in two columns. With Captain Morgan in the lead, they passed the Methodist Church on the left and were soon halfway down the road to the college, which had been converted into the largest war hospital. Now they were headed for the outskirts of town—about two miles from the town square.

In the meantime, Col. Oscar Hugh La Grange had mustered his troops earlier than anyone expected. Since he was familiar with the lay of the land in LaGrange, he had been ordered to direct the assault there. Strategically, he placed some prisoners at the front of their line, with other Confederates interspersed with Union infantry and cavalry. The Colonel was feeling especially aggressive since being awarded "Brevet General" status just a month ago for his meritorious action in war. "Brevet" was an honorary title, and offered no real change in real rank, pay or authority. But it did confer recognition of his battle leadership—knowing how to motivate his men and intimidate his enemies.

Whoever might be waiting for them in LaGrange, they would no doubt be disheartened at the prospect of shooting in the direction of their own kin. But the Colonel didn't think anyone would be waiting. Who was left in LaGrange? As his men poured into the outskirts of the town, the sun was breaking through gauzy gray clouds, lighting the day. They stopped abruptly at Ferrell Gardens where an astonishing sight met them—a sight so unexpected that some of the soldiers fell to their knees. In a moment of inspiration, Mrs. Ferrell had asked her workers to clip the hedge, forming the words *"God Is Love."* Now on this day after Easter, a shaft of sunlight showed the way to heaven from the topiary in Mrs. Ferrell's garden.

Col. La Grange was impatient. "There is no divine presence here, just as there is no one left in LaGrange. We have a job to do and we will not waste another moment on sentiment. Forward! Move out!"

Col. La Grange spurred his bay gelding into a spin, then galloped past the gardens with his men close behind. Minutes later, they came upon the college where Col. La Grange had convalesced as a prisoner of war two years ago. So much had changed, including his toughening as a war commander. Then just at the top of the knoll, they abruptly came to a halt—not quite believing what they were seeing. Below them were two rows of women dressed in bonnets and gowns, the front line kneeling and the back row standing—all with Enfield rifles and muskets aimed at their heads and ready to fire. Col. La Grange saw steady hands, unblinking eyes, and stances of steadfast resolve. No one moved. No one spoke.

The seconds seemed like hours as he met with this, the most vexing conflict of his military career. Col. La Grange dismounted his horse and handed the reins to his next in command. Walking to the center of the street, he motioned for someone from the other side to come forward.

Captain Morgan walked out to the center of the street with Delia by her side. Delia looked straight ahead, instantly shaken. There, in her line of sight, was James Tomlinson, hands tied and thrust forward in front of the enemy line. *Why was he there? Why wasn't he with his unit in the Army of Virginia?* Evidently, he had fought to defend West Point and had been captured with the others. How shocking to see him like this. If the order came to fire, Delia might inadvertently shoot the man who had been her lifelong best friend. Unbidden, the memories came back in a rush of images. He was the one who raced with her on horseback and led the mock raids on Indians. He was always there to make her smile. *But I hate him because of*

Gus! Or do I? Doubt surfaced, fracturing her certainty, and with it, a revelation began to unfold. James left her brother on the battlefield because he was needed by the rest of the brave troops. He made a commitment and stood by it. Wasn't she now doing the very same thing? She had promised *the Nancies* she would stand up for LaGrange. If it meant risking James' life to do it, would she? Like a shooting star exploding into the atmosphere, she knew she had to forgive James. He was only honoring a promise, just as she was doing now.

Col. La Grange surveyed the women's militia and let out an incredulous laugh. "What are you prepared to do? Do you not appreciate how outnumbered you are?"

"So strange that Col. La Grange would take LaGrange," Capt. Morgan said, letting out a laugh of her own. Then she narrowed her eyes, looking directly into his. "I will tell you what we are prepared to do. We are prepared to kill you and defend our homes—or die trying."

"I can see it in those faces. But you won't win," said Col. La Grange.

"Winning is not the thing," said Capt. Morgan. "You could be a force of 3,000 or 300,000. What matters to us is the honor of standing up for all those who fought on our behalf all these years—as well as those you have now placed in harm's way. I assure you, Colonel, we will match the commitment of all our dear men."

Col. La Grange walked back to his front line. He conferred with his officers, fervently whispering, struggling for a solution to this terrible dilemma.

Again, he walked back to the center of the street. "I will be a war hero if I clean up after Gen. Sherman, shutting down all those towns that brought such consternation. But if anyone finds out that I cut down the lives of the extraordinary women facing me now, I will go down in infamy, not glory. I do not want your blood on my record."

"Wonderful! Is this your surrender?" Capt. Morgan inquired

Col. La Grange was appalled. "What on earth are you talking about? I'm offering you a chance to leave quietly."

Delia could not contain herself. "I told you two years ago that I wanted you to know us as human beings. We have feelings and we have tenacity. We will not go quietly or otherwise."

Col. La Grange frowned. "Let me talk with my officers." He turned and walked to the waiting officials to discuss the situation a second time.

Several minutes passed. The resolve of *the Nancies* charged the air with energy.

Colonel LaGrange returned to Captain Morgan in the middle of the street. "I cannot shoot some forty women who are clearly not going to budge."

"Excellent, Colonel. That tells me you have a brain in your head."

Col. La Grange was exasperated. "Well, what do I do?"

"Here's our agreement," said Capt. Morgan. "Listen carefully. You will not harm so much as a hair on the head of any citizen of LaGrange. You will not rob any citizen of LaGrange. And you agree not to burn the houses of the good people who live in LaGrange...your namesake."

"Yes, yes," the Yankee commander said impatiently. "But I cannot tip-toe through LaGrange without doing something that speaks to my war record. I have to destroy *something*—just one thing."

"If you must, then set fire to the depot," said Capt. Morgan. "It's falling down in disrepair anyway. And while you're at it, take the tracks too. They are useless because they don't connect with anything anymore."

"And if I insist on your surrender?"

"I will sound the order to fire." Capt. Morgan turned towards her militia. Delia shouldered her rifle.

"No. No! We can make this agreement without anyone declaring a surrender.

Captain Morgan walked back to her front line and consulted with two of her other officers, Leila Pullen and Augusta Hill. At the conclusion of this brief meeting, she made the trek back to Col. La Grange. "There is just one thing more."

"Oh God, what is it?" Col. La Grange was eager to extricate himself from this ridiculous, yet perilous, predicament.

"We would like you to join us for supper at Ben Hill's Bellevue mansion this evening. Bring your officers and the Confederate soldiers you are holding prisoner. We will come together to celebrate the honoring of this agreement.

"May the rest of my soldiers bivouac on the grounds of the estate?"

"Bellevue would be graced by their presence," said Capt. Morgan.

Colonel La Grange responded with a bow.

Col. La Grange kept his word to the Nancy Harts. The depot was torn apart and set on fire. The railway tracks were pulled up. But no one was harmed. No one was robbed. No house was torched.

When the terms of the agreement were carried out, *the Nancies* departed to Bellevue. They weren't sure they could pull together a fitting dinner party on such short notice, yet managed—in spite of the fact that all the slaves had run off. Mrs. Bull accompanied Mrs. Hill in pouring through her treasured cookbook and found just the right recipes for this unexpected occasion. They decided on a Brunswick stew.

"Addie, dear, this is your chance to show off," her mother told her. "Make something really special. I would like to finally reap the rewards of all those cooking lessons with Effie." She passed Mrs. Hill's cookbook to her youngest daughter.

Uh oh. I'm in trouble, Addie thought. Effie had been a good teacher, certainly. Addie could play the banjo well, but she couldn't cook worth anything. "Perhaps I should have some help, Mother. I mean someone to be my assistant."

"That's a splendid idea, sweetheart. Leila Pullen would surely appreciate learning a dish that would delight a man's stomach as well as his heart."

The blind leading the blind. Addie thought, *Lord help us*. This was going to be a bigger challenge than she had expected, as Leila couldn't cook either. But together, they would have to figure out something.

Shoulder to shoulder, Addie and Leila scanned Mrs. Hill's cookbook searching for a recipe they might be able to pull off.

"Bourbon balls! These sound like a delightful confection, and you don't have to do any actual cooking," said Leila.

Addie wasn't as sure of the choice, but Leila's enthusiasm cemented the decision. Bourbon balls it would be.

Reading through the recipe, they discovered that not all the ingredients were available, and in fact, hadn't been for some years. They would have to make some serious substitutions. There was no Kentucky Bourbon, but there was something called "LaGrange White Lightning"—a local recipe purported to be quite strong. The ladies didn't drink it, of course, but the men seemed to embrace it once brandy and bourbon were impossible to acquire.

By the time the two cooks had completed the substitutions and increased the amounts to serve more people, the recipe was vastly changed.

Addie took a taste of the mixture before adding the liquor. "Ugh, this is terrible," she told Leila, almost spewing the stuff from her mouth.

"Then we will have to adjust," Leila countered, unwilling to let the critical remark spoil her enthusiasm. She poured two cups of liquor into the bowl though the original recipe had only called for half a cup.

Addie smiled. "Oh dear, the soldiers might get tipsy, but I guess they won't be complaining."

As people began arriving, Addie peeked into the large dining room and spotted Dr. Ware. She was pleased to see him at the party. Reportedly, he was still very busy tending patients, and she was glad his load had not been made heavier this day. Leila delivered the first tray of their Bourbon balls to the dining room as Addie caught up with Sallie. She picked up the tray and offered one to her sister. "Pretend you like it," whispered Addie.

Sallie bit into a bourbon ball and wrinkled her nose. "You should stick with music, not cooking."

"Come on, Sister, let's mingle."

Sallie paused when she saw Addie heading toward a group that included Dr. Ware.

"Oh, come on, Sallie. Don't you think it's time?"

As they approached, Dr. Ware was shaking Nancy Morgan's hand. "Capt. Morgan, your troops were among the bravest in the country today. We are all grateful for the courage and commitment of these fine soldiers."

"We couldn't have done it without your help," she said with great warmth.

Sallie took a deep breath. "May I offer my thanks too? You trained us well." She extended her hand to Dr. Ware.

He met her grasp with a gentle squeeze of her hand. "I'm not sure I'm deserving of that. I'm a flawed human being still trying to find my way."

"At least you recognize the shadows in your soul. I have been oblivious to mine for too long," she replied.

Capt. Morgan gushed, "Isn't this grand! Just look around you. What an extraordinary day of reconciliation for all of us."

Col. La Grange joined in. "Capt. Morgan, you have shown me how truly extraordinary women can be, and I am in awe of the courage I encountered on Broad Street today."

"Well, if I do say so, I think *all* the women in Georgia are extraordinary, and I'd like you to meet my friend, Louisa May. She is visiting from Macon and just happened to be staying at Bellevue with one of the Hill girls when history brought all of us together." Mrs. Morgan presented Louisa May to the Colonel. "This is a most courageous man, Louisa May. He has done the right thing at a time when so many of the wrong things are happening to innocent people."

Louisa May was not only impressed with the deeds of Col. Hugh La Grange, but with his dashing good looks as well. His chiseled features; prominent cheekbones, high forehead, and a thin, patrician nose delivered a countenance that was most appealing. Not to mention his short, thick hair with a subtle waviness on top. For a brief moment, she imagined running her fingers through his lustrous mane and reddened at the thought. Yet even in her embarrassment, she couldn't help noticing how large and deep-set the Colonel's eyes were—his face complemented by a well-trimmed mustache and just the hint of a dimple on his chin. In his uniform—even if it was the wrong color for southern sensibilities—this man was positively dazzling to her way of thinking.

"Col. La Grange, where is home for you?" Louisa May purred.

"I come from Wisconsin."

"Oh, my heavens! I have always wanted to know more about Wisconsin. Can you believe this providence? Here is the very man who can tell me all about that interesting state."

Addie rolled her eyes and headed for the kitchen to refill her tray.

In the kitchen Mrs. Hill was still bustling about. "What a splendid spread, Addie. I am so proud of everyone for pulling this together so quickly. Don't take that tray of Bourbon balls before I get to taste one," she called out as Addie turned to leave. "I've been looking forward to this all evening." She popped one of the confections in her mouth and then began to chew quite slowly, turning to Addie's mother with an expression of surprise.

"What's the matter?" asked Mrs. Bull.

"I don't think this is quite my recipe"

Addie's mother took a small bite, which quickly made her cheeks pucker and her eyebrows arch. "Well, Addie, whatever it was you learned from Effie, I guess it wasn't how to cook."

Addie shrugged and smiled, then made a quick exit with her replenished tray.

To her delight, the soldiers loved the LaGrange-style Bourbon balls. When they were gone, they clamored for more. Leila responded quickly. "I'm sorry we've run out of these treats, but Addie has another specialty you are sure to enjoy. She can play any tune you can think of. So let the music begin!"

Addie was glad to take the focus away from her dubious cooking. Once at the keyboard in the grand ballroom, she began to play; later moving to the banjo, and finally to the violin—easily filling musical requests that ranged from country to classical.

James Tomlinson sat up close, clapping his hands and tapping his toes to the rhythm of Addie's exquisite tunes. He watched her adoringly throughout and blew her a kiss when the music ended. At the close of the concert, after the cheering and applause had come to an end, Addie glanced around the room. People were embracing and smiling, but some were tearful as well. James took her hand. "Addie, Col. La Grange is moving on to Macon now and he is taking us with him as prisoners of war." Leaving her hand in his, they walked out to the porch where Delia and Sallie sat watching the soldiers prepare for departure. James caught Delia's eye as he stepped into the night air. "I don't know what to say, Delia."

"I wish you only the best." Delia said gently. "You needn't say anything."

James nodded and offered Addie his arm as they descended the steps, then led her to the formation of soldiers and prisoners.

"Don't say goodbye." Tears pooled in Addie's eyes.

"Then, how about 'You will be in my heart always, Addie Bull.' "

"That will do nicely," she said, dabbing her eyes. Turning, she headed toward the porch, then turning back, waved as James left her once more—maybe once and for all. After the men marched out into the darkness, the sisters looked out over the quiet calm that belied the momentous events of this day.

Addie studied her oldest sister, now so uncharacteristically subdued. "What are you thinking, Delia?"

"I'm thinking I wasted so much time with my towering hatred," said Delia.

"You mean James?" asked Sallie.

"When I saw him in my sights, hands behind his back and helpless, I realized all my hatred just fueled more pain. And that if I could forgive, the hurt would start healing,"

"And did you forgive him?" Addie touched Delia's hand.

"I did, baby sister. And when all this collective hatred melted here tonight, it struck me…" Delia, always so strong, was struggling to find her voice.

Addie and Sallie leaned in close to their sister, whose voice was soft and choked with emotion.

"Forgiveness—that is the bridge to peace, and the faster you get there, the less you will lose." Delia composed herself then smiled at Addie. "And darling sister, it's all right. I know I've lost James."

"Perhaps it's not too late," Addie said quietly.

"No, James loves you. You showed him your compassion, your forgiveness, without hesitation. And if everyone in the country had been quicker to forgive, then think of the souls that would have been spared."

"James didn't kill Gus. He loved him," said Addie.

"I know that now, and I wish you and James the best, God willing this war ever ends.

"Amen!" said Sallie. "Well, we militiawomen have done our part today."

"And speaking of *the Nancies*," said Delia, "I'm so proud of you, Addie, for the woman you've become. And if anybody ever asks about the sharpshooters of The Nancy Hart Militia, I will tell them you were the best."

"Does this mean I won't have to braid your hair or bring you your slippers?"

"Or empty the chamber pot," smiled Delia.

The three sisters began to laugh as they linked arms. It was time for everyone to go home. The Bull sisters headed down the long path with the other *Nancies* towards Broad Street, then across the square, and into open doors and familiar spaces warmed by graceful hearths—into homes still standing, welcoming them back.

Chapter XXVIII

Two weeks after *the Nancies* saved LaGrange, Addie was forced to shoulder her rifle once more as there were now desperate people on every main road. Her family had taken in people whose towns were in ruins and she had been left to look after them while the rest of the family traveled to West Point to help with the homeless there.

Once again, it was Luella Biggs who showed up to warn Addie of impending danger.

"I seen a Bluecoat over yonder. Might be another deserter looking for spoils," said Luella.

Addie had been cautioned by her father to be on the lookout for Yankee renegades. "Well he's come to the wrong place, Luella. We came close to losing this house once, and I'm not about to let one of those damn Bluecoats torch it now."

"I 'spect you mean what you say, Miss Addie."

"If trouble is coming, Luella. You get yourself back in the woods."

"Yessum, but I ain't gon be far, ya hear?"

Addie grabbed her Enfield and stepped out onto the porch. At the end of the driveway, she found a tree to hide behind, waiting in stillness. In the gathering light of dawn she spotted her mark. *There he was—a* Bluecoat! Slumped over and clearly exhausted, he was coming up the hill towards the front gate. Addie steadied her rifle, gauging how much closer he would have to get before she could get off an accurate shot. *Patience. I'll get him before he gets us.* She tensed her finger, primed to squeeze the trigger. *Something's not right. He's wearing gray pants.* She hesitated. As he walked closer, she realized there was something familiar about his form. Just then he lifted his gaze up toward the gate.

"James!" she cried out. Swiftly bringing down her arm, she opened her fingers, letting the rifle fall in the dirt. Stunned and trembling, her knees gave way, and she sat down hard. Closing her eyes, she tried to shut out the gravity of what she had almost done. When she felt his fingers on her face she began to sob.

"I almost shot you!" she said through her tears.

James lowered to the ground, looking into her eyes. Reaching out, he gently touched her shoulder. "Sh, Sh, my sweet Addie. It's all over now. When we got to Macon with Col. La Grange, we heard that General Lee had surrendered at Appomattox. The war is over."

Addie couldn't stop crying. "Why are you wearing half of a Yankee uniform?"

"Col. La Grange let us go as soon he heard the news. Some of his men felt sorry for us having to walk home in rags. Knowing how chilly it is at night, they gave us a few surplus coats."

"Almost got you killed," Addie sniffled.

"Well, you know, when I saw Delia aiming her rifle at the Union troops with me right up front, I thought she might shoot me on purpose. But I also thought she'd miss the shot."

They both laughed. "But I heard you were the sharpshooter in the family, Addie. You wouldn't have missed."

"I guess God had other plans for us," said Addie wiping away the tears with her sleeve.

James looked tenderly at Addie, his expression full of admiration. "What the Nancies did was extraordinary. Weren't you afraid?"

She took a deep breath and let out a sigh. "We were all so scared, but we had our faith, and we had the support of our sisterhood." She paused. "We weren't ready to die for a political position or to free slaves or keep them. But we were all willing to lay down our lives to save what we hold most dear: our families. Love was our strength. There's something else, maybe the most important thing."

"What's that?" asked James.

"In the face of fear, we showed up. Wondrous things can happen if you simply show up."

"Well, it's clear you women have come a long way in four years." James said.

Slowly and deliberately, Addie leaned in close and pressed her lips against his in a long, lingering kiss. When she finally released him, she looked at him sweetly. "Aren't you going to say something?"

"Isn't that awfully forward for a young lady to initiate the first kiss?" James said with a grin.

"Well, you showed up, didn't you?" said Addie smiling back.

"I see what you mean," James chuckled softly. "Wondrous, yes." Standing, he helped Addie to her feet, and they walked together, hand-in-hand, to face the new day.

The rising sun was streaking through the trees, as if announcing an end to the long night of war's despair. Darkness finally stirred. The heaviness of grief shifted. The possibility of hope awakened.

Personal Note By Author Sue Pearson

This novel is based on actual events and real people. Addie Bull is my great grandmother. She and James Tomlinson married after the war, and the last of their four children was Addie Lee Tomlinson, who married Ernest Pearson. Their only child, E.O. Pearson Jr, married Virginia Hobbs, and together they had four children: Marjorie Pearson Bush, Susan Pearson, Nancy Pearson and Jon Pearson.

I wish to thank my great-grandmother, Addie Bull, and my two great aunts, Delia and Sallie, for their bravery and humility. *The Nancies* did not seek recognition for their act of courage, but as their proud and grateful heir, it is an honor to bestow it upon them with the writing of this book. It is my hope that through it, the members of the Nancy Hart Militia will now inspire a new generation who are facing very different challenges, yet like my ancestors, need to reach beyond fear to find courage, peace, and forgiveness.

Author's Notes on the True Story

When my sister, Margie, stopped in to the Troup County Archives to do some research on our family history, Historian Clark Johnson told her of our astonishing connection to the Nancy Hart Militia. Since I have been a professional journalist for 35 years, my sister turned the information over to me, hoping I would do more research and write the little-known story.

With more enthusiasm than I knew what to do with, I made my first trip to LaGrange, GA in 2003. Over the next few years, and with the help of Clark Johnson, also a descendant of one of the Nancies, I poured through hundreds of documents at the Troup County Archives. Among the gems, we found a carefully recorded eye-witness account of the activities of The Nancies. Many years after the war had ended, Leila Pullen, an officer in the militia, addressed a meeting of the Daughters of the Confederacy and detailed the story of the Nancy Hart Militia. Leila's talk was transcribed by the group and placed in the Archives. There were other accounts as well, including an article written by Mrs. Thaddeus Horton for Ladies' Home Journal in November, 1904, (vol. 21,#14).

The Historically Accurate Facts

There were 46 women in the Nancy Hart Militia and most were members of the Methodist Church in LaGrange, Georgia. The "Nancies," as they called themselves, were trained by the only able bodied man of fighting age left in LaGrange: Dr. Augustus Ware. Historical records indicate Dr. Ware had some kind of disability. He applied for service in the Confederate Army several times and was rejected based on this limitation.

In an early target practice one the women did, in fact, accidentally shoot the Bull family's prized bull.

In another incident, a hornet's nest was hit with a bullet, unleashing the full fury of the wasps on the fleeing women.

LaGrange was indeed an important hospital center for the war-wounded since it was located along a rail line and had in residence a large number of doctors.

There is an account of the Easter Sunday 1865 battle of West Point, which is just beyond LaGrange at the Alabama border. A band of soldiers called "Wilson's Raiders" were following orders to destroy railroads and war related businesses in towns in Alabama and Georgia. When the invasion was imminent, West Point citizens telegraphed a message to LaGrange pleading for help. A few old men, young boys, and wounded Confederate soldiers, responded, riding the locomotive from the depot in LaGrange to West Point. A terrible battle followed which resulted in many deaths and considerable destruction in West Point. Most of the remaining Southern fighters were taken prisoner. That night the Yankee commander, Col. Oscar Hugh LaGrange, planned the next invasion which would take place the following day in a march on LaGrange.

A couple of West Point defenders managed to escape, and galloped on horseback through LaGrange warning residents that the Yankees were coming—and urging them to run for their lives.

The next day the Nancies mustered on the lawn of a graceful estate on Broad Street in preparation for facing the invading soldiers. Many of the women had put on layer after layer of dresses so that if, at the end of the day, they had no homes, at least they would have something to wear.

The Nancies marched to the edge of town and formed a line towards the hill where the college stood. At least 1500 soldiers with Wilson's Raiders led by Col. Hugh LaGrange came pouring over the hill. They stopped when they saw the formation of determined women. Col. LaGrange spoke to the leader of the Nancy Hart Militia. He and Captain Nancy Morgan struck a deal: the Nancies would not fire if the Yankees promised not to harm anyone nor burn a single home in LaGrange. Later in the day, the Raiders burned the train depot and pulled up the tracks. The tannery and the jewelry store were burned, but no person was hurt and no home destroyed in the town. The Union officers were invited to supper with the townspeople. The next day Col. La Grange marched his soldiers and his prisoners (many from LaGrange captured in the battle at West Point) to Macon where word of Lee's surrender was soon reported. In response, Col. La Grange released all his prisoners.

The Characters

All of the Nancy Hart Militia members mentioned in the book were real people and documentation exists in the Troup County Archives verifying they were part of the militia. Archived reports verify Sue Pearson descended from the Bull family. Her Great Grandmother was Addie Bull.

Addie Bull's parents were Orville and Martha Bull. They had three daughters and two sons: Adelia, Sallie, Addie, Gus, Orville Jr. The Bulls were well-to-do plantation owners who owned slaves. Gus was considered a rising star on the political scene just as the War Between the States broke out.

James Tomlinson was an artist in LaGrange who learned the new art of photography. He and Gus were both members of the LaGrange Light Guards and went off to war together and fought in the same unit.

My great grandmother, Addie, kept a memory book. Inside are verses penned by friends and family, some directly relating to the war. One verse in particular offers insight into how Gus Bull died during the war. Gus fell in the battle of Seven Pines, Virginia. In the verse we learn he was captured, imprisoned, and died in the prison camp.

Mrs. Hill wrote a popular cookbook much treasured by the ladies of LaGrange.

Leila Pullen's mother worried constantly over her flirting with the wounded soldiers in her care.

Mrs. Ferrell was a master gardener and fashioned intricate topiary, often with spiritual messages.

Dr. Ware did indeed fall in love with one of the Nancies and married Anna Wagnon before the end of the war. He was said to have fathered several mixed race children during his lifetime, and a grandson of that lineage went on to help found the NAACP many years later.

Addie Bull married James Tomlinson in the years following the war. They operated a photographic studio, and had several children, among them Adelaide Lee Tomlinson who married Ernest Pearson. Adelaide and Ernest had an only son, E. O. Pearson Jr. who married Virginia Hobbs. E. O. and Virginia had three daughters, Margie, Sue (the author of the book), Nancy and one son, Jon.

Adelia Bull was a journalist, well-known in LaGrange for her essays.

The Electa Club and the Ladies' Home Society were groups that sprang from the Presbyterian and Baptist churches to help entertain and offer assistance to wounded soldiers.

Other Historical Notes

The profile of the founding and development of the town of LaGrange is accurate. LaGrange was an unusually strong center of education, particularly for women. Many of the families owned estate homes near the town square and plantations in the surrounding countryside. Many owned slaves to serve in the estates and work the plantations.

The Civil War battles and timelines were carefully researched for accuracy.

The story of the Confederate ship *Alabama* in Liverpool is true as are the related characters, James Bullock and Henry Hotze.

Weapons, firing mechanisms, and sharpshooting standards were carefully researched. I visited the site of the Battle of Seven Pines and studied accounts of the fighting where my Great Uncle Gus Bull was wounded. At the Virginia Historical Society in Richmond, I uncovered military summaries of the battle and one dramatic letter written by a Confederate soldier to his brother during a lull in the fighting. His description reveals the emotional horror soldiers experience in the heat of battle. The letter is included in the book by permission of the Virginia Historical Society.

Gratitudes

Special thanks to so many whose support, patience, and enthusiasm guided me in the long journey from inspiration to creation.

This novel would never have been written if my sister, the late Margie Pearson Bush, had not been curious about our family history. Thank you sister dear, for handing me the best story of my long career as a journalist. Historian Forrest Clark Johnson helped her with research at the Troup County Archives in LaGrange, Georgia, delivering the surprising connection between our great grandmother, Addie Bull Tomlinson and the Nancy Hart Militia. Without Clark's guidance and support, this story would never have found the page.

Joe and Debbie Thompson of West Point, GA deserve a shout-out for their help with historical accuracy. Wanda Walker and all the members of the Nancy Hart Club in LaGrange gave me an infusion of energy and enthusiasm.

Thank you to my writing mentor and good friend, Jennifer Basye Sander, whose idea-a-minute expertise kept my writing fires burning. Thanks to Eric Elfman, my most excellent writing coach, who knew I could transcend those early drafts.

Thanks to my children: Matt, Phil, Ty, Evan and Christine for not rolling their eyes over their mother's eight-year obsession to write this novel. My former husband, Rick Atkinson, encouraged me to tackle fiction when others thought it would be too hard. Thanks to all who read and offered helpful comments: Kathy Cairns, Stephanie Skiff, Paula Munier, Christine Kovach, Bill Lanterman, Joan Collins, and Libby Atkinson. A big thank you to editor Maridel Bowes who combines skill, patience and kindness in her work and our friendship.

Thank you Carolynne Smith at Pixel Graphics for a perfectly beautiful book cover.

Hugs and appreciation to my writer friends and spiritual cheerleaders Candy Chand, Marsha Jacobson, Jennifer Forsberg Meyer, Sue Peppers and Mary Witt.

21013827R00158

Made in the USA
San Bernardino, CA
02 May 2015